THE

EVANGELICAL

DILEMMA

Colin D. Standish
President, Hartland Institute

and
Russell R. Standish
Founder, Remnant Ministries

Published and distributed by
Hartland Publications
P.O. Box 1
Rapidan, VA 22733

© 1994, 1996 by Hartland Publications, Rapidan, VA.
98 97 96   5 4 3 2

Printed in United States of America

ISBN 0-923309-28-4

Contents

1	The Authors' Dilemma	5
2	The Historical Dilemma	11
3	The Dilemma of Evangelical Development	19
4	The Dilemma of a Justification-Alone Salvation	23
5	The Dilemma of the Objective Gospel	31
6	The Dilemma of Forensic Justification	41
7	The Dilemma of Unconditionality	47
8	The Dilemma of the "in Christ" Motif	57
9	The Dilemma of the Concept of Original Sin	63
10	The Dilemma of Predestination	69
11	The Dilemma of Irresistible Grace	80
12	The Dilemma of the New-Birth Experience	85
13	The Dilemma of Perfection	91
14	The Dilemma of the Man of Romans Seven	99
15	The Dilemma of the Human Nature of Christ	107
16	The Dilemma of Christ Our Example	115
17	The Dilemma of Acceptance and Assurance	123
18	The Dilemma of Immediate Life After Death	129
19	The Dilemma of the End-Time Judgment	137
20	The Dilemma of Christ, Our Heavenly High Priest	150
21	The Dilemma of the Antichrist	161
22	The Dilemma of the Secret Rapture	170
23	The Dilemma of the Millennium	180
24	The Dilemma of the Lord's Day	187
25	The Dilemma of Dispensationalism	197
26	The Legacy of John Darby	203
27	The Legacy of Cyrus Scofield	210
28	The Dilemma of the Future	220

There is no sanctification
aside from truth,
and it is the truth *that has sanctified*
that leads to unity

THE AUTHORS' DILEMMA

When in 1955 the authors enrolled at the University of Sydney, Australia, they soon became acquainted with a number of religious societies registered with the University. Of the Protestant societies, the dominant two were the Evangelical Union (EU) and the Student Christian Movement (SCM). The differences between these two soon became apparent. The EU, true to its name, attracted young people who were most likely to be fervent church attendees. They had great enthusiasm for proselytizing; they believed in the inerrancy of the Word of God and they subscribed at least in general to the principles of the conservative wing of Protestantism. This Society attracted supporters primarily from the Anglican, Baptist, and Presbyterian Churches. The Anglican Archdiocese of Sydney was the last major bastion of Evangelical (low church) Anglicanism in Australia, and thus a large percentage of the members of the Anglican Church who were students of the University were attracted to this Society. There was also an Anglican Society, which tended to cater to those with Anglo-Catholic (high church) leanings. The Baptist students, as well as some other students including those from the Church of Christ, were naturally attracted to the EU because of their conservative Christian heritage.

The SCM attracted students who were from the more liberal wing of Christendom; those who were more likely to question the inerrancy of the Bible, to support textual criticism and those who saw the Bible as *containing* the Word of God, but not *being* the Word of God. There was a tendency for the SCM to attract those young people who were theoretical in their religion, who enjoyed the academic debate and the criss-cross of theories and speculation concerning the meaning of various aspects of the Bible. This society attracted students from mainstream Protestantism, including the Methodist Church, and some from the Congregationalist Church, and the Presbyterians.

Though the authors joined neither society, they were more attracted to the Fundamentalist approach of the Evangelical Union. The authors came to know some of the members of both groups, and recognized the chasm existing between them. Recognizing the lack of detailed doctrinal orthodoxy among the members supporting the SCM, they were not the least surprised when the Methodist Church, the Congregational Church, and part of the Presbyterian Church joined together in 1977 in what is now known as the Uniting Church of Australia. The more orthodox and more strongly committed Calvinists of the Presbyterian Church have remained separate from the Uniting Church, for to those who joined the Uniting Church it mattered little whether the members supported the concept of predestination, which is common among Presbyterians and some Congregationalists, or whether they accepted the free-will concept of the Methodists. No such issues were allowed to become major considerations. The documents that led to the establishment of the Uniting Church of Australia make it clear that doctrine played a minor role in decision making.

In 1977, at the time of the formation of the Uniting Church, Russell was Deputy Medical Superintendent of a University of Melbourne hospital. The chaplaincy department reported to him. The senior chaplain, an amiable man, was a Presbyterian minister. When Russell inquired of him concerning the basis upon which the Methodists and Presbyterians had resolved their major doctrinal differences, the chaplain replied, "You know, I've never given it a second thought."[1]

However, that which at first surprised and then alarmed the authors, is the evidence that as we have reached into the 1990s, many of those advocating evangelical Protestantism have increasingly accepted the eclecticism and pluralism of the more liberal elements of the Christian church. By pluralism we mean the concept that unity demands less and less emphasis upon a specific creed or doctrinal adherence so that a wide spectrum of beliefs is of equal acceptance to these members.

The Evangelicals of former generations had been staunchly Protestant in every way and had stood strongly in direct opposition to Catholicism and to that church's adherence to church tradition as opposed to the primacy of the Bible. Now it would seem that not even Catholicism represents a threat to the determi-

---

[1] Traditionally Methodism upheld the doctrine of "free will" while Presbyterianism adopted the doctrine of predestination.

nation of many Evangelicals to move toward ecumenical unity. While we see many smaller groups in evangelical Protestantism standing against the ecumenical movement, we see a majority of Evangelicals marching toward pluralism. Many conservative Evangelicals have found common cause with the Roman Catholic Church from which almost half a millennium ago they split. In the United States of America they have been seen to band together with the Roman Catholic tradition on issues including calls from the reestablishment of moral and Christian values in the United States. They appear to have united in their desire to break down the wall of separation between church and state. They have seen a common cause in their opposition to permissive abortion and many other issues. Is it possible that the noble evangelical tradition which is rooted firmly and, we had thought, resolutely in the protestant Reformation has begun to falter seriously, and to lead many Evangelicals toward losing the central focus of their mission? As we see congregation after congregation, church body after church body embracing ecumenism and supporting the concept of a one-world religion that will underpin their hopes for a one-world government, a one-world economy and a one-world social structure, we wonder how long evangelical Protestantism can be sustained.

It would seem to us that the Evangelical movement has no right to exist if it is not in total contradistinction to the Roman Catholic faith from which it so courageously separated at the time of the protestant Reformation. We perceive that many Evangelicals are now warmly embracing the modern ecumenical Bible translations that are proliferating in Christendom. The arguments that separated the protestant Bibles of the European Reformation from the Roman Catholic Bible seem almost to be lost. Nearly all these modern translations are built upon the corrupted, Western Alexandrian Greek manuscripts that were wholly rejected by the Reformers during the sixteenth century. These Greek manuscripts are notorious for their deletions, for their efforts to change the words of the New Testament writers so as to deny the divinity of Jesus Christ, and supporting many other aberrations from the truth. The battle for the Word of God was fierce. The philosophic direction of the early Christian school in Alexandria allowed the intrusion of much paganistic doctrine to pervert Bible truth. The

Protestants accepted the validity of the Eastern Syriac Greek text which evidenced much greater accuracy and thoroughness of transcription, and showed no effort to mutilate the messages of the Apostles.

After careful study of the Codex Vaticanus and the Codex Sinaiticus, the most utilized of the corrupted Western Greek manuscripts, John Burgon, the late-nineteenth century Anglican Dean of Chichester in England, concluded that "In the gospels alone, Codex Vaticanus differs from the Received Text in the following particulars: It omits at least 2,877 words; it adds 536 words; it substitutes 935 words; it transposes 2,098 words; and it modifies 1,132 words; making a total of 7,578 verbal divergences. But the Sinaitic manuscript is even worse for its total divergences in the particulars stated above amount to nearly 9,000" (David Otis Fuller, *True or False*, p. 78).

The protestant Reformers were much drawn to Erasmus' Greek text of 1516 which came from the Syriac manuscripts. It mattered not whether it was the French, or Dutch, or Scandinavian nations, or Hungarian, or English; the Protestants of Europe with absolute consistency chose the superior accuracy of the Eastern Syriac Greek texts from which to translate the Bible into the "vulgar" (vernacular) language. But today, by the multitudes, Evangelicals are accepting the faulted translations taken from the corrupted Western Alexandrian Greek texts. Many proclaim strongly their superiority to the Eastern Syriac text. We watch in wonder how the evangelical Protestants have turned from the powerful stand against "those damnable papist" translations by the protestant Reformers.

It can but come as a matter of dismay to the student of history that there are many Evangelicals today who are willing to accept faulted translations as their basis for faith and practice. This fact becomes even more surprising when we consider the great protestant concept of *sola scriptura* which became the watchcry of evangelical Protestantism as it fought against the Roman Catholic perversion of Christianity. To the early Evangelicals, "the Bible, and the Bible only," was their rule of faith and practice and many evangelical Protestants claimed they had no creed but the Bible.

Thus the preservation and use of those translations which came from the Eastern Syriac tradition were protected with great sacredness.[2]

The Roman Catholics are not always wrong. Indeed, they are not infrequently perceptive. When they saw the 1881 *Revised Version*, the first of the modern Bibles translated by Protestants from the corrupted Western Alexandrian Greek texts, they exclaimed that "it will be the death knell of Protestantism" (*Dublin Review*, 1881).

Is it any wonder then that while so many Evangelicals still proclaim *sola scriptura*, many by their practice and arguments seem to be falling for the concept of *sola theologian*? The moment we consciously or unconsciously move away from an authoritative translation of the Bible as the basis of all faith and practice, we lose our true foundation. The vast majority of theologians are in disagreement with each other. This conflict is one of the great reasons for the pluralism of thought in Evangelicalism today. There is no secure foundation for many. Though the term *sola scriptura* may be mouthed, the real basis of belief is increasingly *sola theologian* where it is possible to choose one theologian or another, thus bringing in diversity of concepts, almost all of which come from the faulted theories of man rather than the clear testimony of the Holy Scriptures.

For the authors of this book, that diversity is a dilemma. For as we approach the purpose of this book to present before our Evangelical friends the clear testimony of God's Word; as we look at areas in evangelical Protestantism that need to be reexamined through the microscope of God's Word, we realize that some of the issues we will address will apply to only some Evangelicals today; and that to others they will be issues that have been resolutely resolved. But in our endeavor to reach the widest audience among evangelical Protestantism we will take up those issues that are increasingly bringing schisms into the once-solid Evangelical community.

---

[2] For a reading in depth on this topic consult *Modern Bible Translations Unmasked*, Russell and Colin Standish, Hartland Publications, Box 1, Rapidan, VA 22733, U.S.A.

We wholeheartedly support the evangelical concept of *sola scriptura*; thus this book will lay its appeal upon the sacred Word. Throughout this book we will cite from the Authorized Version, the Bible of the English Reformation. There will be little dwelling upon the niceties of theological suppositions; and where the concepts of theologians are referred to it will not be as an authority for truth, but rather to point out the areas of dialogue that are the focus of the time. This book is written from a supportive perspective, seeking to help our Evangelical friends face squarely the issues of Protestantism as they are grounded and rooted in God's Holy Word.

THE HISTORICAL DILEMMA

Evangelical Christianity had its foundation in the protestant Reformation. Martin Luther's followers were called Evangelicals to distinguish them from John Calvin's Reformed Church. The Evangelical movement of today traces itself back to the Reformation and sees its roots there. But most Evangelicals do not understand the deeper roots of their theology. It will be surprising to many that some of the roots of evangelical theology antedate the Reformation by more than eleven hundred years. Many of the concepts now espoused by evangelical Protestantism are grounded in the teachings of Augustinian Catholicism. Many Evangelicals, attracted by the Christ-centeredness of their message and the assurance which they believe it brings to them, are unaware of the Catholic roots that have, in many cases, limited and even perverted the direction of their movement.

Today's Evangelicals see their message as being presented as a beautiful extension of Reformation theology in stride with the teachings of Martin Luther and other Reformers. Few who hear this teaching understand the deceptive Roman Catholic heritage of some of the doctrines designed to lull men and women into carnal security and to bind them together for the great day of destruction at the conclusion of the millennium. Yet such doctrines have entered the Evangelical movement by stealth.

By the fourth century of the Christian era the Church was embroiled in theological turmoil. The centrality of Christ as man's Redeemer, and His truth, were all but lost. Almost every wind of doctrine was being preached. Church councils were assembled in desperate and futile efforts to determine orthodoxy. The Church became the arbiter of faith, in place of the Word of God. Each succeeding decree of church councils took the church further away from the simple gospel of Jesus Christ. Out of this theological milieu arose a man who exerted a giant influence in the formulation of theological dogma. Even today this man, Augustine, bishop of Hippo, casts his shadow across Christendom; and his errors have been permitted to darken many corners of evangelical Protestantism.

Augustine was born 354 in north Africa. While his mother was a Christian, his father was a Manichaeist who trained and educated him in Manichaeistic schools. Manichaeism was founded in the third century by Mani, as an offshoot of the ancient Persian religion of Zoroastrianism. It was designed to take the principles of Zoroastrianism and apply them into a perverted form of Christianity. This religious system was uncompromisingly dualistic. It had a special emphasis upon the dualism of light (good) and darkness (evil).

All pagan symbols are symbols of balance. The cross (the balancing of the horizontal and the vertical) is the most ancient and degraded of all pagan symbols. The Star of David, adopted as a symbol by the Jews, is an ancient pagan insignia incorporating the balancing of two triangles. The swastika of the Hindus and the Buddhists is a balancing symbol, as is the Yin and Yang of the Chinese and Koreans. It was this balance that led pagans to create good and bad gods, male and female gods, and male and female priests. It was this concept which encouraged belief that good and evil can reign together. This satanic error had its origin in the Garden of Eden.

Augustine was nurtured in these pagan philosophies. When well into his twenties, he travelled to Italy. There he studied under Ambrose, bishop of Milan, and subsequently accepted Christianity. Augustine was unable to cast off many of the pagan concepts which he had imbibed in his youth. His theological concepts thus were seriously flawed by his early mind set. Yet his doctrinal perspectives were to dominate the training of church leaders until the time of Thomas Aquinas, who lived more than seven hundred years later.

Many of the great theological errors of the Roman Catholic Church were either instigated by Augustine or developed by subsequent theologians who attempted to formulate a consistent theology that would incorporate the Augustinian heresies. The Roman Catholic theologians subsequent to Augustine developed a very consistent and logical theology. But it was built upon wrong premises—premises inimical to the Word of God.

With his pagan mind set, Augustine could not understand the issue of free choice. He saw God as absolute and in total control. A God who permitted man to have freedom of choice was incomprehensible to his pagan presuppositions. Yet he acknowledged that the Bible teaches that some will be saved in the kingdom and some will be lost. To accommodate this truth into his theology, Augustine incorporated the doctrine of predestination. The error of predestination was vigorously challenged in his lifetime. In response, Augustine argued that it was a miracle of the grace of God that any of us should be saved. Thus he suggested that we as erring humans are in no position to question the justice of God in preordaining some to eternal salvation and others to eternal damnation.

This error of predestination logically led to the concept of "once saved, always saved." God, being absolute and unchangeable, arbitrarily decided those who were preordained to salvation and who could never be lost—and those who were preordained to eternal destruction and could never be saved. Naturally this belief gave a presumptuous security to those who believed that they were preordained to salvation. On the other hand, it also led to questions concerning the proclamation of the gospel. Why spread the gospel? Why evangelize? Why proselytize? If God's arbitrary will has predestined men to either salvation or damnation, what was the purpose of evangelism? The answer which satisfied some was, Simply because the Bible mandates it. Augustine's propositions upheld the view that the relationship of man to God is incidental to his salvation. The concept of "once saved, always saved" quickly incorporated the sin-and-live theology.

No longer was victory over sin proclaimed as of any consequence to salvation. Vigorously Augustine argued that it was not possible to gain victory over sin even in the power of Christ. It will be noted that each one of these unscriptural conclusions is a logical deduction from Augustine's false premise based upon his heathen belief that God does not permit man the power of free choice in salvation. These concepts naturally attracted him to the concept of original sin which he quickly popularized. In this doctrine he declared that man is guilty not only of his own sin but, more importantly, he is also guilty of the sin of Adam. Sin is a state of being; not dependent on man's desecration of the Decalogue, though he did suggest that salvation was evidenced in acts of one's life. Initially he claimed that sexual intercourse was the original sin. He had fathered an illegitimate child, exposing his long and unsuccessful battle with sexual desire. This weakness left Augustine to search for a theological basis for his sinful failures. Later he broadened the concept of original sin into other areas. It was due to this concept that Augustine saw the man depicted in Romans 7:14–24 as a fully converted man. Unlike previous understandings which saw the man of Romans seven as an earnest soul struggling and failing in human weakness, Augustine saw him in a saved relationship with God, maybe even man at his best. He ignored the plain testimony of Paul in relationship to this passage.

> For we know that the law is spiritual: but I am carnal, sold under sin. For that which I do I allow not: for what I would, that do I not; but what I hate, that do I. . . . Now then it is no more I that do it, but sin that dwelleth in me. For I know that in me (that is, in my flesh,) dwelleth no good thing: for to will is present with me; but how to perform that which is good I find not. . . . O wretched man that I am! who shall deliver me from the body of this death? (Romans 7:14–24).

Augustine perceived the flesh and the Spirit to be in cosmic tension. Never did he see the triumph of the Spirit over the flesh. He did not understand the legalistic failures of this man nor the complete victory when he surrendered to the love and power of Jesus Christ:

> I thank God through Jesus Christ our Lord. So then with the mind I myself serve the law of God; but with the flesh the law of sin. There is therefore now no condemnation to them which are in Christ Jesus, who walk not after the flesh, but after the Spirit. For the law of the Spirit of life in Christ Jesus hath made me free from the law of sin and death. For what the law could not do, in that it was weak through the flesh, God sending his own Son in the likeness of sinful flesh, and for sin, condemned sin in the flesh: That the righteousness of the law might be fulfilled in us, who walk not after the flesh, but after the Spirit (Romans 8:1–4).

In extant Christian literature Augustine was the first to have proposed the concept that Romans 7:14–24 is a description of a saved man, thus denying the plain import of Scripture. The torment of this man stands in striking contrast with the peace and assurance of God's children so frequently described in Scripture. Not only did Augustine hold Romans seven in the concepts of pagan cosmic tension but he also saw much the same in Galatians chapter five.

> For the flesh lusteth against the Spirit, and the Spirit against the flesh: and these are contrary the one to the other: so that ye cannot do the things that ye would   (Galatians 5:17).

His understanding of this text seemed consistent with what he had deduced from Romans chapter seven. He had ignored the clear testimony of the verses before and after Galatians 5:17.

> This I say then, Walk in the Spirit, and ye shall not fulfill the lust of the flesh. . . . But if ye be led of the Spirit, ye are not under the law   (Galatians 5:16, 18).

It is certain that there is in this passage no mandate for the theological position held by Augustine.

> Now the works of the flesh are manifest, which are these; adultery, fornication, uncleanness, lasciviousness, idolatry, witchcraft, hatred, variance, emulations, wrath, strife, seditions, heresies, envyings, murders, drunkenness, revellings, and such like: of the which I tell you before, as I have told you in time past, *that they which do such things shall not inherit the kingdom of God* (emphasis added). But the fruit of the Spirit is love, joy, peace, longsuffering, gentleness, goodness, faith, meekness, temperance: against such there is no law. And they that are Christ's have crucified the flesh with the affections and lusts. If we live in the Spirit, let us also walk in the Spirit   (Galatians 5:22–25).

Augustine's view of original sin created a dilemma when he considered the Incarnation of Christ. If we were sinners because we were born, it would follow that Christ too was a sinner, for He too was born as we are. Of course, this thought was intolerable. The Bible plainly described Christ as "that holy thing" which was born of Mary (Luke 1:35). Christ could never be described as sinful. Therefore Augustine was forced to conclude by his own logical reasoning that Christ possessed an altogether different nature from that of man. In teaching this view, Augustine postulated that Christ possessed the nature of unfallen man. He thus ignored the plainest evidence of Scripture to the contrary.[1] (Hebrews 2:14–18; 4:15; Romans 1:3). Since Christ was declared to have the human nature of unfallen man, this error led the Catholic Church to espouse the doctrine of the Immaculate Conception, which was fully incorporated into church dogma only in the nineteenth century. This doctrine declared that Mary was born of the Holy Ghost so that she could give birth to a son who possessed an unfallen nature. Thus step by logical step, Augustine's false theology led to the incorporation of numerous unscriptural beliefs into the doctrines of the Roman Catholic Church. Error is never benign. Many of the excesses of the Roman Catholic Church of the Middle Ages flowed forth from these unscriptural doctrines.

But another dilemma arose. Christ was now far removed from man. With Christ's human nature placed above our own, it was difficult to accept Christ as our Mediator since according to Augustine's view, He had not been tempted in the way fallen man was tempted and tested. Neither could there be any expectation that by His power humans could gain victory over sin. Surely if man possessed a nature vastly inferior to the nature in which Christ battled Satan, as Augustine postulated, it would not be possible for man to experience daily victory over sin such as Jesus had on earth. Augustine's inference was that Christ's sinless life was achieved because He held a great advantage over us in that He possessed an unfallen nature, while we were cursed with a fallen nature. Jesus ceased to be truly our example. Jesus thus was not in a position to succor those who are tempted. The Church was compelled to propose mediators other than Jesus. These were men and women who most assuredly did experience and suffer (and yield to) like temptations as we. Mary the mother of Jesus was proclaimed to be a mediator. Numerous saints were created by the Church. These too became recognized as mediators. Upon the priests, who frequently demonstrated themselves to be every bit as given to sin as their parishioners, was bestowed the role of mediator between God and man. One step at a time, the Church, in accepting these pagan concepts, was forced by logical deduction to add error to error in order to substantiate the false premises of Augustine.

---

[1] See Chapter fifteen, The Dilemma of the Human Nature of Christ

It soon became a dictum of the Church that original sin separates man from eternal life. In the very fact of being conceived, man was condemned to eternal torment. These conclusions posed yet another question: How could the guilt of original sin be removed? The church fathers arrived at this solution: By the act of baptism. The question then immediately arose as to the eternal fate of the unbaptized. The answer supplied was terrifying: They were condemned to eternal burning hell. Imagine the impact of such a concept upon parents whose infants had died unbaptized. Infant mortality at the time was high. The anguish of sincere Christian parents of that generation, imagining their children tormented in eternal fire, does not bear contemplation.

The church quickly recognized that it had to supply a solution for this anxiety. Limbo was invented. Limbo certainly was not heaven, but neither was it hell. It was some intermediate place. But even this "solution" did not placate the anguish of the parents. They would never see their little ones again. So the sacrament of infant baptism was introduced as a Catholic dogma. There are extant reports of priests sprinkling water over the abdomens of agonized mothers dying in childbirth and then confidently declaring that both mother and child were assured of heaven.

Though some of Augustine's doctrines had been blunted by Aquinas and Abelard, two theologians of the Middle Ages, most of the theological concepts were still deeply rooted in Catholic theology at the time of the Reformation. Luther reacted more to the excesses of Rome, in the selling of indulgences by Tetzel in an attempt to raise money to complete the building of St. Peter's Basilica, than he did to most of Rome's doctrinal positions. However, out of his study came one of the most beautiful discoveries of Scripture:

The just shall live by faith   (Habakkuk 2:4; Romans 1:17).

Luther had been trained as a monk in the Augustinian monastery at Erfurt. In his own writings he indicated that he had imbibed the words of Augustine before he had so much as set his eyes upon the Scriptures. Thus while Luther was able to throw off almost all the post-Augustinian heresies, he retained many of the Augustinian errors. Luther believed in predestination, "once saved, always saved," the unfallen human nature of Christ, the impossibility for

Christians to consistently obey the law of God, and infant baptism. Thus, in the Protestant reform movement leading to Evangelical Protestantism, Catholicism still retained much influence. Indeed, many of those Augustinian doctrines became more pervasive in the Protestant movement than in Catholicism itself.

Some may ask why the Lutheran church, generally speaking, does not teach predestination today. The answer is simple: after the death of Luther, Melanchthon led the Lutheran community away from predestination. However, John Calvin, the Swiss Reformer who influenced the Dutch Reformed Church, and John Knox, the founder of the Presbyterian Church of Scotland, strongly riveted their Protestantism in predestination. Today throughout many Evangelical communities this doctrine is still key to their concepts of salvation, while the parishioners are almost universally unaware of the Roman Catholic origin of these doctrines. There is no question that Martin Luther led a magnificent Reformation throughout Europe, assisted by other great leaders such as Zwingli, Calvin and Knox. In the plan of God, this Reformation was ever to grow in the unfolding truth to be discovered as God's children marched toward the final climactic events upon the earth.

> But the path of the just is as the shining light, that shineth
> more and more unto the perfect day   (Proverbs 4:18).

The Evangelical community has an urgent responsibility to address the dilemma of its Catholic roots and to discover the human errors that are still inherent in its teachings as a result of its historical development.

THE DILEMMA OF
EVANGELICAL DEVELOPMENT

A s we have indicated, it is usual for evangelical Protestants to trace their roots to the Reformation, especially to that strand of the Reformation that arose out of the teaching of Martin Luther. Calvinism developed its strong roots in doctrines such as predestination, and "once saved, always saved." The adherents of Calvin began to be referred to as the Reform Church. While the Evangelical and Reform traditions continue to remain somewhat separate, there is a blurring of the differences. Modern evangelical theology has tended to merge with Reform theology.

Early after the inception of their faith, Evangelicals held seven basic principles as non-negotiable: (1) They stressed the teaching of the gospel of Jesus Christ as central to their pulpit ministry; (2) They proclaimed that the Scripture is the sole basis of faith and practice; (3) They advocated an active home and foreign missionary outreach that was, by the eighteenth century, to reestablish the concepts of a worldwide Christian thrust; (4) They emphasized that the gospel is justification by faith alone; (5) They preached salvation that is free through the grace of God; (6) They declared an infallible Bible in place of an infallible pope; and (7) They emphasized the priesthood of all believers.

The Reform tradition itself owes much to Luther, for Calvin was greatly influenced by Luther in many areas including total degradation, irresistible grace, "once saved, always saved." These concepts remained strong, especially among hard-core Calvinists even after the Lutheran Church had to a greater extent modified its position. Luther had stressed the sinner's total spiritual impotence and had declared that God's grace is the sole source of faith. He abhorred Erasmus' phrase, "power of applying oneself to grace in Christ," but Melanchthon had striven to uphold the concept of the freedom of the will.

Eventually the Formula of Concord (1595) reaffirmed the total helplessness of humanity and declared that all external calls to salvation reach to all people, and it is possible to fall from grace. These issues were fiercely fought in the latter part of the sixteenth century. Beza, Calvin's pupil, said that Christ died only for the elect. But Beza's pupil, the Dutchman Jacob Arminius, stated that Christ died for all, but that only believers benefit. Grace is not irresistible, and one's actions are necessary for salvation. Thus Arminius presented the concept of salvation that opposed Calvinistic articles of faith. For the last four hundred years or more these two concepts have become the basis of a major division in Protestantism. Those supporting the concepts of Arminius believe that salvation was provided fully and completely through Jesus Christ, but held that man has free will to accept or reject God's proffered salvation.

Those following Calvin's concept, which, as we have seen in the previous chapter, takes its origins from Augustine, bishop of Hippo, believe in total depravity, unconditional election, limited atonement provided for the elect alone, irresistible grace, and the perseverance of the saints. Thus the elect could not be lost irrespective of the patterns of their lives. Works had no part whatsoever in salvation. There were no conditions of redemption. The gospel of salvation involved justification alone. Sanctification, though a good principle, contributed nothing to man's salvation. Rather, it was the evidence of the election of the saints.

Evangelicalism arose in the Church of England during the eighteenth century. John Wesley and others were principally responsible for this movement and thus the Evangelical movement in the Church of England was closely linked with the Methodist movement though it was not part of it, since the evangelical Anglicans remained loyal to the Church of England. It was George Whitefield who introduced the more Calvinistic form of Evangelicalism to the attention of the Anglican movement. In 1846 the Evangelical Alliance (now the World Evangelical Alliance) was formed in London. It included several denominations. It was a reaction led by Anglican Evangelicals to the Catholicizing of the Anglican Church by the Oxford movement begun at Oxford University in the 1830s. The Oxford movement was a vigorous attempt to re-Catholicize the Anglican Church, and probably intended to lead the Church of England back to reunification with the Church of Rome. The goals of that movement soon spread to Cambridge and thus many of the young curates were drawn away from the evangelical goals of the Anglican Church.

The Evangelical Alliance at its formation had eight hundred delegates representing fifty denominations from Europe and America. The American branch of the organization was established in 1867 but later was superseded by the Federal Council of Churches which it had helped establish in 1908. In the 1846 charter, nine doctrines of evangelical Protestantism were enunciated: (1) The divine inspiration, authority and sufficiency of the Scriptures; (2) The right and duty of private judgment in their interpretation; (3) The unity of the Godhead and the trinity of Persons; (4) The utter depravity of human nature; (5) the Incarnation of the Son of God and His atonement for the sins of all men; (6) The justification of sinners by faith alone; (7) The work of the Holy Spirit as sanctifier; (8) The immortality of the soul, the resurrection of the body, and the final judgment of Jesus Christ; and (9) The divine institution of church ministry (*Shorter Oxford Dictionary,* Oxford University Press, 1957, p. 641).

The evangelical revival in the eighteenth century, which flowed over into the nineteenth century, was called Pietism in Europe, Methodism in Britain, and the Great Awakening in America. All these movements rejected church tradition, stressed personal religion, adhered to *sola scriptura,* and denied any reliance upon the sacraments for salvation.

In the early twentieth century, differences between liberal Protestants and fundamental Protestants led to the development of the fundamentalist movement. Fundamentalism developed after World War I, first in the United States where the opposition was mounted against the liberals who attacked the literal inerrancy of Scripture. Indeed, this textual and higher criticism is thought to have its origin among Protestants in some of the theological schools of Germany. But others point out that this modernism began with Catholicism, because Catholic scholars accepted the critical view of the Bible. Pope Leo XIII appeared to encourage these liberal scholars, but then later in his reign condemned this approach. Pope Pius X strongly condemned modernism in 1907. But soon some of these modernist concepts had moved toward Protestantism and were beginning to be taught in Protestant seminaries. The fundamentalist response to this liberal movement soon seemed to merge with the Evangelical movement and often the two words have been used virtually interchangeably.

The National Association of Evangelicals, an interdenominational association in the United States, was formed in 1942. It has usually been seen as an association of conservative Protestant Christians. But over the last thirty years or so a dramatic change has come over the Evangelical movement. It has embraced the Pentecostal and Charismatic movements. It has moved strongly into the ecumenical movement and many Evangelicals are capitulating to the mind set that doctrine should not become an issue and that those things that divide should be put aside so that those things that are in common might be upheld.

It takes little investigation to reveal that every doctrine of the Bible can be seen to be controversial to some significantly large group. While some Evangelicals have stood rigidly opposed to the increasing commonality seen between Roman Catholics and Protestants, the majority of Evangelicals now seem ready to put aside differences of the past in the hope that by the year 2000 we will have unity. Some have even more than casually contemplated a world religion that would incorporate all the pagan religions along with Christianity. Such an association would have been wholly intolerable to Luther and to Calvin. Yet that brand of thinking is increasingly popular and persuasive within the ranks of evangelical Protestantism. All the opposition that has been mounted against it seems to have had little effect upon the major streams of contemporary Evangelicalism. Herein lies a terrible dilemma. There has developed an enormous rift between those faithful to the historic Evangelical movement and those who are capitulating to what many see as the Romanizing of evangelical Protestantism.

THE DILEMMA OF
JUSTIFICATION-ALONE SALVATION

The heart of Luther's enlightenment was the recognition that the gospel teaches that mankind is justified by faith and not by works. This revelation entirely revolutionized Christianity from a false view of salvation, which was built upon the basis of penance and indulgences as a means of obtaining the forgiveness of God and of entering into eternal salvation. This revelation could not have come at a more appropriate time, for in his desperate desire to complete the building of St. Peter's Basilica in Rome, the pope had commissioned Tetzel to sell indulgences in Europe. Not only were these indulgences to cover the sins of the past, but in many cases people were deluded into believing that they would cover the sins committed in the future. With such diabolical and manifest corruption, the hearts of many faithful Christians were crying out for deliverance, and the discovery by Martin Luther of the fundamental truth of salvation was to bring a revival unparalleled in the history of Christianity as men and women broke the shackles of fear and bondage to accept liberty in Christ Jesus.

It took a scholar like Martin Luther, with access to the Scriptures, to understand this principle, not because common people could not understand it, but because the Word of God was virtually unavailable to the common people who had no way of ascertaining truth except through the mouth of the priest. As many of the priests themselves were exceedingly corrupt, and many more ignorant of the Scriptures, there was no way in which the true gospel of Jesus Christ and the free gift of His grace could be understood by men and women. And so in dread and by intimidation many were forced into the payment of large sums of money in the hope of procuring eternal life for themselves or for their deceased loved ones. The fear of hell fire was a constant burden upon their hearts, and many a ruthless priest used this fear mercilessly to force men and women to pay large sums of money to the church to guarantee their salvation. But as if it were not enough, the same fear tactics was used to encourage men and women to extricate their deceased loved ones out of purgatory so that they might have the joy of being transported to heavenly places. Martin Luther, through his study of the Scriptures, liberated millions from such bondage.

The issue of justification by faith became the central theme of the Reformation. It is understandable that many people failed to perceive the proper context of sanctification.

Sanctification was seen through the Roman Catholic doctrine of sacramentalism. The keeping of the seven sacred sacraments was pontificated by the Roman Catholic Church to be essential for salvation. These seven sacred sacraments consist of holy vows, marriage, penance, extreme unction, baptism, confirmation and the Eucharist. Unfortunately, in relating sanctification to sacramentalism the Roman Catholic Church had developed an almost universal view that sanctification is based upon man's work. Certainly sanctification was considered to be an important part of the Christian life and development, and to Luther and other Reformers it went beyond the seven sacred sacraments to include aspects of righteous living. Nevertheless, there is evidence that they were not able to recognize sanctification along with justification as wholly the ministry of Christ for us. Thus it was held that though sanctification is a good principle, it is not part of the gospel of salvation.

Salvation by justification alone became a central pillar of Evangelical Protestantism, and for most Evangelicals today it is still an integral part of their understanding of the gospel. But Evangelicals face a monumental task to prove that sanctification is not part of our qualification for salvation. Indeed, it is impossible to sustain validly this concept from the New Testament. Sanctification is clearly defined in Holy Scripture and cannot be removed from its central place in salvation. Here we are getting to the very heart of Evangelicalism as it faces the difficulty of being unable to sustain what may be the most precious pillar of its foundation.

Geoffrey Paxton, the Australian evangelical theologian, expresses what many Evangelicals believe.

> But the righteousness of faith is not, in whole or in part, the renewal which is present *with* faith. Neither is it that renewal which *follows* faith. The righteousness of faith is never to be

confused with sanctification. It is not sanctification, nor does it include sanctification.   (Geoffrey Paxton, _The Shaking of Adventism,_ p. 45, Zenith Pub. Co., Wilmington, Del, 1977).

With earnestness we want to invite our Evangelical friends to reconsider their belief in a justification-alone salvation. A single Pauline quotation destroys the concept of a justification-alone salvation.

But we are bound to give thanks alway to God for you, breth-ren beloved of the Lord, because God hath from the beginning chosen you to _salvation through sanctification of the Spirit_ and belief of the truth (2 Thessalonians 2:13, emphasis added).

Genuine sanctification is bestowed only when the Holy Spirit directs the life. Another powerful Pauline declaration adds weight to this matter.

But of him are ye in Christ Jesus, who of God is made unto us wisdom, and righteousness, and sanctification, and redemp-tion   (1 Corinthians 1:30).

Remembering that the words _righteous_ and _justify_ come from the same Greek root word, it is demonstrable that Christ came to this earth to provide not only for our justification, but also for our sanctification.

In our youth, as we struggled with the niceties of geometry, we recall that at the end of a theorem or at the end of a geometric problem which we had solved to our satisfaction, and we hoped to that of our teacher, we would end with the letters _Q.E.D._ These letters stood for _quod erat demonstrandum_ which simply means "which was to be demonstrated." If there were no other texts in Holy Writ than these two texts, they would prove beyond any doubt that sanctification is an intimate and integral part of the gospel.

Now the issue of human works arises. What is their relation-ship to sanctification? The Roman Catholic view of sanctification, predicated upon man's works, is not sustainable in the Scriptures. There is not a shred of evidence in the Bible to show that we are sanctified by works. On the contrary, Scripture is emphatic that works play no part whatever as a basis for salvation.

> That in ages to come he might shew the exceeding riches of
> his grace in his kindness toward us through Christ Jesus. For
> by grace are ye saved through faith; and that not of your-
> selves: it is the gift of God   (Ephesians 2:7–8).

Colin recalls listening to an acquaintance deliver the divine service. The preacher made the pronouncement that "To place justification and sanctification together in the gospel is to commit
spiritual adultery." Colin was no less alarmed by the lack of
concern expressed by the congregation than by the words of the
pastor.

At the conclusion of the service, Colin spoke with the pastor,
explaining to him that what he had stated would have been correct
if the faulted view of sanctification held by the preacher had been
correct. He asked Colin what he believed sanctification to be.
Colin responded by saying, "Let us first look at justification.
From your sermon today I perceive you believe that justification
is God's perfect work for man through the death and ministry of
His Son Jesus Christ." Obviously agreeing with that, the pastor
asked Colin for his definition. Colin responded that he too believed in that same wonderful concept of justification, but added,
"It is concerning sanctification that we disagree." Though the
pastor did not say it in overt terms, it was plain that he believed
that sanctification is man's imperfect works for God. The pastor
did not disagree when Colin proposed that definition to him. But
then he asked for Colin's definition of sanctification. Colin replied, "I believe that sanctification, like justification, is God's
perfect work for man through the death and ministry of His Son
Jesus Christ." Many Evangelicals, like that pastor, identify sanctification with the imperfect works of man. There is general agreement in evangelical Protestantism that would accept the concept
that justification is by faith in Jesus Christ alone.

> Therefore being *justified by faith,* we have peace with God
> through our Lord Jesus Christ   (Romans 5:1, emphasis added).

But what most Evangelicals have frequently ignored is the precious truth that just as surely, we are *sanctified* by that same faith
in Jesus Christ. Paul, when making his powerful defense before
King Agrippa, quoted the words of Jesus spoken to him on the
road to Damascus:

> To open their eyes, and to turn them from darkness to light,
> and from the power of Satan unto God, that they may receive
> forgiveness of sins, and inheritance among them which are
> *sanctified by faith* that is in me (Acts 26:18, emphasis added).

The same faith that is essential for our justification is necessary
for our sanctification. There cannot be spiritual adultery in put-
ting together two great aspects of salvation, both of which are
predicated upon the faith of Jesus. But let us go a step further.
Taking into account another Pauline statement concerning justification,

> Much more then, being now *justified by his blood,* we shall
> be saved from wrath through him
> (Romans 5:9, emphasis added).

All Evangelicals agree that we are justified by the blood of Jesus
Christ. His sacrifice alone brings justification to the members of
the human race. But just as surely as we are justified by the death
of our Lord and Saviour Jesus Christ, we are sanctified by that
same death.

> Husbands, love your wives, even as *Christ also loved the*
> *church, and gave himself for it; that he might sanctify and*
> *cleanse it* with the washing of water by the word, that he
> might present it to himself a glorious church, not having spot,
> or wrinkle, or any such thing; but that it should be holy and
> without blemish   (Ephesians 5:25–27, emphasis added).

> Wherefore Jesus also, that he might *sanctify the people with*
> *his own blood,* suffered without the gate
> (Hebrews 13:12, emphasis added).

> By the which will we are *sanctified through the offering of*
> *the body of Jesus Christ* once for all
> (Hebrews 10:10, emphasis added).

The same spilt blood of Jesus that is provided for our pardon and
our forgiveness is also essential for our cleansing and purifying.
We must understand that it is by faith in the blood of Jesus Christ
alone that we can both be justified and sanctified. This truth, so
plainly taught in Scripture, sweeps aside the false view that sanctification is the product of man's works. Most Protestants have
seen works as the *basis* of sanctification rather than the *result* of

sanctification. Without question those who are sanctified by faith will live a life of holiness manifested in obedience to the will of God. Day by day their lives will be surrendered to the dominance of His life.

The indivisible link between justification and sanctification is witnessed throughout the whole of the New Testament. Text after text links the two together. Below is listed a sample of such texts:

> If we confess our sins, he is faithful and just to forgive us our sins [justification], and to cleanse us from all unrighteousness [sanctification]   (1 John 1:9).

> There is therefore now no condemnation to them which are in Christ Jesus [justification], who walk not after the flesh, but after the Spirit [sanctification]   (Romans 8:1).

> For what the law could not do, in that it was weak through the flesh, God sending his own Son in the likeness of sinful flesh, and for sin, condemned sin in the flesh [justification]: that the righteousness of the law might be fulfilled in us, who walk not after the flesh, but after the Spirit [sanctification]
> (Romans 8:3–4).

> Jesus answered, Verily, verily, I say unto thee, Except a man be born of water [justification] and of the Spirit [sanctification], he cannot enter into the kingdom of God   (John 3:5).

Even in the Lord's prayer justification and sanctification are "married" together.

> And forgive us our debts [justification], as we forgive our debtors. And lead us not into temptation, but deliver us from evil [sanctification]: for thine is the kingdom, and the power, and the glory, for ever. Amen   (Matthew 6:12–13).

But the most convincing evidence of the vital role of both justification and sanctification to human salvation is provided in the very last chapter of the last book of the Bible when the final declaration is made concerning the destiny of the inhabitants of the world.

> He that is unjust, let him be unjust still: and he which is filthy, let him be filthy still: and he that is righteous [justified], let him be righteous [justified] still: and he that is holy [sanctified], let him be holy [sanctified] still (Revelation 22:11).

One of the great difficulties in the English language has been the problem of the use of the words *justified* and *righteous* on the one hand, and *sanctified* and *holy* on the other. In the Greek each pair of words is from the same root word. In the English language these pairs appear quite different in their roots and therefore in their spelling. The reason is that English is a hybrid language, incorporating words from many language roots including Old Briton, Latin, Greek, Anglo-Saxon, Jute and French. In most of the romance languages, however, the words *justify* and *righteous* are very similar to each other and the words *sanctification* and *holiness* are closely linked to each other. But it is the Greek in which the New Testament was written that settles the issue. The Greek word most commonly translated "justify" is *dikaioo*. The common word translated "righteous" is *dikaios*. The word *hagiazo* is commonly translated "sanctify" while *hagios* is translated "holy." It is fascinating to note that Revelation 22:11 reads "He that is righteous [*dikaios*], let him be righteous [*dikaioo*] still: and he that is holy [*hagios*], let him be holy [*hagiozo*] still." If this translation were made according to the most common usage, the text would actually read, "He that is righteous, let him be justified still, and he that is holy, let him be sanctified still."

How critical this fact in our understanding of the final declaration of God for His people! Only those who are justified *and* sanctified will be sealed or secured for eternal life. This fact is a very great dilemma for Evangelicals. If we were to hold that all we need for heaven is justification, then it would appear that John was promoting error in this verse. But not the voice of John, but the voice of God is in this declaration. We understand that in taking up the heart of Evangelical concepts of the gospel right from the beginning, we are creating a challenge which no sincere Evangelical can avoid. The Scripture states,

> But the path of the just is as the shining light, that shineth more and more unto the perfect day   (Proverbs 4:18).

It took more than two hundred years for the clear concept of the relationship of justification and sanctification to emerge. The true relationship of sanctification to salvation was strongly proclaimed through the preaching of John Wesley, the British reformer.

Therefore, in summary, let us reiterate the fact that Scripture declares that both justification and sanctification are bestowed through faith in the sacrifice of Jesus. They are inseparable Siamese twins that cannot be rightly torn apart in the understanding of the gospel of salvation. We can draw only one conclusion from the evidence of Scripture, that those who will be saved in the kingdom of God are both justified [pardoned] and sanctified [cleansed of sin].

THE DILEMMA OF
THE OBJECTIVE GOSPEL

T he terms "objective gospel" or "objective salvation" are often used interchangeably. This teaching is linked to the concept of a justification-alone salvation. Well we remember one renowned Evangelical preacher declaring that there is no difference between the drunk in the gutter and the converted man, except that the latter has accepted Christ's salvation. Such a statement indicates the speaker's lack of confidence in the saving grace of God which has transforming power in the life of the Christian. That is the crux of the claim of those promoting an "objective gospel." But such a claim cannot be sustained in the light of Holy Writ. Certainly Scripture does declare that there is no basis either in the works or in the transformed life of the Christian that merits his salvation. Salvation is merited only through the sacrifice of Jesus Christ.[1]

> Neither is there salvation in any other: for there is none other name under heaven given among men, whereby we must be saved (Acts 4:12).

> For by grace are ye saved through faith; and that not of yourselves: it is the gift of God: not of works, lest any man should boast (Ephesians 2:8–9).

But while the only basis of our salvation is the grace of our Saviour, the transformed life is one which loves God and obeys His precepts.

> And shewing mercy unto thousands of them that love me, and keep my commandments (Exodus 20:6).

> Whosoever believeth that Jesus is the Christ is born of God: and every one that loveth him that begat loveth him also that is begotten of him. By this we know that we love the children of God, when we love God, and keep his commandments. For this is the love of God, that we keep his commandments: and his commandments are not grievous (1 John 5:1–3).

---

[1] Evangelicals who proclaim the objective gospel believe that Christ finished His work on Calvary. Tony Campolo, for instance, promotes this concept.

The Scripture is rich in its declaration of the transforming power of the gospel and of the subjective changes in the life of the converted man and woman.

> And such were some of you: but ye are washed, but ye are sanctified, but ye are justified in the name of the Lord Jesus, and by the Spirit of our God   (1 Corinthians 6:11).

> Not by works of righteousness which we have done, but according to his mercy he saved us, by the washing of regeneration, and renewing of the Holy Ghost   (Titus 3:5).

We are assured that Jesus came *to save us from sin,* not in order that we might continue in sin.

> And she shall bring forth a son, and thou shalt call his name Jesus: for he shall save his people from their sins
> (Matthew 1:21).

> What shall we say then? Shall we continue in sin, that grace may abound? God forbid. How shall we, that are dead to sin, live any longer therein?   (Romans 6:1–2).

Paul asserts that the power of the gospel is not unto unrighteousness but unto righteousness.

> For I am not ashamed of the gospel of Christ: for it is the power of God unto salvation to every one that believeth; to the Jew first, and also to the Greek. For therein is the righteousness of God revealed from faith to faith: as it is written, The just shall live by faith. For the wrath of God is revealed from heaven against all ungodliness and unrighteousness of men, who hold the truth in unrighteousness   (Romans 1:16–18).

Salvation is not apart from nor separate from the transformation of man from sin unto righteousness, and from iniquity unto a godly character.

There are many subjective conditions that are set forth in order that we may receive the free gift of the saving sacrifice of Jesus Christ. Some of these conditions are presented below.

> For godly sorrow worketh repentance to salvation not to be repented of: but the sorrow of the world worketh death
> (2 Corinthians 7:10).

That if thou shalt confess with thy mouth the Lord Jesus, and shalt believe in thine heart that God hath raised him from the dead, thou shalt be saved. For with the heart man believeth unto righteousness; and with the mouth confession is made unto salvation   (Romans 10:9–10).

Wherefore, my beloved, as ye have always obeyed, not as in my presence only, but now much more in my absence, work out your own salvation with fear and trembling. For it is God which worketh in you both to will and to do of his good pleasure   (Philippians 2:12–13).

But we are bound to give thanks alway to God for you, brethren beloved of the Lord, because God hath from the beginning chosen you to salvation through sanctification of the Spirit and belief of the truth   (2 Thessalonians 2:13).

For the grace of God that bringeth salvation hath appeared to all men, teaching us that, denying ungodliness and worldly lusts, we should live soberly, righteously, and godly, in this present world   (Titus 2:11–12).

There are those who declare that to place obedience to the commandments of God within the saving acts of God or as a condition of salvation is to be guilty of legalism. Typical of this viewpoint among Evangelicals is this assertion:

Nothing can be more unscriptural in itself, or more pernicious to the souls of men, than the substitution of the gracious work of the Spirit *in* us, for the vicarious work of Christ *for* us as the ground of our pardon and acceptance with God
(James Buchanan, *The Doctrine of Justification,* p. 401).

The problem with the above analysis is that it presents the work of the Holy Spirit in us in contrast to the work of Christ for us. This author has wholly failed to recognize that the gift of Calvary encompasses both the justifying work of Christ for us *and* His sanctifying work in all who believe. How else can we understand the following texts?

And being made perfect, he became the author of eternal salvation unto all them that obey him   (Hebrews 5:9).

> For the time is come that judgment must begin at the house of
> God: and if it first begin at us, what shall the end be of them
> that obey not the gospel of God?   (1 Peter 4:17).

> Here is the patience of the saints: here are they that keep the
> commandments of God, and the faith of Jesus
> (Revelation 14:12).

It is not legalism to humbly obey God's commandments in love to
our Saviour (John 14:15), for countless Scriptures admonish such
obedience under the power of the Holy Spirit. Legalism is the
belief that one's good works *earn* us salvation, thus taking credit
for that which Christ alone has accomplished for us.

Sadly, in a majority of pulpits, pastors are confidently assur-
ing their parishioners that they not only may, but will be saved in
their sins. It is not that these pastors are directly encouraging sin
in the lives of their church members, but they frequently assert
that to hold to any concept that suggests that God's people will
have day-by-day victory through the power of the indwelling Christ
is to deny the free gift of salvation. That assertion is wholly
erroneous, for the free gift of salvation includes not only the
forgiveness of our sins, but also the power to resist the temptations of Satan, thus resulting in a life of purity and of good works.

It is a sad commentary on the present state of Christianity,
that all too many pastors themselves fall into great sin; and in
some cases, their congregations, blinded by the theological principles that these pastors have espoused, are willing to continue to
accept the ministry of profane and unconverted men. We deal
with the issue of the saving grace of Jesus Christ but we often
forget the very meaning of the word *converted.* Conversion is not
simply an objective heavenly record, though that is a reality; the
very word entails a transformation, a metamorphosis from a life
of sin, selfishness, and rebellion to a life of harmony with God,
selflessness, and righteousness.

Thus conversion accomplishes, not a mere modification of
one's former life, but a total transformation; for the Holy Spirit
now dwells within and empowers the life. There are those who
claim that unless we persistently and deliberately reject the salva-

tion of Christ we will all be saved. They place no emphasis upon the acceptance of salvation, the acceptance of the ministry of Christ in the life.

The chief editor of the New International Version (NIV) of the Bible illustrates this view when he states that the NIV "shows that great error which is so prevalent today in some orthodox Protestant circles, namely the error that regeneration depends upon faith . . . and that in order to be born again man must first accept Jesus as Savior" (Edwin Palmer, *The Holy Spirit,* p. 83). But such a view is not sustained by God's Word.

> How shall we escape, if we neglect so great salvation; which at the first began to be spoken by the Lord, and was confirmed unto us by them that heard him   (Hebrews 2:3).

The very words of Jesus Himself demand a response from the individual.

> And the Spirit and the bride say, Come. And let him that heareth say, Come. And let him that is athirst come. And whosoever will, let him take the water of life freely
> (Revelation 22:17).

There must be an active acceptance of Christ and His power in our lives before we can be saved. There is much cheap "grace," easy "salvation" in evangelical Protestantism today. But that kind of "salvation" certainly was not taught by Jesus.

> Then said Jesus unto his disciples, Verily I say unto you, That a rich man shall hardly enter into the kingdom of heaven. And again I say unto you, It is easier for a camel to go through the eye of a needle, than for a rich man to enter into the kingdom of God. When his disciples heard it, they were exceedingly amazed, saying, Who then can be saved?
> (Matthew 19:23–25).

> Then said one unto him, Lord, are there few that be saved? And he said unto them, Strive to enter in at the strait gate: for many, I say unto you, will seek to enter in, and shall not be able   (Luke 13:23–24).

> Not every one that saith unto me, Lord, Lord, shall enter into the kingdom of heaven; but he that doeth the will of my Father which is in heaven   (Matthew 7:21).

What is difficult for many Christians to understand is that while salvation is wholly of God through Christ, and that we are not in any way saved by our own works of righteousness, nevertheless true salvation brings the revitalizing of the character.

> Not by works of righteousness which we have done, but according to his mercy he saved us, by the washing of regeneration, and renewing of the Holy Ghost   (Titus 3:5).

> For by grace are ye saved through faith; and that not of yourselves: it is the gift of God: not of works, lest any man should boast. For we are his workmanship, created in Christ Jesus unto good works, which God hath before ordained that we should walk in them   (Ephesians 2:8–10).

For salvation to be authentic there are accompanying good works.

> But, beloved, we are persuaded better things of you, and things that accompany salvation, though we thus speak. For God is not unrighteous to forget your work and labour of love, which ye have shewed toward his name, in that ye have ministered to the saints, and do minister. And we desire that every one of you do shew the same diligence to the full assurance of hope unto the end: that ye be not slothful, but followers of them who through faith and patience inherit the promises
> (Hebrews 6:9–12).

> Wherefore lay apart all filthiness and superfluity of naughtiness, and receive with meekness the engrafted word, which is able to save your souls. But be ye doers of the word, and not hearers only, deceiving your own selves. For if any be a hearer of the word, and not a doer, he is like unto a man beholding his natural face in a glass: for he beholdeth himself, and goeth his way, and straightway forgetteth what manner of man he was. But whoso looketh into the perfect law of liberty, and continueth therein, he being not a forgetful hearer, but a doer of the work, this man shall be blessed in his deed. If any man among you seem to be religious, and bridleth not his tongue, but deceiveth his own heart, this man's religion is vain. Pure religion and undefiled before God and the Father is this, To visit the fatherless and widows in their affliction, and to keep himself unspotted from the world   (James 1:21–27).

But Scripture does present objective truths:

(1) Jesus died to save the world.

> And said unto the woman, Now we believe, not because of thy saying: for we have heard him ourselves, and know that this is indeed the Christ, the Saviour of the world   (John 4:42).

> And if any man hear my words, and believe not, I judge him not: for I came not to judge the world, but to save the world
> (John 12:47).

> For God sent not his Son into the world to condemn the world; but that the world through him might be saved
> (John 3:17).

(2) God's grace is exceedingly abundant to every sinner.

> For if by one man's offence death reigned by one; much more they which receive abundance of grace and of the gift of righteousness shall reign in life by one, Jesus Christ. . . . Moreover the law entered, that the offence might abound. But where sin abounded, grace did much more abound
> (Romans 5:17, 20).

> And the grace of our Lord was exceeding abundant with faith and love which is in Christ Jesus   (1 Timothy 1:14).

(3) God's love for the whole human race is unconditional.

> For God so loved the world, that he gave his only begotten Son, that whosoever believeth in him should not perish, but have everlasting life   (John 3:16).

> For if, when we were enemies, we were reconciled to God by the death of his Son, much more, being reconciled, we shall be saved by his life   (Romans 5:10).

> The Lord hath appeared of old unto me, saying, Yea, I have loved thee with an everlasting love: therefore with lovingkind-ness have I drawn thee   (Jeremiah 31:3).

> Behold, what manner of love the Father hath bestowed upon us, that we should be called the sons of God: therefore the world knoweth us not, because it knew him not   (1 John 3:1).

(4) Man is justified and sanctified through the blood of Jesus.

> Much more then, being now justified by his blood, we shall be saved from wrath through him   (Romans 5:9).

> Wherefore Jesus also, that he might sanctify the people with
> his own blood, suffered without the gate   (Hebrews 13:12).

> By the which will we are sanctified through the offering of
> the body of Jesus Christ once for all   (Hebrews 10:10).

These objective truths, however, require the subjective response
of each individual before salvation can become a reality. The
objective aspects of the gospel are never divorced from the subjective aspects. Thus Evangelicals have rightly noted these truly
objective truths of salvation, but have failed to acknowledge that
the gospel is not complete without the subjective experiences of
salvation. We must remind ourselves of these crucial texts:

> And being made perfect, he became the author of eternal
> salvation unto all them that obey him   (Hebrews 5:9).

> For the grace of God that bringeth salvation hath appeared to
> all men, teaching us that, denying ungodliness and worldly
> lusts, we should live soberly, righteously, and godly, in this
> present world   (Titus 2:11–12).

> But we are bound to give thanks alway to God for you, breth-
> ren beloved of the Lord, because God hath from the beginning
> chosen you to salvation through sanctification of the Spirit
> and belief of the truth   (2 Thessalonians 2:13).

> Wherefore, my beloved, as ye have always obeyed, not as in
> my presence only, but now much more in my absence, work
> out your own salvation with fear and trembling. For it is God
> which worketh in you both to will and to do of his good
> pleasure   (Philippians 2:12–13).

> For godly sorrow worketh repentance to salvation not to be
> repented of: but the sorrow of the world worketh death
>   (2 Corinthians 7:10).

> For with the heart man believeth unto righteousness; and with
> the mouth confession is made unto salvation   (Romans 10:10).

The transformation of life brought by the gospel is wonderfully
demonstrated in the experience of Zacchaeus. Zacchaeus had lived
a life of selfishness, of deceit and of dishonesty. But when confronted with the call of Jesus upon his life, Zacchaeus' transformation was evident to all who were present.

> And Zacchaeus stood, and said unto the Lord; Behold, Lord, the half of my goods I give to the poor; and if I have taken any thing from any man by false accusation, I restore him fourfold. And Jesus said unto him, This day is salvation come to this house, forsomuch as he also is a son of Abraham. For the Son of man is come to seek and to save that which was lost   (Luke 19:8–10).

The demonstration by Zacchaeus was consistent with the message of Paul.

> And being made perfect, he became the author of eternal salvation unto all them that obey him   (Hebrews 5:9).

None of us will be saved unless the love of Christ is in our heart. This love will be manifest in our love for our fellow men, and in works of righteousness. Without these there is no salvation. The concept that salvation is purely an objective act accomplished on Calvary and recorded in the books of heaven, falls short of the glorious concepts that are taught in the Word of God. Thus it is said of Jesus:

> That he would grant unto us, that we being delivered out of the hand of our enemies might serve him without fear, in holiness and righteousness before him, all the days of our life. And thou, child, shalt be called the prophet of the Highest: for thou shalt go before the face of the Lord to prepare his ways; to give knowledge of salvation unto his people by the remission of their sins, through the tender mercy of our God; whereby the dayspring from on high hath visited us, to give light to them that sit in darkness and in the shadow of death, to guide our feet into the way of peace   (Luke 1:74–79).

Salvation will not come to men and women unless they have the Holy Spirit in their lives. This salvation is built upon their love of the truth and their submission to the indwelling power of the grace of God.

To give eternal life and a heavenly home to those who persist in sin would be to thwart the plan of salvation, which is designed to rid the universe of sin and sinners. God never manipulates. At His coming He will not force a sinner into sinlessness. We may

seek God's power to overcome sin only in these days of probation. God in His wisdom gives us the choice. For those who will
to obey, He supplies the power.

The foundation of our salvation is devoid of any contribution
of our own; nevertheless God's plan for His people is the purifi-
cation of their hearts so that their heavenly citizenship will be
assured. No unregenerate sinner will ever enter the kingdom of
heaven.

The transforming power of God's grace was abundantly seen
in the life of our maternal grandfather, John Bailey (1865–1949).
For well over half a century Grandfather strenuously opposed
God's call upon His life. His violent Irish temper was exacerbated
by his heavy alcohol consumption. Our dear grandmother, Alice,
a faithful servant of God, suffered much domestic persecution for
her faith until her death in 1942. But God is not willing that any
should perish, and in 1947, Grandfather yielded his life to his
heavenly Father. As teenage lads, we lived with him, since our
parents cared for Grandfather. What a change of character the
Holy Spirit wrought in his life! He even remembered for the very
first time that his grandsons had a birthday. Our memory is of a
loving Grandfather and our praise goes to our God.

THE DILEMMA OF
FORENSIC JUSTIFICATION

Many terms have been used to describe justification as an objective act of God, independent from any subjective human element. Believing this doctrine, men proclaim that neither confession nor repentance, neither belief nor the new birth experience nor any response whatever from humans is required before justification is appropriated to every human. Terms used include: forensic, judicial, legal, universal, corporate and temporary justification. Those who believe in a forensic justification adamantly reject the concept that justification in any way refers to being "made righteous." The proponents of forensic justification hold that the justified one is "accounted righteous" or "declared righteous" through the death of Jesus Christ. Proponents of this view usually state that when Jesus died we were all in Christ, and all were legally justified. Manifestly if our justification was bestowed two thousand years ago, no subjective element could be involved.

If our God were to justify us and grant us salvation against our will, He would be a manipulator of man's conscience. The very fact that sin entered heaven is proof beyond dispute that God grants freedom of the will to all.

There can be no question that justification is God's perfect work for man through the death and ministry of His Son Jesus Christ. True Christians believe in that concept. Most agree that there is no merit in any human works. But does justification take place irrespective of the transformation of the life of the individual? It must be kept in mind that those who are advocating forensic justification are proclaiming that salvation is granted by justification *alone*. Thus it is held that there is no subjective element necessary for our salvation. This belief creates a serious dilemma. Taking the concepts of forensic justification together with justification-alone salvation, we are forced to conclude that universally all humanity was saved by the death of Christ on Calvary. We must then reckon with the concepts of universalism, which would logically argue that ultimately every human being will be saved. But the Bible insists that the majority of mankind will be lost.

> Enter ye in at the strait gate: for wide is the gate, and broad is the way, that leadeth to destruction, and many there be which go in thereat: because strait is the gate, and narrow is the way, which leadeth unto life, and few there be that find it
> (Matthew 7:13–14).

> Marvel not at this: for the hour is coming, in the which all that are in the graves shall hear his voice, and shall come forth; they that have done good, unto the resurrection of life; and they that have done evil, unto the resurrection of damnation (John 5:28–29).

> And whosoever was not found written in the book of life was cast into the lake of fire (Revelation 20:15).

Some, who recognize that in the light of these and many other texts there can be no concept of universal salvation, have postulated that the only way we can lose salvation is to reject persistently and consciously the justification that was accomplished on Calvary. In so doing, they reject any aspect of salvation that requires active acceptance of the saving grace of Jesus Christ. But while the Bible presents a salvation that is freely offered, that salvation can be appropriated only by the acceptance or receiving of that salvation.

> And if it seem evil unto you to serve the Lord, choose you this day whom ye will serve; whether the gods which your fathers served that were on the other side of the flood, or the gods of the Amorites, in whose land ye dwell: but as for me and my house, we will serve the Lord (Joshua 24:15).

> And Elijah came unto all the people, and said, How long halt ye between two opinions? if the Lord be God, follow him: but if Baal, then follow him (1 Kings 18:21).

> And the Spirit and the bride say, Come. And let him that heareth say, Come. And let him that is athirst come. And whosoever will, let him take the water of life freely
> (Revelation 22:17).

> For if by one man's offence death reigned by one; much more
> they which receive abundance of grace and of the gift of
> righteousness shall reign in life by one, Jesus Christ
>   (Romans 5:17).

Let it not be forgotten that the five foolish virgins lost salvation,
yet they still earnestly desired it. The Bible states that even after
the door of mercy was closed they still sought entry to God's
kingdom.

> Afterward came also the other virgins, saying, Lord, Lord,
> open to us. But he answered and said, Verily I say unto you, I
> know you not   (Matthew 25:11–12).

They lost salvation because they failed to meet the heart conditions God in His wisdom has set for the receipt of His grace. They
did not lose salvation because they willfully and persistently rejected salvation. This fact is true of many Christians who will fail
to receive eternal life.

> Not every one that saith unto me, Lord, Lord, shall enter into
> the kingdom of heaven; but he that doeth the will of my
> Father which is in heaven. Many will say to me in that day,
> Lord, Lord, have we not prophesied in thy name? and in thy
> name have cast out devils? and in thy name done many won-
> derful works? And then will I profess unto them, I never
> knew you: depart from me, ye that work iniquity
>   (Matthew 7:21–23).

These texts in no way negate the truth that God has chosen each
of us. But as in any covenant or contract, both sides must ratify
the agreement. There are those who proclaim that there are no
conditions for the reception of salvation. But the Bible is rich in
examples of the conditions for the bestowal of salvation.

> Blessed is the man that endureth temptation: for when he is
> tried, he shall receive the crown of life, which the Lord hath
> promised to them that love him   (James 1:12).

> Hearken, my beloved brethren. Hath not God chosen the poor
> of this world rich in faith, and heirs of the kingdom which he
> hath promised to them that love him?   (James 2:5).

But as it is written, Eye hath not seen, nor ear heard, neither have entered into the heart of man, the things which God hath prepared for them that love him   (1 Corinthians 2:9).

For since the beginning of the world men have not heard, nor perceived by the ear, neither hath the eye seen, O God, beside thee, what he hath prepared for him that waiteth for him
(Isaiah 64:4).

Henceforth there is laid up for me a crown of righteousness, which the Lord, the righteous judge, shall give me at that day: and not to me only, but unto all them also that love his appearing   (2 Timothy 4:8).

For God so loved the world, that he gave his only begotten Son, that whosoever believeth in him should not perish, but have everlasting life   (John 3:16).

And they said, Believe on the Lord Jesus Christ, and thou shalt be saved, and thy house   (Acts 16:31).

For as the heaven is high above the earth, so great is his mercy toward them that fear him   (Psalm 103:11).

Like as a father pitieth his children, so the Lord pitieth them that fear him   (Psalm 103:13).

But if we walk in the light, as he is in the light, we have fellowship one with another, and the blood of Jesus Christ his Son cleanseth us from all sin   (1 John 1:7).

And, behold, one came and said unto him, Good Master, what good thing shall I do, that I may have eternal life? And he said unto him, Why callest thou me good? there is none good but one, that is, God: but if thou wilt enter into life, keep the commandments   (Matthew 19:16–17).

Blessed are they that keep his testimonies, and that seek him with the whole heart. They also do no iniquity: they walk in his ways   (Psalm 119:2–3).

But the mercy of the Lord is from everlasting to everlasting upon them that fear him, and his righteousness unto children's children; to such as keep his covenant, and to those that remember his commandments to do them (Psalm 103:17–18).

> Not by works of righteousness which we have done, but according to his mercy he saved us, by the washing of regeneration, and renewing of the Holy Ghost   (Titus 3:5).

Thus Scripture sets forth many subjective conditions for the provision of salvation. As seen above these include enduring temptation, love to God, waiting for God's coming, loving Christ's appearing, belief in Christ, fearing God, walking in the light, keeping the commandments, seeking God with the whole heart, doing no iniquity, walking in God's ways and being washed by the washing of regeneration.

The confusion comes because of an unwarranted extrapolation from the truth. The truth makes it wholly evident that Jesus died for the sins of the whole world.

> And he is the propitiation for our sins: and not for ours only, but also for the sins of the whole world   (1 John 2:2).

> Herein is love, not that we loved God, but that he loved us, and sent his Son to be the propitiation for our sins
> (1 John 4:10).

> And we have seen and do testify that the Father sent the Son to be the Saviour of the world   (1 John 4:14).

It is the will of God that all men be saved.

> Who will have all men to be saved, and to come unto the knowledge of the truth   (1 Timothy 2:4).

> The Lord is not slack concerning his promise, as some men count slackness; but is longsuffering to us-ward, not willing that any should perish, but that all should come to repentance
> (2 Peter 3:9).

The concept of forensic justification falls short of the gospel in the light of the very message that Jesus preached.

> Now after that John was put in prison, Jesus came into Galilee, preaching the gospel of the kingdom of God, and saying, The time is fulfilled, and the kingdom of God is at hand: repent ye, and believe the gospel   (Mark 1:14–15).

There are subjective elements to salvation.

He that covereth his sins shall not prosper: but whoso
confesseth and forsaketh them shall have mercy
(Proverbs 28:13).

If we confess our sins, he is faithful and just to forgive us our
sins, and to cleanse us from all unrighteousness (1 John 1:9).

The concept of a salvation that does not involve the least confession, repentance and forsaking of sin is an empty gospel that
cannot be sustained from the Word of God, nor can it lead men
and women into the eternal fellowship of God. It is a most dangerous deception, for it convinces men and women that their salvation is assured while they are yet in their sins. Surely Evangelicals
must soberly address the fateful consequences of such a teaching.

THE DILEMMA OF
UNCONDITIONALITY

I
t is a common practice among many Evangelicals to emphasize that salvation is unconditional; that all humanity was
saved corporately on Calvary. But such a conclusion is so
contrary to scriptural evidence that it is hard to understand how
so many texts of the clearest and most unequivocal nature could
be put aside to hold such a view. Many offer a single text as the
basis for this conclusion.

> Therefore as by the offence of one judgment came upon all
> men to condemnation; even so by the righteousness of one the
> free gift came upon all men unto justification of life
> (Romans 5:18).

When Romans 5:18 is read in context, it provides powerful evidence against the notion of unconditional salvation. Salvation is
provided to those only who receive (or accept) it. This is set forth
plainly in Romans 5:17.

> For if by one man's offence death reigned by one; much more
> they which *receive* abundance of grace and of the gift of
> righteousness shall reign in life by one, Jesus Christ
> (Romans 5:17, emphasis added).

The implication of this text is that those who choose not to receive
the grace of God and the gift of righteousness, will not reign with
Christ. As indicated, at first glance it may appear that Romans
5:18 supports the concept that all humanity was saved uncondi-
tionally on Calvary. The Bible frequently talks in these universali-
ties, showing that God has done everything possible for the salvation of the human race. For example:

> For therefore we both labour and suffer reproach, because we
> trust in the living God, who is the Saviour of all men, spe-
> cially of those that believe   (1 Timothy 4:10).

Texts such as these have provided superficial support for the
Universalists who believe that everyone will be saved. Some even
believe that Lucifer and his evil angels will ultimately be saved.
But those who accept the plain words of Scripture discover that

neither Satan and his evil angels nor unregenerate human beings will be saved. An understanding of the words of Jesus spoken just prior to His crucifixion assist us to understand how we may apply texts such as Romans 5:18.

> Now is the judgment of this world: now shall the prince of this world be cast out. And I, if I be lifted up from the earth, will draw all men unto me   (John 12:31–32).

Manifestly Christ's death on Calvary did not grant salvation to any one. Rather it provided the opportunity to all mankind to accept God's merciful salvation, and exhibited such matchless love for every individual that every searching soul in beholding Christ, and Him crucified, is drawn to Him.

Not all have been drawn to God, but provision has been made through the grace of God and the sacrifice of Jesus *for* all men. This understanding must not be misinterpreted. There are conditions of salvation. One has but to read the best-known and most beloved text of the Scripture to understand this fact.

> For God so loved the world, that he gave his only begotten Son, that whosoever believeth in him should not perish, but have everlasting life   (John 3:16).

Salvation is not opened to all, but it is open to those who believe on Jesus. Genuine belief incorporates thorough repentance.

> I tell you, Nay: but, except ye repent, ye shall all likewise perish   (Luke 13:3).

When Jesus preached the gospel of the kingdom, He combined belief and repentance together as the basis of the acceptance of His salvation.

> Now after that John was put in prison, Jesus came into Galilee, preaching the gospel of the kingdom of God, and saying, The time is fulfilled, and the kingdom of God is at hand: repent ye, and believe the gospel   (Mark 1:14–15).

Many state correctly that good works provide no basis for man's salvation, and in no way does humanity merit his salvation. This truth is uncontestable, for there is no basis nor foundation for salvation other than the death and ministry of our Lord and Saviour Jesus Christ. Well might we question the role of good works in salvation. God details conditions that have been laid down which point man to take hold of the free gift of salvation. These conditions add nothing to the merit of Jesus Christ. They are not the ground for man's salvation; for man could contribute nothing because of his sinful and degraded life. For some, this provides a divine paradox. But like all the biblical mysteries it is founded in and upon the infinite knowledge, wisdom and truthfulness of God. Generations of Christians have asserted that salvation is assured to those who love Jesus with the whole heart. This truth is undeniable. Scripture verifies the truth that love is the great condition of salvation.

> Blessed is the man that endureth temptation: for when he is tried, he shall receive the crown of life, which the Lord hath promised to them that love him   (James 1:12).

> Hearken, my beloved brethren, Hath not God chosen the poor of this world rich in faith, and heirs of the kingdom which he hath promised to them that love him?   (James 2:5).

> But as it is written, Eye hath not seen, nor ear heard, neither have entered into the heart of man, the things which God hath prepared for them that love him   (1 Corinthians 2:9).

Thus the Bible does not teach a conditionless salvation. Indeed, Christ taught in the parable of the pearl of great price that to possess Christ is to receive the free gift which costs our all. This appears to be paradoxical. Those who indicate that we have nothing to do other than to accept the gift are not consistent nor in harmony with divine revelation. We must love Christ fully or salvation is not our possession. The love of Christ can be manifested only when we have allowed the Holy Spirit to take from our lives the love of self and the love of the world. Some Christians have, in accepting the condition of love for Christ, entirely misunderstood what such love entails. In this way they have expressed a sentimental attachment to their Saviour, believing that a life that does not conform with His example is still compatible with meeting the condition of love. No concept could be more misleading and damaging to the Christian's blessed hope. We shall examine other conditions for salvation as laid down in the Scripture, in order to explore the real meaning of that love for Christ which meets the great condition.

Paul's words cited above are taken from the words of Isaiah. Isaiah sets out another condition which is synonymous with love.

> For since the beginning of the world men have not heard, nor perceived by the ear, neither hath the eye seen, O God, beside thee, what he hath prepared for him that waiteth for him
>   (Isaiah 64:4).

Thus to truly love Christ requires diligent expectancy of Christ's return. Paul verifies this truth.

> Henceforth there is laid up for me a crown of righteousness, which the Lord, the righteous judge, shall give me at that day: and not to me only, but unto all them also that love his appearing   (2 Timothy 4:8).

Commitment to Christ presupposes a dedicated desire to see the Lord return. It cannot be said of a man that he truly loves Christ unless he wholeheartedly believes in Him. Love without true belief is not love at all. Thus belief is set forth as a condition of salvation.

> And they said, Believe on the Lord Jesus Christ, and thou shalt be saved, and thy house   (Acts 16:31).

Now we must again keep in mind the all-encompassing nature of true belief.

> Whosoever believeth that Jesus is the Christ is born of God: and every one that loveth him that begat loveth him also that is begotten of him. By this we know that we love the children of God, when we love God, and keep his commandments. For this is the love of God, that we keep his commandments: and his commandments are not grievous. For whatsoever is born of God overcometh the world: and this is the victory that overcometh the world, even our faith. Who is he that overcometh the world, but he that believeth that Jesus is the Son of God?   (1 John 5:1–5).

The devils have counterfeited every divine virtue. They have a counterfeit belief; but it will not save them.

> Thou believest that there is one God; thou doest well: the devils also believe, and tremble   (James 2:19).

In the text quoted earlier (1 John 5:1–5) it will be noted that genuine belief includes seven elements, without which belief would be counterfeit. The elements are:

1. The new birth experience
2. Love to God
3. Love to our fellow man
4. Keeping the commandments
5. Overcoming the world
6. Victory in the life
7. Faith

To possess merely an intellectual assent to the fact that Jesus died for the sins of the world is of no more value as a condition for salvation than is the belief that the devils possess.

Further, no one meets the great condition unless he fears [obeys] God. Therefore the very first words of God's everlasting gospel are "Fear God" (Revelation 14:7). Such fear is consistently defined in the Old Testament in terms of obedience.

> And he said, Lay not thine hand upon the lad, neither do thou any thing unto him: for now I know that thou fearest God, seeing thou hast not withheld thy son, thine only son from me
> (Genesis 22:12).

> That thou mightest fear the Lord thy God, to keep all his statutes and his commandments, which I command thee, thou, and thy son, and thy son's son, all the days of thy life; and that thy days may be prolonged   (Deuteronomy 6:2).

> Therefore thou shalt keep the commandments of the Lord thy God, to walk in his ways, and to fear him (Deuteronomy 8:6).

> And now, Israel, what doth the Lord thy God require of thee, but to fear the Lord thy God, to walk in all his ways, and to love him, and to serve the Lord thy God with all thy heart and with all thy soul, to keep the commandments of the Lord, and his statutes, which I command thee this day for thy good?
> (Deuteronomy 10:12–13).

No chapter of Scripture so emphatically explores the condition of fearing God more than does the one-hundred-third Psalm. Just examine three of these verses.

> For as the heaven is high above the earth, so great is his
> mercy toward them that fear him   (Psalm 103:11).

> Like as a father pitieth his children, so the Lord pitieth them
> that fear him   (Psalm 103:13).

> But the mercy of the Lord is from everlasting to everlasting
> upon them that fear him, and his righteousness unto children's
> children   (Psalm 103:17).

Other conditions, each further illuminating the meaning of true
love for Jesus, are set forth in Scripture. Only two of these are
illustrated below.

(1) To walk as Christ walked:

> But if we walk in the light, as he is in the light, we have
> fellowship one with another, and the blood of Jesus Christ his
> Son cleanseth us from all sin   (1 John 1:7).

(2) To serve Jesus with the whole heart:

> And Samuel said unto the people, Fear not; ye have done all
> this wickedness: yet turn not aside from following the Lord,
> but serve the Lord with all your heart   (1 Samuel 12:20).

Many Christians joyfully embrace one or other of the conditions
as set forth in Scripture while tragically relying upon a limited
perception of one condition to excuse the meeting of other conditions. Indeed one condition above all others is ignored by the
majority of Christians, and that is obedience to God's commandments.

As youths we were walking down the main street of our city,
Newcastle, Australia, when we happened upon a band of very
zealous folk preaching on the street corner. These good people
called themselves Gospel Fishermen. The recurring theme of the
speaker was the great promise, "Believe on the Lord Jesus Christ
and thou shalt be saved" (Acts 16:31). Often the speaker urged,
"Only believe." One cannot doubt that his assurance was true, for
Scripture surely sets this forth as a condition for salvation. After
some time one of the assistants came over to us and commenced
to labor with us. When we indicated that we believed that true
Christians would keep the commandments of God and gave as our

evidence Revelation 14:12, the text suddenly enraged the evange-list. He started away from us claiming that to keep the law was to go to hell. But the Scripture clearly places this matter in another light.

> If ye love me, keep my commandments   (John 14:15).

> And the dragon was wroth with the woman, and went to make war with the remnant of her seed, which keep the com-mandments of God, and have the testimony of Jesus Christ
> (Revelation 12:17).

> Here is the patience of the saints: here are they that keep the commandments of God, and the faith of Jesus
> (Revelation 14:12).

> Blessed are they that do his commandments, that they may have right to the tree of life, and may enter in through the gates into the city   (Revelation 22:14).

The dialogue between Christ and the rich young ruler explains the centrality of commandment-keeping to the life of the saints.

> And, behold, one came and said unto him, Good Master, what good thing shall I do, that I may have eternal life? And he said unto him, Why callest thou me good? there is none good but one, that is, God: but if thou wilt enter into life, keep the commandments   (Matthew 19:16–17).

Some have presented an interpretation of Matthew 19:16–17 in a way which does not do justice to its meaning. This school of thought suggests that Jesus set before this young man an unattain-able goal in order to bring him to a full dependence upon Christ for salvation. Such an interpretation does violence to Scripture. It cannot be denied that Christ sought to destroy this young man's self-reliance and point him to Himself as the only hope for salva-tion. However, in urging obedience, Christ was promising its real-ity if he would abrogate self entirely. To suggest that Christ expected this man to continue in sin would be to deny the possibil-ity of full reliance upon Christ. The whole concept has neither logical nor scriptural merit. To accept such a premise would be to deny the possibility of meeting the great condition for the power of the indwelling Christ. If we cannot keep the commandments, then by the testimony of John 14:15 we cannot love Christ. Obedience to the law, and love of Jesus, are synonymous terms. To obey means to love and to love means to obey. Yet how many claim love without obedience. Today too many say, Well, we can't obey. What we must do is to serve Jesus with our whole heart. Such people do not perceive that to serve Jesus is to obey Him.

> Blessed are they that keep his testimonies, and that seek him
> with the whole heart. They also do no iniquity: they walk in
> his ways   (Psalm 119:2–3).

A wholehearted relationship with Jesus encompasses a life of love and obedience. The above scripture assures us that walking in Jesus' way indicates a Spirit-filled obedience. The same is true of those who fear God.

> But the mercy of the Lord is from everlasting to everlasting
> upon them that fear him, and his righteousness unto children's
> children; to such as keep his covenant, and to those that
> remember his commandments to do them (Psalm 103:17–18).

The gentleman who many years ago in Newcastle urged upon us the need to "only believe," was denying that such belief involves obedience, and thus was proposing a counterfeit belief. That such a counterfeit exists is made plain in the Scriptures. As we documented earlier,

> The devils also believe, and tremble   (James 2:19).

Since the devils have no hope whatever of salvation, their faith must be a formal belief which does not guarantee salvation. Full commandment-keeping, though not the basis of salvation, is a condition of salvation, and so we return to the great condition. Equally it may be stated that obedience is the great condition to be fitted for heaven; for obedience to, and love for God are synonymous virtues. Frequently in Scripture these two conditions are emphasized together. They are even enshrined in the Decalogue itself as great conditions in the second commandment.

> And showing mercy unto thousands of them that love me, and
> keep my commandments   (Exodus 20:6).

No true believer can validly deny the possibility of complete obedience (which is love for God) as an essential condition to heavenly fitness. To deny is either to misunderstand God's precious mercy or to make His sacrifice on Calvary ineffective for our lives. For Calvary provides both forgiveness for repentant sinners and power to live victoriously. In the book of Deuteronomy these two great conditions, either separately or unitedly are upheld before literal Israel several times.

> Know therefore that the Lord thy God, he is God, the faithful God, which keepeth covenant and mercy with them that love him and keep his commandments to a thousand generations
> (Deuteronomy 7:9).

> Therefore thou shalt love the Lord thy God, and keep his charge, and his statutes, and his judgments, and his commandments, alway   (Deuteronomy 11:1).

> Ye shall walk after the Lord your God, and fear him, and keep his commandments, and obey his voice, and ye shall serve him, and cleave unto him   (Deuteronomy 13:4).

> If thou shalt keep all these commandments to do them, which I command thee this day, to love the Lord thy God, and to walk ever in his ways; then shalt thou add three cities more for thee, beside these three   (Deuteronomy 19:9).

> Thou hast avouched the Lord this day to be thy God, and to walk in his ways, and to keep his statutes, and his commandments, and his judgments, and to hearken unto his voice
> (Deuteronomy 26:17).

> The Lord shall establish thee an holy people unto himself, as he hath sworn unto thee, if thou shalt keep the commandments of the Lord thy God, and walk in his ways
> (Deuteronomy 28:9).

As Joshua spoke to God's people he brought together many aspects of the great condition. These requirements are no less to be found in spiritual Israel than they were in literal Israel.

> But take diligent heed to do the commandment and the law,
> which Moses the servant of the Lord charged you, to love the
> Lord your God, and to walk in all his ways, and to keep his
> commandments, and to cleave unto him, and to serve him
> with all your heart and with all your soul   (Joshua 22:5).

God in His immeasurable love for us has not left us in the least
doubt as to His requirements. The elements of the plan of salvation are simple. We have sinned, the wages of which is eternal
death. Nothing we can ever do after the commission of our first
sin can ever merit salvation or contribute to it in any way. Had
God's love not provided His Son as our substitute, our lives
would be hopeless, irrespective of the quality of the course of our
lives subsequent to the first sin. But God did make freely available to all, salvation through the merits of Christ. However, there
are conditions for our salvation, which are met through the power
of the indwelling Christ in our lives. While these provide no merit
or basis for man's salvation, we cannot be saved without them.

> And this is love, that we walk after his commandments. This
> is the commandment, That, as ye have heard from the begin-
> ning, ye should walk in it   (2 John 6).

For this condition too God provides. Without His power we cannot in the least serve or obey Him. Thus not only is the merit for
the provision of salvation all His, but so too is all the power for
meeting the great condition. Thus Jesus not only demonstrates His
infinite love to the universe through His death, but provides the
divine power to prove that man united with divinity can keep all
of God's divine precepts. The meeting of these conditions on earth
is a sacred testimony to the saving power of the perfect life that
our Saviour lives out in the experience of every son and daughter
of God.

THE DILEMMA OF
THE "IN CHRIST" MOTIF

F or many Evangelicals the "in Christ" motif is the central theme of the apostle Paul's theology. It is true that on a significant number of occasions Paul uses the term "in Christ."

Salute Andronicus and Junia, my kinsmen, and my fellow prisoners, who are of note among the apostles, who also were *in Christ* before me   (Romans 16:7, emphasis added).

And was unknown by face unto the churches of Judaea which were *in Christ*   (Galatians 1:22, emphasis added).

Therefore if any man be *in Christ,* he is a new creature: old things are passed away; behold, all things are become new
      (2 Corinthians 5:17, emphasis added).

For he hath made him to be sin for us, who knew no sin; that we might be made the righteousness of God *in him*
      (2 Corinthians 5:21, emphasis added).

The issue of the "in Christ" motif revolves around the belief that Adam was responsible for the guilt of all men and Jesus is responsible for the salvation of all men, and that human consent plays no part in either.

For as in Adam all die, even so in Christ shall all be made alive   (1 Corinthians 15:22).

Nevertheless death reigned from Adam to Moses, even over them that had not sinned after the similitude of Adam's transgression, who is the figure of him that was to come. But not as the offence, so also is the free gift. For if through the offence of one many be dead, much more the grace of God, and the gift by grace, which is by one man, Jesus Christ, hath abounded unto many. And not as it was by one that sinned, so is the gift: for the judgment was by one to condemnation, but the free gift is of many offences unto justification. For if by one man's offence death reigned by one; much more they which receive abundance of grace and of the gift of righteousness shall reign in life by one, Jesus Christ. Therefore as by

> the offence of one judgment came upon all men to condemna-
> tion; even so by the righteousness of one the free gift came
> upon all men unto justification of life   (Romans 5:14–18).

It is frequently argued that the whole human race was in Adam
when he sinned because each one of us is a genetic descendant of
Adam. It is further argued that in a mysterious way, when Jesus
died on the cross we were all in Christ so that "in Christ" we paid
the penalty for our sins. This concept is blasphemy. The Scripture
does not confirm it nor imply it. When we look at the fifth chapter
of Romans used as a basis for this theology we read,

> But God commendeth his love toward us, in that, while we
> were yet sinners, Christ died for us   (Romans 5:8).

> For if, when we were enemies, we were reconciled to God by
> the death of his Son, much more, being reconciled, we shall
> be saved by his life   (Romans 5:10).

Each passage clearly states that Christ died that we might be
reconciled to God so that the love of God might be understood by
each one of us and that Jesus might be our sin bearer. In no more
beautiful way is this truth expressed than in the fifty-third chapter
of Isaiah:

> But he was wounded for our transgressions, he was bruised
> for our iniquities: the chastisement of our peace was upon
> him; and with his stripes we are healed   (Isaiah 53:5).

In no way, actually, genetically, or mystically, did we have anything to do with the price paid for our redemption. To imply that
we were in Christ mystically when He died so that in that sense
we paid the penalty for our own sins is surely an abomination and
blasphemy. Inevitably the term "in Christ" is used to refer to
justification. Paul and other Bible writers also refer to the "Christ
in" concept. Nevertheless, the "Christ in" concept is seen by many
Evangelicals as outside the saving grace of Jesus. Let us look
more closely at this whole situation. What was Paul talking about
when he talked about "in Christ"?

> Therefore if any man be in Christ, he is a new creature: old
> things are passed away; behold, all things are become new
> (2 Corinthians 5:17).

The dilemma of Evangelicals who emphasize the "in Christ" motif, is that Paul does not talk about the objective gospel that they also espouse, but rather he explains that if we are *in Christ* we are new creatures, the old habits are passed away, and we are now in newness of life. There must be an entire transformation of character, a total subjective change of heart. This fact surely demonstrates the completeness of the new-birth experience. Paul also identifies the "Christ in" concept as central to salvation.

> To whom God would make known what is the riches of the glory of this mystery among the Gentiles; which is *Christ in you,* the hope of glory: whom we preach, warning every man, and teaching every man in all wisdom; that we may present every man perfect *in Christ Jesus*
> (Colossians 1:27–28, emphasis added).

It will be seen that Paul, in this reference, uses both *Christ in* and *in Christ* as essential and complementary aspects of salvation. One cannot be "in Christ" if Christ is not in him. Similarly the reverse is equally true.

There is no appropriate way in which the concepts of *in Christ* and *Christ in* can be separated one from another, any more than justification and sanctification can be separated. Thus Christ in His discourses frequently placed the two concepts together.

> He that eateth my flesh, and drinketh my blood, dwelleth *in me,* and *I in him* (John 6:56, emphasis added).

> Even the Spirit of truth; whom the world cannot receive, because it seeth him not, neither knoweth him: but ye know him; for *he dwelleth with you, and shall be in you*
> (John 14:17, emphasis added).

> At that day ye shall know that I am in my Father, and *ye in me, and I in you* (John 14:20, emphasis added).

> *Abide in me, and I in you.* As the branch cannot bear fruit of itself, except it abide in the vine; no more can ye, except ye abide in me (John 15:4, emphasis added).

> If *ye abide in me, and my words abide in you,* ye shall ask what ye will, and it shall be done unto you
> (John 15:7, emphasis added).

> *I in them, and thou in me,* that they may be made perfect in
> one, and that the world may know that thou hast sent me, and
> hast loved them, as thou hast loved me
> > (John 17:23, emphasis added).

Not only does John record these significant statements of Jesus,
but he himself emphasized them in his first epistle.

> And he that keepeth his commandments *dwelleth in him, and*
> *he in him.* And hereby we know that he abideth in us, by the
> Spirit which he hath given us (1 John 3:24, emphasis added).

> Hereby know we that we *dwell in him, and he in us,* because
> he hath given us of his Spirit. And we have seen and do
> testify that the Father sent the Son to be the Saviour of the
> world. Whosoever shall confess that Jesus is the Son of God,
> *God dwelleth in him, and he in God.* And we have known and
> believed the love that God hath to us. God is love; and he that
> dwelleth in love *dwelleth in God and God in him*
> > (1 John 4:13–16, emphasis added).

Paul emphasizes the "in Christ" concept, and he also emphasizes
the "Christ in" you concept. In his beautiful way he says,

> But now *in Christ Jesus* ye who sometimes were far off are
> made nigh by the blood of Christ
> > (Ephesians 2:13, emphasis added).

This same beautiful message is seen when Paul speaks concerning
"Christ in" us:

> For it is God which worketh *in you* both to will and to do of
> his good pleasure   (Philippians 2:13, emphasis added).

> But ye are not in the flesh, but in the Spirit, if so be that the
> Spirit of God dwell *in you.* Now if any man have not the
> Spirit of Christ, he is none of his
> > (Romans 8:9, emphasis added).

> I am crucified with Christ: nevertheless I live; yet not I, but
> *Christ liveth in me:* and the life which I now live in the flesh I
> live by the faith of the Son of God, who loved me, and gave
> himself for me   (Galatians 2:20, emphasis added).

Frequently the argument of Paul in the book of Hebrews is used. Paul states that Levi, yet unborn, was in the loins of Abraham when Abraham returned tithe to Melchisedec. Paul uses this fact as a basis for demonstrating that the High Priestly ministry of Melchisedec was a higher ministry than the Levitical priesthood. It is an interesting argument, and it does reflect upon the thinking of the Israelites in their relationship of forebear to descendant. But it is a text which cannot be used to claim that all humanity was *in Christ* when He died. Nor is it possible to use this text to teach the error that each one bore the penalty for his or her sins *in Christ* on Calvary. Every evidence of the Scripture declares that Christ was alone when He bore that penalty. No one else shared the unbelievable anguish of that moment.

> I have trodden the winepress alone; and of the people there was none with me: for I will tread them in mine anger, and trample them in my fury; and their blood shall be sprinkled upon my garments, and I will stain all my raiment
>
> (Isaiah 63:3).

If we were to say that we were all "in Christ" and we paid the penalty, then Jesus did not pay the penalty alone. It took the perfect Son of God to die for each one of us—the Righteous for the unrighteous, the Guiltless for the guilty, the Sinless for the sinner, the Just for the unjust, the Holy for the unholy.

Tragically the belief that we were *in Christ* when He died leads to the concept that every human being was justified and saved on Calvary. While there are those who claim that we can lose that salvation by rejecting it, there is no evidence in such a gospel that we have to actively accept the salvation that God has offered to us. Yet the words of Scripture are clear that we need not reject salvation to lose it, we need only to neglect it.

> How shall we escape, if we neglect so great salvation; which at the first began to be spoken by the Lord, and was con- firmed unto us by them that heard him   (Hebrews 2:3).

In the illustration of the vine and the branch of John 15, we have a special picture of the situation. Those who are in a saving rela- tionship with Jesus are both *in Christ* as well as possessing *Christ in them,* through the indwelling of the Holy Spirit. The vine and branch are both in each other, and when they are separated the branch is destined to die. And so it is with salvation. An undue emphasis on the *in Christ* motif, dissociating this concept from "Christ in" us, is an imbalance and a denial of the fullness of the role of Christ in the plan of salvation. Such a limitation of the provisions of Christ's sacrifice can lead only to many souls being lost from the kingdom of heaven. Eternity is at stake. This is not a trivial matter nor a nicety of theological debate, it is a matter of eternal life and eternal destination.

THE DILEMMA OF
THE CONCEPT OF ORIGINAL SIN

T he concept of original sin was popularized in Augustinian theology. This concept held that we not only inherited the weakness of Adam and the natural tendency and inevitable inclination to follow into pathways of sin, but we are also actually condemned for the sin of Adam.

> The early Church Fathers contained nothing very definite about original sin. . . . It is especially in Augustine that the doctrine of original sin comes to fuller development. According to him the nature of man, both physical and moral, is totally corrupted by Adam's sin, so that he cannot do otherwise than sin. This inherited corruption of original sin is a moral punishment for the sin of Adam   (Louis Berkof, *Systematic Theology,* Grand Rapids, Michigan, Erdmanns Publishing, pp. 244, 245).

> Natural man has true freedom to choose between several alternatives, although, given his condition as a sinner subject to concupiscence, and as a member of this "mass of damnation," all the alternatives open to him are sin. The option not to sin does not exist   (Justo L. Gonzalez, *A History of Christian Thought,* vol. 2, Nashville: Abingdon Press, 1971, p. 44).

The Jesuit professor, Dr. Peter de Rosa, has recorded that,

> In this, Gregory [Pope Gregory VI] took St. Paul literally: "In Adam all have sinned." This means from the first moment of a person's existence there is guilt. This is not a personal taint, but a taint of nature and so unavoidable. The nature derives from the parents. From the beginning the baby's soul is polluted by this original, this inherited sin. Gregory was not blind to the problems this raised. For example, parents were cleansed from original sin in baptism. How could they hand on original sin to their babies? He answers: Though holy themselves, they handed on corrupt nature by sex, desire galvanized by lust. Babies are born as the damned fruit of the lust of their redeemed parents. From the first they are the offspring of Gehenna or Hell; they are justly children of wrath because they are sinners. If they die unbaptized, they are

condemned to everlasting torments for the guilt of their birth
alone. Existence is itself a state of sin; to be born is to be
qualified for eternal punishment
(Peter de Rosa, *Vicars of Christ,* Corgi Books, 1989, p. 452).

There is no question that when Adam sinned, death passed upon
all men.

For all have sinned, and come short of the glory of God
(Romans 3:23).

When Adam and Eve sinned, their unfallen nature was changed to
a fallen nature in which was inscribed on every cell of their
bodies, death; for every cell and the body itself were destined to
death. That fallen nature has been inherited by all their progeny,
so that outside of the return of Jesus Christ, the resurrection of the
faithful dead, and the transformation that will take place at the
Second Coming of Jesus, all humanity is destined to eternal
oblivion.

For this corruptible must put on incorruption, and this mortal
must put on immortality. So when this corruptible shall have
put on incorruption, and this mortal shall have put on immortality, then shall be brought to pass the saying that is written,
Death is swallowed up in victory   (1 Corinthians 15:53–54).

There are those who strongly argue that we sin because we are
sinners. That is the logical deduction of the principle of original
sin. But the Bible does not sustain such a premise. Rather the
Bible insists that our guilt results from our own acts of sin.

Then it shall be, because he hath sinned, and is guilty
(Leviticus 6:4).

For whosoever shall keep the whole law, and yet offend in
one point, he is guilty of all. For he that said, Do not commit
adultery, said also, Do not kill. Now if thou commit no adultery, yet if thou kill, thou art become a transgressor of the law
(James 2:10–11).

John puts it simply in the clearest definition possible.

Whosoever committeth sin transgresseth also the law: for sin
is the transgression of the law   (1 John 3:4).

Paul, recognizing that we can only keep the commandments of God by the faith of Jesus, declared:

> And he that doubteth is damned if he eat, because he eateth not of faith: for *whatsoever is not of faith is sin*
> (Romans 14:23, emphasis added).

Now God is just. If we sin through ignorance it is not accounted to us as sin.

> Therefore to him that knoweth to do good, and doeth it not, to him it is sin (James 4:17).

> And the times of this ignorance God winked at; but now commandeth all men every where to repent: Because he hath appointed a day, in the which he will judge the world in righteousness by that man whom he hath ordained; whereof he hath given assurance unto all men, in that he hath raised him from the dead (Acts 17:30–31).

Jesus Himself fully endorsed such a concept.

> Jesus said unto them, If ye were blind, ye should have no sin: but now ye say, We see; therefore your sin remaineth
> (John 9:41).

> If I had not come and spoken to them, they had not had sin: but now they have no cloke for their sin (John 15:22).

If all humanity have the sin of Adam, then Jesus could never have uttered these words, for surely all would be guilty of sin irrespective of their ignorance. We must be thankful that we serve a compassionate God. God has compassion upon those who are ignorant.

> Who can have compassion on the ignorant, and on them that are out of the way; for that he himself also is compassed with infirmity (Hebrews 5:2).

If that ignorance has been the result of deliberate negligence of the principles of God, then there is no mercy.

> How shall we escape, if we neglect so great salvation; which at the first began to be spoken by the Lord, and was confirmed unto us by them that heard him (Hebrews 2:3).

All members of the human race had wandered away from
God and therefore were outside of the provisions of salvation. We
would all be lost had not God, through Christ, intervened in our
behalf.

> All we like sheep have gone astray; we have turned every one
> to his own way; and the Lord hath laid on him the iniquity of
> us all   (Isaiah 53:6).

> As it is written, There is none righteous, no, not one
>   (Romans 3:10).

> But we are all as an unclean thing, and all our righteousnesses
> are as filthy rags; and we all do fade as a leaf; and our
> iniquities, like the wind, have taken us away   (Isaiah 64:6).

These texts in no wise confirm the concept of original sin. They
simply recognize cause and effect. Because we are born with
sinful natures, we are destined to rebel against God, choose the
way of Satan, and accumulate our own life of sin, requiring the
saving grace of Christ to redeem us from the punishment we so
justly deserve. All human beings are born with a sinful human
nature—a nature that is attracted to sin. Even when converted and
surrendered to Christ we still possess this nature. But through the
power of Christ it is subdued and we live in the power of the
Spirit.

> Knowing this, that our old man is crucified with him, that the
> body of sin might be destroyed, that henceforth we should not
> serve sin. For he that is dead is freed from sin
>   (Romans 6:6–7).

> For the law of the Spirit of life in Christ Jesus hath made me
> free from the law of sin and death   (Romans 8:2).

When Christ gathers His saints to His kingdom, our nature is
transformed into a sinless nature.

> For this corruptible must put on incorruption, and this mortal
> must put on immortality. So when this corruptible shall have
> put on incorruption, and this mortal shall have put on immor-
> tality, then shall be brought to pass the saying that is written,
> Death is swallowed up in victory   (1 Corinthians 15:53–54).

It is not the nature that we have that will determine our eternal destiny. Our eternal destiny is determined by the acceptance of Christ; and as we confess and repent of our sins, Christ forgives; and as we lay hold on His power we gain victory over the temptations of Satan. This requires a daily resubmission of our lives to God, requiring the first moments of our waking time to rededicate our lives to Christ and call upon Him for power so that as the day continues in that power, we can have victory over Satan.

> Submit yourselves therefore to God. Resist the devil, and he will flee from you   (James 4:7).

Contrast the situations of the wicked and the righteous in terms of the carnal mind and the spiritual mind. While both the wicked and the righteous continue to have a sinful nature, those with the carnal mind are slaves to that nature and cannot in this state gain victory over sin. Indeed most do not have the desire to do so. Those with a spiritual mind have daily surrendered their lives and their wills to Jesus Christ and have gained victory over sin. While we retain the carnal mind we cannot find victory. That is why the man of Romans 7 had such a failed experience.

> For we know that the law is spiritual: but I am carnal, sold under sin. For that which I do I allow not: for what I would, that do I not; but what I hate, that do I   (Romans 7:14–15).

In the same passage of Scripture Paul clarifies the destiny of those who retain a carnal mind on the one hand, and of those who have allowed Christ to develop within them a spiritual mind on the other hand.

> For to be carnally minded is death; but to be spiritually minded is life and peace. Because the carnal mind is enmity against God: for it is not subject to the law of God, neither indeed can be. So then they that are in the flesh cannot please God. But ye are not in the flesh, but in the Spirit, if so be that the Spirit of God dwell in you. Now if any man have not the Spirit of Christ, he is none of his. And if Christ be in you, the body is dead because of sin; but the Spirit is life because of righteousness. But if the Spirit of him that raised up Jesus from the dead dwell in you, he that raised up Christ from the dead shall also quicken your mortal bodies by his Spirit that dwelleth

in you. Therefore, brethren, we are debtors, not to the flesh, to live after the flesh. For if ye live after the flesh, ye shall die: but if ye through the Spirit do mortify the deeds of the body, ye shall live. For as many as are led by the Spirit of God, they are the sons of God   (Romans 8:6–14).

No text more quickly destroys the original sin concept than those texts which declare that no one will be lost for someone else's sin. When Moses expressed his willingness to be blotted out of the book of life if it could save the children of Israel, God's answer was explicit.

And Moses returned unto the Lord, and said, Oh, this people have sinned a great sin, and have made them gods of gold. Yet now, if thou wilt forgive their sin—; and if not, blot me, I pray thee, out of thy book which thou hast written. And the Lord said unto Moses, Whosoever hath sinned against me, him will I blot out of my book   (Exodus 32:31–33).

The prophet Ezekiel sets forth exactly the same principle.

The soul that sinneth, it shall die. The son shall not bear the iniquity of the father, neither shall the father bear the iniquity of the son: the righteousness of the righteous shall be upon him, and the wickedness of the wicked shall be upon him
(Ezekiel 18:20).

The human race has not inherited the guilt of Adam, because each person is responsible for his own sin. He neither bears the guilt of another nor does another bear his guilt, except it be Christ who bore the guilt of sinners upon Calvary. To teach otherwise is to diminish man's own guilt, and has the effective result of absolving man from the responsibility to avail himself of the fullness of the power of the gospel to seek God's full restoration of moral strength.

THE DILEMMA OF
PREDESTINATION

The concept of the divine predestination of the saved was central to the theology of Augustine. It proved to be a very tenacious and powerful error in Catholicism and subsequently in Protestantism. Unquestionably the prestige of Luther and Calvin, both of whom espoused this doctrine, is such that modern-day adherents to this doctrine believe that it has strong Protestant roots. There are biblical texts which, on superficial reading, seem to support the Augustinian concept. Such texts, if they did in fact support the notion of predestination, would contradict the overwhelming testimony of Scripture which emphasizes human choice as essential to the reception of God's saving grace. God, however, is not the author of confusion. Scripture is *never* contradictory.

John Calvin, himself, acknowledged the unanswered questions of the doctrine of predestination.

> If it be evidently the result of the Divine will, that salvation is freely offered to some, and others are prevented from attaining it—this immediately gives rise to important and difficult questions, which are incapable of any other explanation, than by the establishment of pious minds in what ought to be received concerning election and predestination—a question, in the opinion of many, full of perplexity; for they consider nothing more unreasonable, than that, to the common mass of mankind, some should be predestinated to salvation and others to destruction (John Calvin, *Institutes of the Christian Religion,* Vol. III, p. 140).

Calvin believed this was the reason some did not have the gospel preached to them, while others rejected the gospel when they heard it. He could not grasp the import that those who reject the gospel do so because of a conscious decision, nor could he understand that God judges the heathen who have not heard the gospel according to their response to the Holy Spirit's promptings.

> For when the Gentiles, which have not the law, do by nature
> the things contained in the law, these, having not the law, are
> a law unto themselves: which shew the work of the law writ-
> ten in their hearts, their conscience also bearing witness, and
> their thoughts the mean while accusing or else excusing one
> another   (Romans 2:14–15).

In dealing with the predestinarian dilemma we must also look at
its concomitant concept of "once saved, always saved." This concept states that once we are saved by Christ we can never lose
that salvation. Here are some of the texts that have been used to
support this Augustinian concept.

> Having predestinated us unto the adoption of children by Jesus
> Christ to himself, according to the good pleasure of his will
>   (Ephesians 1:5).

> In whom also we have obtained an inheritance, being predes-
> tinated according to the purpose of him who worketh all things
> after the counsel of his own will   (Ephesians 1:11).

> What then? Israel hath not obtained that which he seeketh
> for; but the election hath obtained it, and the rest were blinded
>   (Romans 11:7).

> And except that the Lord had shortened those days, no flesh
> should be saved: but for the elect's sake, whom he hath cho-
> sen, he hath shortened the days   (Mark 13:20).

In examining these texts we want to do two things. First, we want
to examine the way in which Scripture uses the words *chosen,
election,* and *predestination;* and then evaluate those texts which
make it plain that God is not an arbitrary God, a God who manipulates the human race. He is a God who has given to man
reason and decision-making capacities, the ability to choose, to
accept and to reject. We understand this clearly in everyday life,
but God has not limited our ability to choose and decide to the
common activities of life. This gift pertains also to the capacity of
each person to choose Christ or Satan as his Lord, to decide to
follow a course of right or wrong, to believe truth or error, to
accept salvation or destruction, eternal life or eternal death. Once
a choice is made for Christ it affects even the smallest decisions
of life. Our choice for Christ will affect what we eat and drink, it

will affect the clothes we wear, it will affect the kind of car we purchase, it will affect how we use our money and how we use our discretionary time. It affects our conversation and what we read. Indeed there is nothing that is not affected by our surrender to Jesus Christ. Some of the many texts which bear significant relevance to this issue demand examination.

> He that killeth an ox is as if he slew a man; he that sacrificeth a lamb, as if he cut off a dog's neck; he that offereth an oblation, as if he offered swine's blood; he that burneth incense, as if he blessed an idol. Yea, they have chosen their own ways, and their soul delighteth in their abominations. I also will choose their delusions, and will bring their fears upon them; because when I called, none did answer; and when I spake, they did not hear: but they did evil before mine eyes, and chose that in which I delighted not (Isaiah 66:3–4).

Men who do wrong have *chosen* their own ways. As a result the Lord permits delusions to come upon them. He has called them but they have not responded, for they continue to choose to do evil. This is the basic understanding of God's calling and His choosing. God calls but He chooses only those who obey Him. He rejects all those who have rejected His call upon their lives. Thus Jesus could say,

> So the last shall be first, and the first last: for many be called, but few chosen   (Matthew 20:16).

> For many are called, but few are chosen   (Matthew 22:14).

The biblical concept of election is a concept that is built upon the *conditions* of salvation. As we have emphasized earlier, those conditions save no man, for we are saved only by the death, resurrection and ministry of Jesus Christ. But human choices decide whether or not the free salvation of God is accepted in the life. That is consistent with the promise that God gave to the eunuchs in the days of the prophet Isaiah.

> For thus saith the Lord unto the eunuchs that keep my sabbaths, and choose the things that please me, and take hold of my covenant; Even unto them will I give in mine house and

within my walls a place and a name better than of sons and of
daughters: I will give them an everlasting name, that shall
not be cut off   (Isaiah 56:4–5).

This truth parallels Paul's explanation to the Roman believers.

And he that searcheth the hearts knoweth what is the mind of
the Spirit, because he maketh intercession for the saints according to the will of God. 28 And we know that all things
work together for good to them that love God, to them who
are called according to his purpose. 29 For whom he did
foreknow, he also did predestinate to be conformed to the
image of his Son, that he might be the firstborn among many
brethren. 30 Moreover whom he did predestinate, them he
also called: and whom he called, them he also justified: and
whom he justified, them he also glorified (Romans 8:27–30).

Verse 28 expresses one of the conditions of God's calling. It is a
calling to those who love God. It is also noted in verse 29 that
these calls are made according to the foreknowledge of God. Now
theologians have debated for centuries over the issue of foreknowledge as opposed to predestination. There are those who
claim that if God has foreknowledge, then He has total control,
for the destiny of God cannot be otherwise. But indeed foreknowledge in no way demands that God has intervened or made an
arbitrary decision in terms of the human race. Foreknowledge
simply recognizes that God knows how every human being will
respond to His free gift of salvation and to the ministry of the
Holy Spirit. Such foreknowledge does not imply a causal relationship where God determines or ordains the fate of His creation.
Judas did not have to betray Christ. He chose through his own
decision-making powers to betray his Lord and Saviour. He had
not responded to the full dominance of Christ's love in his life.

Yet our God who sees the future as clearly as He sees the
past and the present, knew from the days of eternity. Thus the
Lord could prophesy Judas' fateful decision.

Yea, mine own familiar friend, in whom I trusted, which did
eat of my bread, hath lifted up his heel against me
                                                (Psalm 41:9).

But as we read Christ's loving pleas to Judas we can but recognize that as with all humanity, Christ treated Judas as if He did not possess such foreknowledge. Only our God could demonstrate such love. Another example of human choice is witnessed through the record of Paul.

> For Demas hath forsaken me, having loved this present world, and is departed unto Thessalonica   (2 Timothy 4:10).

Demas chose the love of this present world above the love of God. It was his personal decision. God most certainly did not impose that choice upon him. Christ has chosen the entire human race, but we still must make our choice to accept His calling. When Jesus told the disciples that He had chosen them, He included Judas with the rest of the disciples, but tragically Judas did not fully respond to Him.

> Ye have not chosen me, but I have chosen you, and ordained you, that ye should go and bring forth fruit, and that your fruit should remain: that whatsoever ye shall ask of the Father in my name, he may give it you (John 15:16).

The concept that Christ ordained some to eternal salvation and others to eternal destruction is a false theory built upon pagan concepts of a god in total and unwavering control. This concept leaves the human race without power to decide or to choose. God gives us unequivocal evidence that we must make choices along the pathway to salvation. This power of decision is His gift to us.

> And Elijah came unto all the people, and said, How long halt ye between two opinions? If the Lord be God, follow him: but if Baal, then follow him   (1 Kings 18:21).

> And if it seem evil unto you to serve the Lord, choose you this day whom ye will serve; whether the gods which your fathers served that were on the other side of the flood, or the gods of the Amorites, in whose land ye dwell: but as for me and my house, we will serve the Lord   (Joshua 24:15).

Jesus opens his heart to all men.

> In the last day, that great day of the feast, Jesus stood and cried, saying, If *any man* thirst, let him come unto me, and drink   (John 7:37, emphasis added).

> Come unto me, *all* ye that labor and are heavy laden, and I
> will give you rest   (Matthew 11:28, emphasis added).

In the sermon on the mount, Jesus specifies the choices that we
must make. Our decisions determine whether we accept the free
gift of God's salvation.

> Enter ye in at the strait gate: for wide is the gate, and broad is
> the way, that leadeth to destruction, and many there be which
> go in thereat: because strait is the gate, and narrow is the
> way, which leadeth unto life, and few there be that find it
> (Matthew 7:13–14).

> Not every one that saith unto me, Lord, Lord, shall enter into
> the kingdom of heaven; but he that doeth the will of my
> Father which is in heaven. Many will say to me in that day,
> Lord, Lord, have we not prophesied in thy name? and in thy
> name have cast out devils? and in thy name done many won-
> derful works? And then will I profess unto them, I never
> knew you: depart from me, ye that work iniquity
> (Matthew 7:21–23).

It will be noted that those who have failed to receive the gift of
eternal life will be those who continue to sin. The sin and live
theology that is so prevalent in Evangelicalism today is certainly
the deception of Satan as he seeks to gather all whom he can
under his banner. The promises of God are too clear. God has not
preordained some to eternal salvation, while others are capri-
ciously condemned to eternal destruction.

> Wherefore he is able also to save them to the uttermost that
> come unto God by him, seeing he ever liveth to make inter-
> cession for them   (Hebrews 7:25).

> The Lord is not slack concerning his promise, as some men
> count slackness; but is longsuffering to us-ward, not willing
> that any should perish, but that all should come to repentance
> (2 Peter 3:9).

> And the Spirit and the bride say, Come. And let him that
> heareth say, Come. And let him that is athirst come. And
> whosoever will, let him take the water of life freely
> (Revelation 22:17).

When we understand these things, we can understand the wonderful counsel of Peter in his second letter.

> According as his divine power hath given unto us all things that pertain unto life and godliness, through the knowledge of him that hath called us to glory and virtue. Whereby are given unto us exceeding great and precious promises: that by these ye might be partakers of the divine nature, having escaped the corruption that is in the world through lust. And beside this, giving all diligence, add to your faith virtue; and to virtue knowledge; and to knowledge temperance; and to temperance patience; and to patience godliness; and to godliness brotherly kindness; and to brotherly kindness charity. For if these things be in you, and abound, they make you that ye shall neither be barren nor unfruitful in the knowledge of our Lord Jesus Christ. But he that lacketh these things is blind, and cannot see afar off, and hath forgotten that he was purged from his old sins. Wherefore the rather, brethren, give diligence to make your calling and election sure: for if ye do these things, ye shall never fall: for so an entrance shall be ministered unto you abundantly into the everlasting kingdom of our Lord and Saviour Jesus Christ   (2 Peter 1:3–11).

Here is recorded what is sometimes called Peter's ladder. A careful examination of this text leads to the conclusion that if we do not "climb" this ladder we will lose our calling and election and fail to obtain eternal life. Peter's ladder, in many ways, is similar to the fruit of the Spirit.

> But the fruit of the Spirit is love, joy, peace, longsuffering, gentleness, goodness, faith, meekness, temperance: against such there is no law. And they that are Christ's have crucified the flesh with the affections and lusts   (Galatians 5:22–24).

If we do not grow in these Christian attributes we are blind, we have forgotten to be purged from our sins, and Peter calls for diligence to make our calling and election sure, that we might attain of everlasting life. If God predetermined our lives it would be worthless for Peter to offer the advice given. Now we can understand Paul's and Peter's concept of election. Paul cites the condition of election.

> Paul, a servant of God, and an apostle of Jesus Christ, accord-
> ing to the faith of God's elect, and the acknowledging of the
> truth which is after godliness   (Titus 1:1).

Faith, truth and godliness—there is no election without these char-
acteristics. In God's power they must be exercised by the believers. To the church in Colosse Paul wrote,

> Put on therefore, as the elect of God, holy and beloved, bow-
> els of mercies, kindness, humbleness of mind, meekness,
> longsuffering; forbearing one another, and forgiving one an-
> other, if any man have a quarrel against any: even as Christ
> forgave you, so also do ye. And above all these things put on
> charity, which is the bond of perfectness
>   (Colossians 3:12–14).

Those who feel eternal security while they are living a life of sin
and selfishness face terrible tragedy on the day of the Lord when
they realize they are lost for eternity. Peter presents the true understanding of God's election according to His foreknowledge, for
such election comes through sanctification of the Spirit and obedience.

> Elect according to the foreknowledge of God the Father,
> through sanctification of the Spirit, unto obedience and sprin-
> kling of the blood of Jesus Christ: Grace unto you, and peace,
> be multiplied   (1 Peter 1:2).

Again we must emphasize that it is not obedience that saves, but
those who have accepted the fullness of the sacrifice of Christ in
their lives have sought Christ not only for forgiveness, but have
asked Him to transform their lives so that they may live lives in
daily conformity to the will of God.

There is another implication worthy of our investigation. The
Bible offers clear testimony that those who once followed in the
pathway of righteousness, but who have returned to their lives of
worldliness and sin, will not be saved. The Bible most decidedly
does not teach the error of "once saved, always saved." Consider
these passages of Scripture:

> But when the righteous turneth away from his righteousness,
> and committeth iniquity, and doeth according to all the abomi-
> nations that the wicked man doeth, shall he live? All his

righteousness that he hath done shall not be mentioned: in his trespass that he hath trespassed, and in his sin that he hath sinned, in them shall he die (Ezekiel 18:24).

Again, when a righteous man doth turn from his righteousness, and commit iniquity, and I lay a stumblingblock before him, he shall die: because thou hast not given him warning, he shall die in his sin, and his righteousness which he hath done shall not be remembered; but his blood will I require at thine hand (Ezekiel 3:20).

Therefore, thou son of man, say unto the children of thy people, The righteousness of the righteous shall not deliver him in the day of his transgression: as for the wickedness of the wicked, he shall not fall thereby in the day that he turneth from his wickedness; neither shall the righteous be able to live for his righteousness in the day that he sinneth. When I shall say to the righteous, that he shall surely live; if he trust to his own righteousness, and commit iniquity, all his righteousnesses shall not be remembered; but for his iniquity that he hath committed, he shall die for it. . . . When the righteous turneth from his righteousness, and committeth iniquity, he shall even die thereby (Ezekiel 33:12–13, 18).

For it is impossible for those who were once enlightened, and have tasted of the heavenly gift, and were made partakers of the Holy Ghost, and have tasted the good word of God, and the powers of the world to come, if they shall fall away, to renew them again unto repentance; seeing they crucify to themselves the Son of God afresh, and put him to an open shame (Hebrews 6:4–6).

For if we sin wilfully after that we have received the knowledge of the truth, there remaineth no more sacrifice for sins, but a certain fearful looking for of judgment and fiery indignation, which shall devour the adversaries
(Hebrews 10:26–27).

For if after they have escaped the pollutions of the world through the knowledge of the Lord and Saviour Jesus Christ, they are again entangled therein, and overcome, the latter end is worse with them than the beginning. For it had been better for them not to have known the way of righteousness, than, after they have known it, to turn from the holy commandment delivered unto them. But it is happened unto them according

to the true proverb, The dog is turned to his own vomit again;
and the sow that was washed to her wallowing in the mire
(2 Peter 2:20–22).

There is an urgent need for those Evangelicals who hold to the
concept of divine predestination and who proclaim the concept of
"once saved, always saved" to reevaluate them in the light of the
Scripture. Our relationship with Christ is a day by day relationship as we surrender to Jesus asking Him to take our lives and
through His ministration to give us victory over every Satanic
deception.

Our God is able through Christ to keep us from falling and to
present us faultless before the throne of God (Jude 24). To hold to
the doctrine of predestination is to deny the infinite love of God.
What a monster God would be if the overwhelming majority of
the inhabitants of the world were preordained to eternal burning
torment, when they had not the slightest opportunity to choose
salvation. Such persons without the choice to be born or not,
without a choice once they are born, to have to suffer, not for a
thousand years, a million years, a billion years or even a trillion
years, but forever and ever and ever in the excruciating agony of
hell fire at the arbitrary decision of a god, would be the most
telling evidence against the biblical truth that God is love, which
could ever be provided. There is but one god who would desire
thus to treat poor mortals, and that is the one who styled himself
the god of this world—Satan, himself. Tragically, myriads over
the centuries have rejected Christ because they saw in this the
concept of an arbitrary and wholly fiendish god when, had they
been taught the truth, they would have known that God is love
(1 John 4:8).

In recent times Colin has twice travelled on airplanes with
evangelical ministers. In both conversations, the concepts of predestination and eternal burning torment have been discussed. While
both affirmed their belief in these teachings, neither seemed to
have given the slightest consideration to the diabolical consequences
of such teaching. We serve a God who so loved the world that
whosoever believeth in him should not perish but have everlasting
life (John 3:16). The very heart of the gospel dispels any concept
of an arbitrary god, for such a god might induce servitude be-

cause of fear, but never grateful obedience because of the reciprocation of love. Surely the linkage of predestination with eternal burning punishment is one of the most vulnerable doctrines of Evangelicalism, one screaming out for redress. That all Scripture denies predestinarian theology provides the pressing motivation for such a change lest more clear-thinking men and women reject this shameful caricature of our dear Saviour.

THE DILEMMA OF
IRRESISTIBLE GRACE

T he concept of irresistible grace is central to the Calvinistic principles of salvation. This belief is demanded by the adherence to predestination and to "once saved, always saved." To those to whom the Lord has called, according to this position, the grace of God is irresistible and therefore all who are so chosen are saved and can never be lost, irrespective of their life histories. Of course Scripture testifies to the certainty that grace has been provided for all humanity.

> For the grace of God that bringeth salvation hath appeared to all men (Titus 2:11).

It is this grace which enables any human being to experience the desire to turn to God and to accept His salvation. When man sinned, his whole character changed from that of goodness to evil. And had not God specifically intervened in his behalf, and placed His grace in the pathway of each human being, all would have been totally in allegiance to Satan and would have been lost for eternity. It was shortly after man sinned that God gave the promise:

> And I will put enmity between thee and the woman, and between thy seed and her seed; it shall bruise thy head, and thou shalt bruise his heel (Genesis 3:15).

Upon the fall of man, God placed in us an enmity for Satan that was no longer natural. Thus through the grace of God, provision was made so that every human being who accepted the leadership and saving power of God through Christ would be saved. There is no other way that salvation can take place.

> For by grace are ye saved through faith; and that not of yourselves: it is the gift of God: not of works, lest any man should boast (Ephesians 2:8–9).

> Neither is there salvation in any other: for there is none other name under heaven given among men, whereby we must be saved (Acts 4:12).

When Paul asked for a special intervention by God in his physical dilemma, God answered that His grace was sufficient.

> And lest I should be exalted above measure through the abundance of the revelations, there was given to me a thorn in the flesh, the messenger of Satan to buffet me, lest I should be exalted above measure. For this thing I besought the Lord thrice, that it might depart from me. And he said unto me, My grace is sufficient for thee: for my strength is made perfect in weakness. Most gladly therefore will I rather glory in my infirmities, that the power of Christ may rest upon me
> (2 Corinthians 12:7—9).

When Adam and Eve stood naked in the Garden of Eden, God provided not only sufficient strength, but exceeding abundant strength for them.

> For if by one man's offence death reigned by one; much more they which receive abundance of grace and of the gift of righteousness shall reign in life by one, Jesus Christ
> (Romans 5:17).

> Moreover the law entered, that the offence might abound. But where sin abounded, grace did much more abound
> (Romans 5:20).

> And the grace of our Lord was exceeding abundant with faith and love which is in Christ Jesus   (1 Timothy 1:14).

Even though we now have nearly six billion people in the world, God's grace remains "exceedingly abundant" for every human being. We need that grace for our justification.

> That being justified by his grace, we should be made heirs according to the hope of eternal life   (Titus 3:7).

Grace is essential for our salvation.

> For the grace of God that bringeth salvation hath appeared to all men, teaching us that, denying ungodliness and worldly lusts, we should live soberly, righteously, and godly, in this present world; looking for that blessed hope, and the glorious appearing of the great God and our Saviour Jesus Christ; who gave himself for us, that he might redeem us from all iniquity, and purify unto himself a peculiar people, zealous of good works   (Titus 2:11–14).

Yet though God has provided grace for every human being, there are conditions placed upon the bestowal of grace that leads to salvation.

> Surely he scorneth the scorners: but he giveth grace unto the
> lowly   (Proverbs 3:34).

> But he giveth more grace. Wherefore he saith, God resisteth
> the proud, but giveth grace unto the humble   (James 4:6).

> Likewise, ye younger, submit yourselves unto the elder. Yea,
> all of you be subject one to another, and be clothed with
> humility: for God resisteth the proud, and giveth grace to the
> humble   (1 Peter 5:5).

While the grace of God is available to all human beings, and while all benefit from it, in that every heartbeat and every breath we take is a gift of the grace of God, giving us probationary time whereby we may accept the provisions of God's salvation; these facts do not support the claim that we cannot resist that grace. For that reason Paul admonished those to whom he spoke to continue in the grace of God.

> Now when the congregation was broken up, many of the Jews
> and religious proselytes followed Paul and Barnabas: who,
> speaking to them, persuaded them to continue in the grace of
> God   (Acts 13:43).

The fact that Paul realized that this grace was not irresistible is recorded in his second epistle to the Corinthians.

> We then, as workers together with him, beseech you also that
> ye receive not the grace of God in vain. (For he saith, I have
> heard thee in a time accepted, and in the day of salvation
> have I succoured thee: behold, now is the accepted time; be-
> hold, now is the day of salvation.) Giving no offence in any
> thing, that the ministry be not blamed: but in all things ap-
> proving ourselves as the ministers of God, in much patience,
> in afflictions, in necessities, in distresses, in stripes, in im-
> prisonments, in tumults, in labours, in watchings, in fastings;
> by pureness, by knowledge, by longsuffering, by kindness, by
> the Holy Ghost, by love unfeigned, by the word of truth, by
> the power of God, by the armour of righteousness on the right
> hand and on the left, by honour and dishonour, by evil report
> and good report: as deceivers, and yet true; as unknown, and

yet well known; as dying, and behold, we live; as chastened, and not killed; as sorrowful, yet alway rejoicing; as poor, yet making many rich; as having nothing, and yet possessing all things (2 Corinthians 6:1–10).

Paul also knew it was possible to fall from the grace of God.

Looking diligently lest any man fail of [margin: fall from] the grace of God; lest any root of bitterness springing up trouble you, and thereby many be defiled (Hebrews 12:15).

But I keep under my body, and bring it into subjection: lest that by any means, when I have preached to others, I myself should be a castaway (1 Corinthians 9:27).

Peter also emphasized that saving grace could be lost.

For if after they have escaped the pollutions of the world through the knowledge of the Lord and Saviour Jesus Christ, they are again entangled therein, and overcome, the latter end is worse with them than the beginning. For it had been better for them not to have known the way of righteousness, than, after they have known it, to turn from the holy commandment delivered unto them. But it is happened unto them according to the true proverb, The dog is turned to his own vomit again; and the sow that was washed to her wallowing in the mire
(2 Peter 2:20–22).

In apostolic times there were those who were trying to use the concept of grace in much the same way it is used today: as a cover for sin, and to sustain ungodly behavior. Jude boldly attacked this heresy, showing again that there is true grace and there is a counterfeit grace.

For there are certain men crept in unawares, who were before of old ordained to this condemnation, ungodly men, turning the grace of our God into lasciviousness, and denying the only Lord God, and our Lord Jesus Christ (Jude 4).

The Lord has not given to His people grace to cover sin; but rather, grace to forgive sin and to cleanse His faithful saints from sin.

Do we then make void the law through faith? God forbid: yea, we establish the law (Romans 3:31).

The concept of irresistible grace is untenable, in the light of the Word of God. Unfortunately, like so many of the other dilemmas that we are addressing in this book, these concepts arose from men, principally Augustine; enunciating a false concept contrary to Scripture, and then attempting to bring all other concepts into logical agreement with the original false concept. This tactic leads to a wholly unbiblical gospel. It also leads many to throw aside any concept of grace that provides power for victory over sin. The belief that grace is provided through Christ not only for our forgiveness, but also for victorious Christian living, is frequently labeled "legalism." But Paul contrasts a salvation built upon the grace of God, and a salvation built upon the keeping of the Law. We are saved only through the grace of Christ, but the condition of accepting grace's free gift is through obedience to the will of God. Not only does God mandate such obedience, but through Christ He provides the power for obedience to become a reality in our lives. No one need be confused by this doctrine, because it is the grace of God that enables converted Christians to live godly in this present world (Titus 2:12).

Especially since the influence of John Nelson Darby, the founder of the Plymouth Brethren Church, upon American Protestantism in the latter part of the nineteenth century; and the influence of Cyrus Ingerson Scofield, the editor of the Scofield Reference Bible, in the early part of the twentieth century, evangelical Protestants have strengthened their belief in the disjunction of law and grace. But surely this separation results only in the destruction of both. It is a broken law which requires the grace of God, which flows from the sacrifice of Jesus on Calvary for our salvation. That grace provides the avenue by which humble, confessing and repentant lawbreakers can obtain divine pardon *and* restoration. How great and all-sufficient is the mighty grace of our heavenly Father!

THE DILEMMA OF
THE NEW-BIRTH EXPERIENCE

The evening dialogue between Jesus and Nicodemus is centered around the most critical aspects of salvation. Nicodemus thought to flatter Jesus by addressing Him as "Rabbi." Jesus did not wear the garb of a rabbi, neither had He studied in the rabbinical schools. In Christ's day there were three levels of rabbis, each with its own distinctive dress. But no doubt Jesus was dressed in the simple garb of the Galilean.

Jesus swept aside Nicodemus' vain flattery, and reached the very heart of his need. Jesus responded to his unexpressed question with the answer,

> Verily, verily, I say unto thee, Except a man be born again, he cannot see the kingdom of God   (John 3:3).

Nicodemus responded:

> How can a man be born when he is old? can he enter the second time into his mother's womb, and be born? (John 3:4).

No doubt Nicodemus was taken aback by Christ's words, since the term "born again" was used among the Jews exclusively to refer to those proselytized from the Gentiles. He was not just an ordinary Jew. He prided himself in being a Pharisee; and not just an ordinary Pharisee, but a leader in the Sanhedrin. No doubt this pride contributed to his awkward response, which he undoubtedly recognized as totally inappropriate. Jesus again ignored Nicodemus' response, penetrating to the core of the need of Nicodemus.

> Jesus answered, Verily, verily, I say unto thee, Except a man be born of water and of the Spirit, he cannot enter into the kingdom of God   (John 3:5).

Jesus was talking clearly about conditions of salvation. Colin once listened to an evangelical theologian who argued vigorously that the new birth and conversion were not coincidental. "Conversion," said the theologian, "took place well before the new-birth experience." He explained that conversion was the insemination of truth and pointed to the length of gestation in human beings and even in elephants as an indication that conversion comes much before we are born again. But this analogy cannot be accepted as truth, for Jesus says that we cannot see the kingdom of God unless we are born again (John 3:3). No one would rightly argue that at conversion we are not in a saved relationship with Jesus. Therefore the new birth must take place at conversion. This exposition of the gospel by Jesus Christ lies directly in contrast to the concept of an objective salvation. When we are converted we experience the new birth. Conversion and the new birth both include our justification. Being born of water refers to our repentance which leads to justification.

> Then said Paul, John verily baptized with the baptism of repentance, saying unto the people, that they should believe on him which should come after him, that is, on Christ Jesus
> (Acts 19:4).

> When John had first preached before his coming the baptism of repentance to all the people of Israel   (Acts 13:24).

> John did baptize in the wilderness, and preach the baptism of repentance for the remission of sins. . . . I indeed have baptized you with water: but he shall baptize you with the Holy Ghost   (Mark 1:4, 8).

> I indeed baptize you with water unto repentance: but he that cometh after me is mightier than I, whose shoes I am not worthy to bear: he shall baptize you with the Holy Ghost, and with fire   (Matthew 3:11).

Just as surely, the baptism of the Holy Spirit pinpoints sanctification, for it is the Holy Spirit that sanctifies unto obedience and perfection of character.

> And we are his witnesses of these things; and so is also the Holy Ghost, whom God hath given to them that obey him
> (Acts 5:32).

Yet many evangelical spokesmen greatly de-emphasize the transformation brought about by the new birth. Here is one instance.

> We do not deny the regeneration of the believer. But the believer is not the primary locus of the new birth. The primary locus of the new birth is Jesus Christ. Regeneration in

Christ, not in the believer, is the fundamental focus of the New Testament"

(Paxton, G., *Present Truth,* June 1979, p. 19).

While Christ is the central focus of the New Testament, it is His saving and transforming power in the lives of all who believe in Him, which is brought to the fore.

Seeing ye have purified your souls in obeying the truth through the Spirit unto unfeigned love of the brethren, see that ye love one another with a pure heart fervently: being born again, not of corruptible seed, but of incorruptible, by the word of God, which liveth and abideth for ever   (1 Peter 1:22–23).

This new birth encompasses the whole of the "In Christ" experience.

Therefore if any man be in Christ, he is a new creature: old things are passed away; behold, all things are become new
(2 Corinthians 5:17).

Paul especially emphasizes that transformation of character is the sure product of conversion.

For in Christ Jesus neither circumcision availeth any thing, nor uncircumcision, but a new creature   (Galatians 6:15).

In Paul's letter to Titus, while denying that our works have anything to do with our salvation, nevertheless, he clearly related our new birth to regeneration and the renewal of our life.

Not by works of righteousness which we have done, but according to his mercy he saved us, by the washing of regeneration, and renewing of the Holy Ghost   (Titus 3:5).

The ordinance of baptism is the symbol of the washing away of sin and coming to newness of life. Paul expresses this fact beautifully in the sixth chapter of Romans.

1 What shall we say then? Shall we continue in sin, that grace may abound? 2 God forbid. How shall we, that are dead to sin, live any longer therein? 3 Know ye not, that so many of us as were baptized into Jesus Christ were baptized into his death? 4 Therefore we are buried with him by baptism into death: that like as Christ was raised up from the dead by the glory of the Father, even so we also should walk in newness

of life. 5 For if we have been planted together in the likeness of his death, we shall be also in the likeness of his resurrection: 6 knowing this, that our old man is crucified with him, that the body of sin might be destroyed, that henceforth we should not serve sin. 7 For he that is dead is freed from sin
(Romans 6:1–7).

This passage clearly sets forth the fact that the new birth includes:

(1) Victory through Christ over sin (verses 2 and 6)
(2) The born-again Christian walks in newness of life (verse 4)

Baptism is the public acknowledgment that we have died to sin and become alive to forgiveness and the sanctifying power of Jesus Christ. Thus it was Jesus who declared that salvation is predicated upon genuine belief and baptism.

He that believeth and is baptized shall be saved; but he that believeth not shall be damned (Mark 16:16).

Many Evangelicals have failed to understand the full implication of genuine belief, as it is set forth by John.

Whosoever believeth that Jesus is the Christ is born of God: and every one that loveth him that begat loveth him also that is begotten of him. By this we know that we love the children of God, when we love God, and keep his commandments. For this is the love of God, that we keep his commandments: and his commandments are not grievous. For whatsoever is born of God overcometh the world: and this is the victory that overcometh the world, even our faith. Who is he that overcometh the world, but he that believeth that Jesus is the Son of God? (1 John 5:1–5).

True belief encompasses our love for God and our love for our fellow men, the keeping of the commandments of God, overcoming the world, and victory through the faith of Jesus. When we understand true belief, we recognize that it encompasses more, vastly more, than an intellectual assent. These are issues that have never been thoroughly addressed by the overwhelming majority of Evangelicals. But Scripture is absolutely adamant on these issues. The Bible teaches that those who are born again have victory over sin in their lives.

Whosoever is born of God doth not commit sin; for his seed remaineth in him: and he cannot sin, because he is born of God   (1 John 3:9).

We know that whosoever is born of God sinneth not; but he that is begotten of God keepeth himself, and that wicked one toucheth him not   (1 John 5:18).

These great salvation principles were enunciated by Paul to the Roman believers.

But ye are not in the flesh, but in the Spirit, if so be that the Spirit of God dwell in you. Now if any man have not the Spirit of Christ, he is none of his. And if Christ be in you, the body is dead because of sin; but the Spirit is life because of righteousness. But if the Spirit of him that raised up Jesus from the dead dwell in you, he that raised up Christ from the dead shall also quicken your mortal bodies by his Spirit that dwelleth in you. Therefore, brethren, we are debtors, not to the flesh, to live after the flesh. For if ye live after the flesh, ye shall die: but if ye through the Spirit do mortify the deeds of the body, ye shall live   (Romans 8:9–13).

Once again we see not the slightest evidence of the "sin and live" theology so commonly heard among Evangelicals today. Rather do we see that salvation is predicated upon the wonderful power of God, His strength and sacrifice. Those who claim that salvation was secured two thousand years ago on Calvary without the regeneration of the human being under the power of the indwelling Christ, and through the Holy Spirit's ministration, are far from the truth of Paul and the other Bible writers. This theme is reiterated in many parts of the Pauline presentations.

Buried with him in baptism, wherein also ye are risen with him through the faith of the operation of God, who hath raised him from the dead. And you, being dead in your sins and the uncircumcision of your flesh, hath he quickened together with him, having forgiven you all trespasses
                                                   (Colossians 2:12–13).

> If ye then be risen with Christ, seek those things which are above, where Christ sitteth on the right hand of God. Set your affection on things above, not on things on the earth. For ye are dead, and your life is hid with Christ in God
>
> (Colossians 3:1–3).

It is essential that evangelical Christians reassess the centrality of the new-birth experience to salvation. There must be no continued denial that conversion is the new-birth experience. There must be an understanding that the new-birth experience encompasses both our justification, and that through the death and ministry of Jesus we may have forgiveness of sins and victory over sin in our lives.

For Christians to be assured of the new-birth experience independent of the great transforming power of the gospel within their lives, is to perpetrate a tragic deception. With the return of Jesus near at hand, our plea is to preach the fullness of the saving power of the gospel of Calvary, so plainly set forth in Scripture.

THE DILEMMA OF
PERFECTION

There are two words in the English language that are often used synonymously, when indeed in the spiritual sense they have significantly different meanings. These words, *perfection* and *perfectionism,* have long been a point of misunderstanding by even earnest Christians. It is certainly wrong to equate them.

Perfectionism is rightly applied only to certain groups which have arisen from time to time, who claim that they have received holy (unfallen) flesh similar to that of Adam before the fall, so that it is impossible for them to sin. In the biblical sense, the word perfection means a sanctified life gaining victory over the temptations of Satan through the power of the indwelling Christ. Biblical perfection in no wise implies that humans this side of the return of Jesus will attain to holy flesh, nor does it exclude the possibility of falling back into sin. Victory over Satan's temptations for one day does not guarantee victory for the next day; for only those who are completely surrendered to Christ each day can have renewed victory daily.

Paul sets forth perfection as the goal of every Christian.

And he gave some, apostles; and some, prophets; and some, evangelists; and some, pastors and teachers; for the perfecting of the saints, for the work of the ministry, for the edifying of the body of Christ: till we all come in the unity of the faith, and of the knowledge of the Son of God, unto a perfect man, unto the measure of the stature of the fulness of Christ: that we henceforth be no more children, tossed to and fro, and carried about with every wind of doctrine, by the sleight of men, and cunning craftiness, whereby they lie in wait to deceive; but speaking the truth in love, may grow up into him in all things, which is the head, even Christ
(Ephesians 4:11–15).

All scripture is given by inspiration of God, and is profitable for doctrine, for reproof, for correction, for instruction in righteousness: that the man of God may be perfect, throughly furnished unto all good works   (2 Timothy 3:16–17).

> Therefore leaving the principles of the doctrine of Christ, let
> us go on unto perfection; not laying again the foundation of
> repentance from dead works, and of faith toward God
> (Hebrews 6:1).

This call to character perfection is consistent with the call of
Jesus to His hearers.

> Be ye therefore perfect, even as your Father which is in heaven
> is perfect   (Matthew 5:48).

It is important not to misunderstand this call to perfection. Some
have said that it is an impossible call, because we can never have
the infinite perfection of God; and a law which reflects the infinite
character of God must therefore require infinite perfection. But
God alone has infinite knowledge, a maturity of perfection built
upon all the infinite wisdom of the universe. Some have claimed
that if we do not have such infinite knowledge, and therefore an
infinitely perfect response to the law of God, it is still sin. But it is
obvious that if this be true, then the angels are also sinners,
because they too lack the infinite wisdom of God; and it would
also hold that the saints would continue in sin after their redemption. A perfect person is simply keeping the law of God, both in
deed and in thought. The attainment of Christian character perfection through the presence of the indwelling Holy Spirit is not a
finishing point in character development. Christ in His great mercy
grants us the status of perfection when we live up to all the light
of His will which He has provided at any given time in our lives.
As we continue to live the Christian life, Christ entrusts us with
greater knowledge of His will, and empowers the willing Christian
to meet the requirements of this new knowledge. Thus we advance
from one level to the next, being perfect at each stage. God's
Word specifically declares that when He has not entrusted us with
a knowledge of His will in a certain area, He does not count that
matter as a breach of His law.

> Jesus said unto them, If ye were blind, ye should have no sin:
> but now ye say, We see; therefore your sin remaineth
> (John 9:41).

> If I had not come and spoken unto them, they had not had
> sin: but now they have no cloke for their sin   (John 15:22).

> And the times of this ignorance God winked at; but now
> commandeth all men every where to repent   (Acts 17:30).

> Therefore to him that knoweth to do good, and doeth it not, to
> him it is sin   (James 4:17).

Some assume that temptation is sin; but there is a great difference between temptation on the one hand, and sins of the mind on the other hand. When temptations are harbored or cherished, then, and only then, do they become sin. But when, through the power of Jesus, temptations are repelled, there is no sin. The contemplation of evil is clearly defined as sin by Scripture.

> Whosoever hateth his brother is a murderer: and ye know that
> no murderer hath eternal life abiding in him   (1 John 3:15).

> But I say unto you, That whosoever looketh on a woman to
> lust after her hath committed adultery with her already in his
> heart   (Matthew 5:28).

Temptation is neither sin, nor evidence that the person has retained iniquity in his heart. Christ had the most evil thought possible—to worship Satan—placed in His mind (Matthew 4:9), but He did not for a moment cherish the temptation, and thus remained "without sin" (Hebrews 4:15). We will have evil thoughts presented to our minds so long as Satan is free to tempt us. Further, our *old life* of sin may also be responsible for temptation. Our response to those evil thoughts determines whether or not we commit sin. When we come to Christ, we not only have an inherited sinful nature but we have been further seriously weakened by the many habits developed by sinful practice. While the mind no longer serves sin, yet these past experiences serve as further areas through which Satan tempts us. But we have been promised powerful victory over all the cultivated, as well as the inherited tendencies to evil. If under God's controlling power we resist temptation, we need not fear the consequences, nor need we doubt God's cleansing power to mortify the deeds of the body, and to implant the divine nature within us. Thus James could confidently say:

> Blessed is the man that endureth temptation: for when he is
> tried, he shall receive the crown of life, which the Lord hath
> promised to them that love him   (James 1:12).

What a blessed assurance this is! Our Lord does not allow His surrendered people to fall victim to Satan's temptations.

> There hath no temptation taken you but such as is common to man: but God is faithful, who will not suffer you to be tempted above that ye are able; but will with the temptation also make a way to escape, that ye may be able to bear it
> (1 Corinthians 10:13).

Those who hold to the view that everything is sin unless it meets the infinite will of God, hold to what is sometimes called the "high" definition of sin. If, under this definition, sin is meeting the standard of the infinite will of God, then it is logical for these people to declare that it is impossible to have victory over sin. Unfortunately, in so doing, they then go beyond their false definition of sin and use this "high" definition as an excuse to deny the possibility of victory over sin as it is defined in the Bible.

> Whosoever committeth sin transgresseth also the law: for sin is the transgression of the law   (1 John 3:4).

Once one accepts that eternity is offered to men who continue in sins of limitations, it is understandable that those with such a belief see no reason to suspect that they cannot be saved while persisting in sins that directly transgress God's law. The "high" definition of sin is used to downgrade the standard of obedience which God requires, while paradoxically the "low" standard of sin elevates the requirement of obedience demanded by God. The "high" definition is used to deny that:

> He that saith he abideth in him ought himself also so to walk, even as he walked   (1 John 2:6).

On the other hand, the "low" definition of sin, built upon 1 John 3:4, points men and women to Christ as their example of obedience. In reality, if man believes that God does not provide power to overcome all sin, he is inclined to the conclusion that God cannot give the power to overcome any sin. Few people there are who will tell us which sins God has the power to overcome in the believer, and which ones He does not.

Some suggest a temporal factor. God can give victory over all sin some of the time. Once again we are entitled to know when God can give victory and when He cannot, or when He does not.

Strangely, some who teach the "high" definition of sin claim that Christ makes no provision for deliberate sin after conversion. They hasten to assure the congregations that David was in a saved relationship when he perpetrated his awful act of murder and adultery.

The punishment of Korah, Dathan, and Abiram has sometimes been used as an example of non-forgiveness of deliberate sins. But such evidence cannot be sustained in the light of God's forgiveness of deliberate acts of sin by Adam, Abraham, Jacob, David, Peter and many others. The plain message of God is that He can and does forgive, and is desirous of giving victory over all sins all the time. It is not for man's glorification, but that God's character may be vindicated, and that the false claims of Satan that fallen man cannot gain victory over sin may be put to rest. We do have the promise that if we sin, there is still forgiveness.

> My little children, these things write I unto you, that ye sin not. And if any man sin, we have an advocate with the Father, Jesus Christ the righteous (1 John 2:1).

The issue facing evangelical Protestantism is not a new one. Controversy existed between the teachings of John Wesley, who believed in Christian perfection, and Count Von Zinzendorf, who claimed to battle this concept of perfection with fire and sword because he did not believe that we could overcome sin. Wesley's response was fascinating:

> I say, why so vehement? Why are those who oppose salvation from sin, few excepted, so eager? In God's name, why are you so fond of sin? What has it ever done for you? What good is it ever likely to do for you in this world, or in the world to come? And why are you so violent against those who hope for a deliverance from it?
> (John Wesley, *The Works of Wesley,* Volume 6, page 1).

More than two hundred years later, the same battle rages in Protestantism. As we have noted earlier, the dispute really goes back to Augustine and his concept of original sin. So that many, who are afraid of the concept of perfection, fear that such a concept will lead them into looking to their own works for salvation. That is certainly a hazard that must be avoided constantly. But to those who understand the principles of perfection clearly, it is a concept that requires of them that they look constantly to Jesus, because "by beholding Christ we become changed." In grand language, John the apostle reports that he and others beheld the glory of Jesus.

> And the Word was made flesh, and dwelt among us, (and we beheld his glory, the glory as of the only begotten of the Father,) full of grace and truth   (John 1:14).

This beholding also was a mighty theme of John the Baptist.

> The next day John seeth Jesus coming unto him, and saith, Behold the Lamb of God, which taketh away the sin of the world   (John 1:29).

The perfection of character that has not one shred of legalism in it, results when through Christ's power we behold, meditate upon, contemplate and exemplify the life of Jesus Christ. As we choose to behold Him, our characters are transformed, our life becomes one of selflessness, and His life becomes our life. This is in marked contrast to the concept of perfectionism. There have been members of groups in past history who, under that concept of perfectionism, have done unbelievable acts of iniquity while still claiming to be living perfect lives. The perfection that man has is not one of which he can boast, for it is all the work of Christ in him. More than that, it is not one that the true Christian dare acknowledge, for in so doing, it would be the pitfall leading him back into a life of sin. It must be left to divine evaluation. The example of Job is a faithful example to us all.

> And the Lord said unto Satan, Hast thou considered my servant Job, that there is none like him in the earth, a perfect and an upright man, one that feareth God, and escheweth evil?   (Job 1:8).

Job was perfect in God's power because he "eschewed evil" and "sinned not." Yet he did not possess the slightest inkling that he was perfect. Humility, and the knowledge that God was ever revealing new insights concerning His law, prevented any proud claim to perfection.

Job made not the slightest boast of his character perfection.

If I speak of strength, lo he is strong: and if of judgment, who shall set me a time to plead? If I justify myself, mine own mouth shall condemn me: if I say, I am perfect, it shall also prove me perverse. Though I were perfect, yet would I not know my soul: I would despise my life   (Job 9:19–21).

Yet Job could say,

That thou enquirest after mine iniquity, and searchest after my sin? Thou knowest that I am not wicked; and there is none that can deliver out of thine hand   (Job 10:6–7).

It is to this selfless, unboasting perfection that God calls us.

Depart from evil, and do good; seek peace, and pursue it
(Psalm 34:14).

Depart from evil, and do good; and dwell for evermore
(Psalm 37:27).

Let him eschew evil, and do good; let him seek peace, and ensue it   (1 Peter 3:11).

Then like Job we will say,

Whom, though I were righteous, yet would I not answer, but I would make supplication to my judge   (Job 9:15).

Some suggest that God has neither the power nor the intent to bring victory over temptation. That is to deny the power of God. Genuine character perfection is more than being made perfect _in_ Christ, it is being made perfect _by_ Christ. God at the end of time will have a people who have so beheld Christ that they have been transformed into His image. They will be a declaration of the saving power of Christ, to men and to angels. Any claims that such concepts of perfection are legalistic are false, for such character perfection is provided through the grace and ministry of Jesus Christ.

We make an earnest plea to our Evangelical friends. Here is a truth so central to human salvation, that to ignore it, deny it, or reject it, will lead untold myriads to eternal destruction. We know that is not the goal of Evangelicals, but it is the sole basis of the final agonizing rejection of those who were confidently assured of salvation, but who will be lost eternally.

> Not every one that saith unto me, Lord, Lord, shall enter into the kingdom of heaven; but he that doeth the will of my Father which is in heaven. Many will say to me in that day, Lord, Lord, have we not prophesied in thy name? and in thy name have cast out devils? and in thy name done many wonderful works? And then will I profess unto them, I never knew you: depart from me, ye that work iniquity
>
> (Matthew 7:21–23).

These precious lost souls have not done the will of the Father and have not claimed Christ's victorious power. Let us tell the world of Christ's all-sufficient power.

THE DILEMMA OF
THE MAN OF ROMANS SEVEN

L ooking through the eyes of the pagan concepts contained in Manichaeism, Augustine saw the man described in Romans chapter seven as a converted man, a man struggling, though saved. Since that time myriads, including large segments of evangelical Protestantism, have used the seventh chapter of Romans as a biblical defense of the claim that we are saved in our sins. Paul's theme is not difficult to discern, and is succinctly summed up as follows:

> For that which I do I allow not: for what I would, that do I not; but what I hate, that do I. . . . For I know that in me (that is, in my flesh,) dwelleth no good thing: for to will is present with me; but how to perform that which is good I find not. For the good that I would I do not: but the evil which I would not, that I do (Romans 7:15, 18–19).

The struggle between the Spirit and the flesh, as recorded in Romans chapters seven and eight, and in Galatians chapter five, greatly attracted the mind of Augustine, bishop of Hippo, because of his predisposition to the pagan concept of the balance of all cosmic forces within the universe. In Romans chapter seven Augustine perceived a cosmic tension between good and evil:

> I find then a law, that, when I would do good, evil is present with me. For I delight in the law of God after the inward man: But I see another law in my members, warring against the law of my mind, and bringing me into captivity to the law of sin which is in my members (Romans 7:21–23).

Augustine saw an unresolvable conflict, a conflict where the flesh and the Spirit were ever in battle, with neither gaining the final victory or ascendancy. He saw a similar struggle in Galatians.

> For the flesh lusteth against the Spirit, and the Spirit against the flesh: and these are contrary the one to the other: so that ye cannot do the things that ye would (Galatians 5:17).

Thus Augustine came to the conclusion that even the converted man, whom he believed to be predestined of God to eternal life, would continue to sin throughout his life, unable to have victory over the works of the flesh. Others have claimed that Romans chapter seven does not represent man at his worst, but man at his best. One scholar expressed this view in the following words: "In short, Romans 7:14–25 . . . Paul is not describing himself at his worst, but himself at his best" (R. Brinsmead, *Present Truth,* Vol. 4, No. 1, p. 61). But we have a number of grave problems with such a concept. The man of Romans chapter seven lacks even the slightest indication of the peace and contentment of those who are followers of Jesus Christ. It is little wonder that with unresolved frustration, he cries out in great despair and helplessness,

> O wretched man that I am! who shall deliver me from the
> body of this death?   (Romans 7:24).

The question of course that must be settled is whether Paul is here illustrating the experience of a regenerate Christian, or of a man who has as yet not given himself unreservedly to Christ. While man's reasoning cannot settle any scriptural question, nevertheless, it would seem strange indeed if a man fully possessed by the Spirit of God, one who has fully surrendered self, were still doing the works of self. Further, if Christ had already become supreme in the life of this poor wretch, why does he not declare that Christ *has* delivered him, rather than cry out, "Who shall deliver me?", looking to Christ as his future deliverer? One cannot see in the plaintive cry of this tormented soul the absolute assurance so central to the theme of evangelical Protestantism. How different the turmoil of spirit and the repeated dejection of this man, from the calm victories of the redeemed who submit totally to God. Where is the confident assurance that Job expresses in his most pitiful dilemma?

> For I know that my redeemer liveth, and that he shall stand at
> the latter day upon the earth   (Job 19:25).

Where is the calm assurance of Paul as he faced the executioner's block?

For I am now ready to be offered, and the time of my departure is at hand. I have fought a good fight, I have finished my course, I have kept the faith: Henceforth there is laid up for me a crown of righteousness, which the Lord, the righteous judge, shall give me at that day: and not to me only, but unto all them also that love his appearing (2 Timothy 4:6–8).

In Romans chapter seven we witness a man emotionally tormented and tortured. How do we reconcile a life of continued obedience with that of the man of Romans seven, who lived a life of continual disobedience? They are clearly not one and the same person. The problem of this man is plainly seen in the statement of Paul in verses seventeen and twenty.

Now then it is *no more I that do it, but sin that dwelleth in me.* . . . Now if I do that I would not, it is *no more I that do it, but sin that dwelleth in me* (Romans 7:17, 20)

How do we reconcile this man with the man of Galatians 2:20?

I am crucified with Christ: nevertheless I live; yet not I, but Christ liveth in me: and the life which I now live in the flesh I live by the faith of the Son of God, who loved me, and gave himself for me (Galatians 2:20).

We cannot reconcile them, for one is described as a converted man and the other a man who is unconverted. Christ cannot reside in the life that is in bondage to Satan and sin. It is impossible. Now lest we be misunderstood, we make it clear that this man is not an atheist, an agnostic, nor is he a man who is indifferent to the claims of Christ upon his life. He sincerely and earnestly wants to be saved. He is doing everything he knows to do, to measure up to the standard of salvation. But this man is trapped in the awful clutches of legalism, so common among many earnest but unsurrendered people. This man wants to be saved; he wants to live a life in harmony with the Lord; he wants to do good; but in his human strength he has failed miserably, and has reached a culminating crisis. He reaches the conviction at last, that he is wholly unable to live the life of a Christian. But with wonderful assurance, this man finds the answer to his agonizing dilemma.

I thank God through Jesus Christ our Lord (Romans 7:25).

Only through the daily total surrender of his life to Christ will he ever live the life of a converted Christian. Only through the power of Jesus can he have victory and peace. We have spent many years in the study of psychology and, in the case of Russell, psychiatry as well, and full well we know the helpless misery of guilt. We understand that a large percentage of the psychiatric beds of hospitals could be closed if men and women were not suffering from the emotional trauma resulting from guilt. God has the only satisfying answer to guilt. The man of Romans seven has reached a state of neurotic despair. People have committed suicide when in this strait. Others, convinced that Christianity does not work for them, have severed any connection with Christianity, accepting that they will try to find a little pleasure out of this life and take the consequences of the life to come. Still others have decided that they can continue to sin and somehow find a way of entrance into the kingdom. But Paul gives the only true answer, that of victory through Christ. This answer is magnificently brought out in the eighth chapter of Romans as Paul continues his discourse on this subject.

> There is therefore now no condemnation to them which are in Christ Jesus, who walk not after the flesh, but after the Spirit. For the law of the Spirit of life in Christ Jesus hath made me free from the law of sin and death. For what the law could not do, in that it was weak through the flesh, God sending his own Son in the likeness of sinful flesh, and for sin, condemned sin in the flesh: that the righteousness of the law might be fulfilled in us, who walk not after the flesh, but after the Spirit   (Romans 8:1–4).

To hypothesize that the man of Romans seven could be a converted man is to deny the internal evidence of Paul's arguments here.

> For we know that the law is spiritual: but I am carnal, sold under sin   (Romans 7:14).

When we consider this wretched man who recognizes that he is carnal, sold under sin, in slavery and bondage to a life of defeat, we must compare his plight with the message of Romans 8:6.

> For to be carnally minded is death; but to be spiritually minded
> is life and peace   (Romans 8:6).

Before finding Christ as the sole answer to his life, this man is carnally minded and therefore on the broad road that leads to destruction. While he retains the carnal mind, he will never have peace. That peace comes to those who love the law of God.

> Great peace have they which love thy law: and nothing shall
> offend them   (Psalm 119:165).

Likewise, when we examine Galatians chapter five, we find exactly the same situation. To extract verse seventeen out of its context is to do grave disservice to the inspired counsel that Paul is giving.

> For the flesh lusteth against the Spirit, and the Spirit against
> the flesh: and these are contrary the one to the other: so that
> ye cannot do the things that ye would   (Galatians 5:17).

Let us look at verse sixteen.

> This I say then, Walk in the Spirit, and ye shall not fulfil the
> lust of the flesh   (Galatians 5:16).

Here the great victory that God wants for His children is presented. Verse eighteen confirms it.

> But if ye be led of the Spirit, ye are not under the law
>   (Galatians 5:18).

So that we cannot in any way misunderstand his message, Paul contrasts the *works* of the flesh with the *fruit* of the Spirit. Some have carelessly claimed that if evil is defined in terms of our acts of sin, then righteousness must be defined in terms of acts also. But Paul, while defining evil in terms of works, defined righteousness in terms of fruit. The Holy Spirit transforms the character in harmony with the righteousness of Christ. From a holy life flow good works.

> Now the works of the flesh are manifest, which are these;
> Adultery, fornication, uncleanness, lasciviousness, idolatry,
> witchcraft, hatred, variance, emulations, wrath, strife, seditions,
> heresies, envyings, murders, drunkenness, revellings,
> and such like: of the which I tell you before, as I have also

> told you in time past, that they which do such things shall not
> inherit the kingdom of God. But the fruit of the Spirit is love,
> joy, peace, longsuffering, gentleness, goodness, faith, meek-
> ness, temperance: against such there is no law. And they that
> are Christ's have crucified the flesh with the affections and
> lusts   (Galatians 5:19–24).

It will be seen that evil of every kind will lead to eternal destruction, but that when Jesus reigns in our lives we will have fruit
unto salvation. Salvation now! peace and contentment now! victory now! as opposed to the torment of those seeking salvation
through their own efforts. The man of Romans seven finds victory
only when he has acknowledged that he cannot be victorious of
himself; that he must have the power of the indwelling Christ in
his life. Once he has accepted Christ and has surrendered the
totality of his will to Him, then he is indeed "a new creature: old
things are passed away; behold, all things are become new"
(2 Corinthians 5:17). To hold the Augustinian view that Romans
chapter seven deals with the converted man is a most dangerous
pathway. It gives "security" to those who have no victory at all; it
emasculates God's power and does not invite dependence upon
Christ for strength to obey. Thousands of Christians are being
deluded into a totally false assurance by this indefensible interpretation.

If only Romans chapter seven were studied in the context of
the chapters before and after it, there would be no problem. The
sixth chapter of Romans makes plain the fact that a man who has
crucified self is free from sin and no longer is a slave to it.

> Knowing this, that our old man is crucified with him, that the
> body of sin might be destroyed, that henceforth we should not
> serve sin. For he that is dead is freed from sin
>   (Romans 6:6–7).

Every man is dead. We are either dead *in* trespasses and sin and
thus a slave to sin; or we are, in Christ's strength, dead *to* sin and
thus freed from it. The man of Romans seven falls into the first
category, the man of Romans eight into the second. It is clearly a
travesty of scriptural interpretation to proclaim the manifest error

that a man who is a slave to sin has reached the highest plane of Christian liberty. The carnally minded man cannot be accepted by God.

> Because the carnal mind is enmity against God: for it is not subject to the law of God, neither indeed can be. So then they that are in the flesh cannot please God   (Romans 8:7–8).

How could a man who is at enmity with God, who cannot please Him, and who minds the things of the flesh, have reached the acme of spiritual experience? Of course, there are still severe tests for the victorious Christian, but Romans seven depicts struggle and failure, while Romans eight depicts unbroken victory which ends in the great crescendo of the last few verses.

> Who shall separate us from the love of Christ? shall tribulation, or distress, or persecution, or famine, or nakedness, or peril, or sword? As it is written, For thy sake we are killed all the day long; we are accounted as sheep for the slaughter. Nay, in all these things we are more than conquerors through him that loved us. For I am persuaded, that neither death, nor life, nor angels, nor principalities, nor powers, nor things present, nor things to come, nor height, nor depth, nor any other creature, shall be able to separate us from the love of God, which is in Christ Jesus our Lord   (Romans 8:35–39).

It is helpful to understand that the term "sold under sin" is of Old Testament origin. On each occasion that it is used in the Old Testament it is applied to lost sinners. Never once is it used to describe one saved. Two instances of the use of this term are illustrated:

> And Ahab said to Elijah, Hast thou found me, O mine enemy? And he answered, I have found thee: because thou hast sold thyself to work evil in the sight of the LORD
> (1 Kings 21:20).

> And they caused their sons and their daughters to pass through the fire, and used divination and enchantments, and sold themselves to do evil in the sight of the LORD, to provoke him to anger   (2 Kings 17:17).

It was with the background knowledge of these Old Testament passages that Paul wrote Romans seven.

The power of Christ in the life provides liberation from the enslavement to sin.

> For the law of the Spirit of life in Christ Jesus hath made me free from the law of sin and death   (Romans 8:2).

As we compare Romans 7:17 and 20 with Galatians 2:20, we see the contrast. The unconverted man is controlled by indwelling sin; the converted man is fully empowered by Christ. The former has continual defeat; the second, continual victory. The former is a man in despair, the latter a man at peace. When this understanding of Romans chapters seven and eight is clearly assimilated, it will lead the believer to a daily surrender of his will to Jesus Christ, praying for Christ to take his life and work His miracle of salvation in him. It will be in this understanding that we will fulfill the counsel of James:

> Submit yourselves therefore to God. Resist the devil, and he will flee from you   (James 4:7).

This submission must be the daily practice of our lives. How far such Pauline truth is from the teachings in most contemporary evangelical pulpits! We are not dealing here with peripheral issues. Eternity is at stake, in how we understand and respond to these central pillars of human salvation.

THE DILEMMA OF

THE HUMAN NATURE OF CHRIST

God's Word defines plainly that Christ took upon Himself our fallen, sinful nature.

Concerning his Son Jesus Christ our Lord, which was made of the seed of David according to the flesh   (Romans 1:3).

For what the law could not do, in that it was weak through the flesh, God sending his own Son in the likeness of sinful flesh, and for sin, condemned sin in the flesh: that the righteousness of the law might be fulfilled in us, who walk not after the flesh, but after the Spirit   (Romans 8:3–4).

Forasmuch then as the children are partakers of flesh and blood, he also himself likewise took part of the same; that through death he might destroy him that had the power of death, that is, the devil; and deliver them who through fear of death were all their lifetime subject to bondage. For verily he took not on him the nature of angels; but he took on him the seed of Abraham. Wherefore in all things it behoved him to be made like unto his brethren, that he might be a merciful and faithful high priest in things pertaining to God, to make reconciliation for the sins of the people. For in that he himself hath suffered being tempted, he is able to succour them that are tempted   (Hebrews 2:14–18).

But when the fulness of the time was come, God sent forth his Son, made of a woman, made under the law, To redeem them that were under the law, that we might receive the adoption of sons   (Galatians 4:4–5).

While taking upon Himself our fallen nature, He in no way participated in our sin.

For we have not an high priest which cannot be touched with the feeling of our infirmities; but was in all points tempted like as we are, yet without sin   (Hebrews 4:15).

Jesus by His life gained victory over sin, and by His resurrection gained victory over the results of sin—death. We might well ask how Evangelicals were led to the false view that Christ came in the pre-fall nature of Adam, when the Bible plainly teaches that He accepted sinful human nature. Once again, this error can be traced to Augustinian theology.

Augustine and his followers had a gigantic problem. Having assumed that we sin because we are sinners as a result of original sin, they were confronted with the fact that there is no way that Christ can be referred to as a sinner. Therefore, in order to support his false hypothesis, Augustine was prepared to postulate that Christ had an altogether different nature from that of the rest of the human race; otherwise He, too, would have been a sinner. Thus they rejected the clear testimony of the Word of God that we are sinners because "all have sinned and come short of the glory of God" (Romans 3:23). They also appear to have ignored the clearest definition possible for sin:

> Whosoever committeth sin transgresseth also the law: for sin
> is the transgression of the law   (1 John 3:4).

Having ignored this definition, the adherents of Augustinian doctrine found it necessary to incorporate in their theology a Christ who had taken upon Himself the nature of unfallen man. As a result, they placed "Christ" wholly outside the deeper experience of humanity. Paul clarifies the humanity with which Christ came to this earth.

> Who, being in the form of God, thought it not robbery to be
> equal with God: but made himself of no reputation, and took
> upon him the form of a servant, and was made in the likeness
> of men: And being found in fashion as a man, he humbled
> himself, and became obedient unto death, even the death of
> the cross   (Philippians 2:6–8).

Some have incorrectly argued that this text, together with Romans 8:3, refers to Christ "like man" or in the "likeness" of sinful flesh. But the word translated "like" is the Greek word *homoioma* from which today we get the word "homogeneity" meaning "of the same order." Christ was made of the same order "as man" or "He was made of the same order as sinful flesh." True understanding of the human nature of Christ leads us to a much fuller understanding of the wonderful sacrifice that Jesus made in behalf of humanity. It would indeed have been of unbelievable humiliation for the Son of God to have taken upon Himself the nature of created angels. It certainly would also have been an even greater condescension to have taken upon Himself the nature of Adam before his transgression. But to take upon Himself the nature of fallen humanity was the ultimate evidence of His identification with the human race. The only divine strength He had was not resident within Himself, as it would have been if He had taken upon Himself unfallen nature, but His strength was from His Father alone.

> I can of mine own self do nothing: as I hear, I judge: and my judgment is just; because I seek not mine own will, but the will of the Father which hath sent me   (John 5:30).

Representative of the beliefs of some Evangelicals is the following:

> For centuries Christians have argued about the human nature of Christ. Some have believed that He could have sinned, but did not. Others, including this writer, that He could not have sinned   (Martin, W. *The Kingdom of the Cults,* Minneapolis: Bethany House, 1985, p. 433).

It has been argued that though Jesus took the physical form of a degenerate human being, He did not take the spiritual form of such. But this reasoning would demand an allegiance to the Greek pagan concept of the dichotomy of body and soul—that the body is evil and the soul is pure. This Greek philosophy easily found a nesting place within apostate Christianity through the acceptance of Augustinian concepts. But there is not one shred of evidence in the Word of God that Jesus took other than our own nature, and it was through the power of His heavenly Father that He was able to resist every temptation of Satan. Indeed, not for one incipient moment during his life did Christ ever lose His relationship with God. In one sense alone was He different from the rest of humanity. Matthew states,

> Now the birth of Jesus Christ was on this wise: When as his mother Mary was espoused to Joseph, before they came together, she was found with child of the Holy Ghost
> (Matthew 1:18).

And Luke records:

> And the angel answered and said unto her, The Holy Ghost
> shall come upon thee, and the power of the Highest shall
> overshadow thee: therefore also that holy thing which shall be
> born of thee shall be called the Son of God   (Luke 1:35).

There is no human way to explain the conception of Jesus as a
result of the overshadowing of the Holy Spirit, yet in faith we
accept that Mary indeed was a virgin, having never had sexual
relationships with any man. This fact allowed the babe to be
totally overshadowed by the Holy Spirit, thus beginning His life
and ending His life in complete conformity to the will of God.
However, the same experience of Jesus from His conception is
ours when, in the new-birth experience, we are born of the Spirit.
Some have rationally argued that Luke 1:35 placed Jesus in an
altogether different experience from that of normal humanity, because it was declared that Jesus was "that holy thing." This view,
of course, is a reference to His unbroken life of sanctification.
However, a simple comparison of scripture with scripture from
the same author, Luke, demonstrates that this term was not unique
even to the perfect Son of God.

> (As it is written in the law of the Lord, Every male that
> openeth the womb shall be called holy to the Lord;)
> (Luke 2:23).

While undoubtedly this statement had a unique application to
Christ, who indeed never once failed to repulse the persistent
temptations of Satan, nevertheless as it is noted by Luke, every
male that was born was considered holy unto the Lord. Contem-
plating this fact, we can well understand another text sometimes
used to support the concept that Christ had altogether a different
nature from ours.

> For such an high priest became us, who is holy, harmless,
> undefiled, separate from sinners, and made higher than the
> heavens   (Hebrews 7:26).

This text, however, is referring to Jesus in His High Priestly
ministry after His ascension, and after He had been received by
the Father. However, it would not be incorrect to apply this text in
part to Jesus before His crucifixion, for indeed, unlike the rest of

the human race, He remained "undefiled and separate from sinners" in that He was without sin, although upon earth He was not made higher than the heavens.

Let us look at this issue in greater depth. Christ possessed a dual nature, human and divine. Many, following part of the Augustinian package of falsehood, teach that Christ's human nature was unfallen, having misunderstood the true human nature of our Saviour. Yet Augustine's position was established upon the false premise of man's original sin, which naturally led him to wrongly postulate that Christ could not have inherited man's fallen nature. Many times, inconclusive statements have been used to deny the certainty of conclusive statements of Inspiration which establish the human nature of Christ. There is little doubt that this topic has been greatly weakened by serious errors of judgment by many who claim to be dividers of the truth.

We developed a carnal nature because we each have sinned. But when we are transformed by the new birth, our carnal mind is replaced by the spiritual mind.

> For they that are after the flesh do mind the things of the flesh; but they that are after the Spirit the things of the Spirit. For to be carnally minded is death; but to be spiritually minded is life and peace. Because the carnal mind is enmity against God: for it is not subject to the law of God, neither indeed can be. So then they that are in the flesh cannot please God. But ye are not in the flesh, but in the Spirit, if so be that the Spirit of God dwell in you. Now if any man have not the Spirit of Christ, he is none of his. And if Christ be in you, the body is dead because of sin; but the Spirit is life because of righteousness: But if the Spirit of him that raised up Jesus from the dead dwell in you, he that raised up Christ from the dead shall also quicken your mortal bodies by his Spirit that dwelleth in you. Therefore, brethren, we are debtors, not to the flesh, to live after the flesh. For if ye live after the flesh, ye shall die: but if ye through the Spirit do mortify the deeds of the body, ye shall live   (Romans 8:5–13).

Because Christ was plagued by the weaknesses of His fallen nature, it was far harder for Him to obey than it was for our first parents in the Garden of Eden. But by the constant infilling of the

Holy Spirit, indeed He did obey, and obey perfectly. When these facts are appreciated, any concept that Christ had an advantage over us entirely loses its force.

We might well ask why Christ's nature is so important to our understanding of the gospel. What we believe colors our understanding of truth. In order to support the false concept that man cannot obey the commandments of the Word, it was necessary to postulate that Christ, who we all agree did obey perfectly, had a nature which cannot be ours. For if Christ obeyed in a nature that could be ours, there would be no excuse for sinning, and a central theme of most evangelical Protestants is that we will continue to sin until the return of Jesus. If Christ had the same fallen nature as ours, the theory that a Spirit-filled man cannot obey God's law would collapse. But the Bible speaks unequivocally of Christ's nature and declares it to be identical with ours.

> And the Word was made flesh, and dwelt among us, (and we beheld his glory, the glory as of the only begotten of the Father,) full of grace and truth   (John 1:14).

Here, as in other passages to which we will be referring, the common Greek word *sarx* is used for flesh. In some translations *sarx* is translated as nature. The flesh or nature of Christ was no different from that of ordinary human beings. Paul clearly states:

> Concerning his Son Jesus Christ our Lord, which was made of the seed of David according to the flesh   (Romans 1:3).

Note that Paul does not compare Christ's human nature with Adam's. Had he done so he would have given some credence to the concept that Christ took upon Himself the nature of the pre-fall Adam. But he goes back just as far as David, a man who unfortunately, though referred to as "a man after mine own heart" (Acts 13:22), had many tragic blots upon his human life. This fact, that Christ was born of fallen human flesh, is confirmed too in Paul's writings to the Hebrews.

> Forasmuch then as the children are partakers of flesh and blood, he also himself likewise took part of the same; that through death he might destroy him that had the power of death, that is, the devil; and deliver them who through fear of death were all their lifetime subject to bondage. For verily he

> took not on him the nature of angels; but he took on him the
> seed of Abraham. Wherefore in all things it behoved him to
> be made like unto his brethren, that he might be a merciful
> and faithful high priest in things pertaining to God, to make
> reconciliation for the sins of the people. For in that he himself
> hath suffered being tempted, he is able to succour them that
> are tempted   (Hebrews 2:14–18).

It will be noted here that He was born of the seed of Abraham.
Abraham has been acknowledged as the father of the faithful.
Nevertheless he was also a man who seriously flawed his life's
experience by faithlessness in respect to the promise of God in the
birth of his son, and in lying to the king of Egypt. There is no
doubt that Paul understood that Christ took upon Himself our
human nature. Indeed, one of the most powerful statements of the
saving grace of Jesus again confirms this truth.

> There is therefore now no condemnation to them which are in
> Christ Jesus, who walk not after the flesh, but after the Spirit.
> For the law of the Spirit of life in Christ Jesus hath made me
> free from the law of sin and death. For what the law could not
> do, in that it was weak through the flesh, God sending his
> own Son *in the likeness of sinful flesh*, and for sin, con-
> demned sin in the flesh: that the righteousness of the law
> might be fulfilled in us, who walk not after the flesh, but after
> the Spirit   (Romans 8:1–4, emphasis added).

Here we see that Christ came in the likeness of sinful flesh and
condemned sin in the flesh [*sarx*] so that the righteousness of the
Law might be fulfilled in us who walk not after the flesh, but after
the Spirit. This text in a most remarkable way places the nature of
Christ in the context of the victory we too can have, if day by day
and moment by moment our whole strength is secured in the
power of the Divine. When we understand this promise, there is
no excuse for sinning. But even more powerfully, Paul gives us an
understanding of the human nature of Christ in his letter to the
Galatians.

> Even so we, when we were children, were in bondage under
> the elements of the world: But when the fulness of the time
> was come, God sent forth his Son, made of a woman, made
> under the law, to redeem them that were under the law, that
> we might receive the adoption of sons   (Galatians 4:3–5).

Here it will be seen that Christ is made under the law that He might redeem those who are under the law. There is no disputing the fact that Christ was made under the law so that He could redeem us who were under the bondage of the law. Consequently, Paul could write so confidently of the high priestly ministry of Christ for each of us.

> For we have not an high priest which cannot be touched with the feeling of our infirmities; but was in all points tempted like as we are, yet without sin   (Hebrews 4:15).

To understand what Christ was willing to do for each one of us that we might be saved, reveals the love that draws us to Him. It draws us to Him, and with a deeper and greater understanding of what it meant for God to give His only begotten Son to the human race that we might have eternal life. In the illumination of this truth, we can understand the following texts with a depth of meaning not otherwise comprehended.

> But God commendeth his love toward us, in that, while we were yet sinners, Christ died for us. . . . For if, when we were enemies, we were reconciled to God by the death of his Son, much more, being reconciled, we shall be saved by his life
> (Romans 5: 8, 10).

Now linking this truth from Romans 8:1–4 with the final call to the human race in Revelation chapter 3, no question remains as to the reason that Christ overcame in man's sinful nature. Jesus overcame in our sinful nature to provide strength for us to overcome Satan's temptations.

> To him that overcometh will I grant to sit with me in my throne, even as I also overcame, and am set down with my Father in his throne   (Revelation 3:21).

THE DILEMMA OF
CHRIST OUR EXAMPLE

Most Evangelicals strongly acknowledge the substitutionary role of Jesus through His sacrifice on Calvary. A minority, however, have accepted the moral-influence theory in which it is held that only a pagan god would require the death of his son to appease his wrath. But the emphasis upon the appeasement of a wrathful god does not do justice to our understanding of Christ's saving grace. The moral influence supporters believe that Christ came to be our example, but not our substitute. But, though we might not fully understand it, sin demands the death of the sinner; and only Christ our Creator could die as our substitute that we might live.

> And almost all things are by the law purged with blood; and without shedding of blood is no remission   (Hebrews 9:22).

As we investigate the Scriptures, it is evident that Jesus is both our Substitute and our Example. The failure of many Evangelicals to put Christ's substitutionary and exemplary roles together diminished the fullness of the gospel of our Lord.

When man sinned in Eden, he forged a separation which could be bridged only by divine grace. Mankind was hopeless and destined to eternal oblivion, but in the midst of despair God unfolded a provision, conceived before the foundation of the world, whereby helpless men could again face the future with hope.

> And I will put enmity between thee and the woman, and between thy seed and her seed; it shall bruise thy head, and thou shalt bruise his heel   (Genesis 3:15).

The mystery of the Incarnation, the ministry and sacrificial provisions of Christ began to be revealed step by step. As the years passed, further light unveiled more facets of the much-looked-for Redeemer.

> And Abel, he also brought of the firstlings of his flock and of the fat thereof. And the LORD had respect unto Abel and to his offering   (Genesis 4:4).

And Enoch also, the seventh from Adam, prophesied of these, saying, Behold, the Lord cometh with ten thousands of his saints   (Jude 14).

And Noah builded an altar unto the LORD; and took of every clean beast, and of every clean fowl, and offered burnt offerings on the altar   (Genesis 8:20).

And God said, Sarah thy wife shall bear thee a son indeed; and thou shalt call his name Isaac: and I will establish my covenant with him for an everlasting covenant, and with his seed after him   (Genesis 17:19).

Seeing that Abraham shall surely become a great and mighty nation, and all the nations of the earth shall be blessed in him
                                                       (Genesis 18:18).

The LORD hath sworn in truth unto David; he will not turn from it; Of the fruit of thy body will I set upon thy throne
                                                       (Psalm 132:11).

Therefore the Lord himself shall give you a sign; Behold, a virgin shall conceive, and bear a son, and shall call his name Immanuel   (Isaiah 7:14).

For unto us a child is born, unto us a son is given: and the government shall be upon his shoulder: and his name shall be called Wonderful, Counseller, The mighty God, The everlasting Father, The Prince of Peace   (Isaiah 9:6).

And there shall come forth a rod out of the stem of Jesse, and a Branch shall grow out of his roots   (Isaiah 11:1).

Behold, the days come, saith the LORD, that I will raise unto David a righteous Branch, and a King shall reign and prosper, and shall execute judgment and justice in the earth
                                                       (Jeremiah 23:5).

But perhaps to no one in pre-Christian times was the ministry and mission of Christ so fully revealed as to Isaiah.

Surely he hath borne our griefs, and carried our sorrows: yet we did esteem him stricken, smitten of God, and afflicted. But he was wounded for our transgressions, he was bruised for our iniquities: the chastisement of our peace was upon him; and with his stripes we are healed   (Isaiah 53:4–5).

The need for the sacrifice of the Son of God has long been a mystery to many. It must be kept in mind that Lucifer's heavenly challenge was a direct attack upon Christ's creatorship of this world. He challenged God's judgment in that he was not included in the counsels of creation. What Lucifer could not achieve in heaven, he sought by ruthless deception to achieve with earth's first inhabitants. When Adam yielded to his temptations, Satan assumed the title of the prince of this world, claiming the eternal allegiance of humanity. Through Satan's successful deceptions, sin became epidemic for all mankind, and with this came the inevitability of death.

> Wherefore, as by one man sin entered into the world, and death by sin; and so death passed upon all men, for that all have sinned   (Romans 5:12).

> For all have sinned, and come short of the glory of God
> (Romans 3:23).

> For the wages of sin is death; but the gift of God is eternal life through Jesus Christ our Lord   (Romans 6:23).

The redemption of man could be achieved only by the second Adam (Christ) taking man's place and redeeming his failure. Christ was man's Creator, and He alone could be man's Recreator. Lucifer's challenge was directed against Christ; and therefore Christ, and only He, could redeem lost man. Undoubtedly the angels would have gladly taken Christ's place, but it was not possible. Christ, by His perfect life on earth, gained complete victory over sin, and by His death and resurrection gained victory over the result of sin—death. In so doing, He drew men to Himself and forever falsified Satan's claim against the character of God before the entire universe. But more than that, He paid the supreme penalty on behalf of all humanity.

The Bible is emphatic in presenting this great theme. Therefore we must reject as unscriptural and untrue the moral-influence theory, which sees Christ as man's supreme Example, but not his substitute. But in so doing we must also reject the claims of many Evangelicals who see Christ as our Substitute but not man's example. Christ was both *Substitute* and *Example*.

As we have stated, there are those who recoil from the substitutionary work of Christ, wrongly interpreting it as portraying God as bloodthirsty, requiring a blood sacrifice to appease His anger, in much the same way that pagans seek to appease their gods. But Christ's sacrifice was not made to appease an angry God. This concept is Satan's counterfeit. Christ's sacrifice for man's salvation revealed not an angry God, but a God who demonstrated His limitless love for a rebellious people. The laws of the universe declared the inevitability of eternal death to every sinner. After the fall, Satan claimed the imprisonment of man in sin and death. The life of Christ, His victory over death, gave man freedom from sin and death that could be achieved by no other means.

> But now is Christ risen from the dead, and become the firstfruits of them that slept. For since by man came death, by man came also the resurrection of the dead. For as in Adam all die, even so in Christ shall all be made alive.
>
>   (1 Corinthians 15:20–22).

Without Christ, man is eternally helpless and hopeless, but he has been invited to look upon his crucified Lord and live. Jesus became our Substitute that we might have eternal life.

> For this is my blood of the new testament, which is shed for many for the remission of sins   (Matthew 26:28).

> So Christ was once offered to bear the sins of many; and unto them that look for him shall he appear the second time without sin unto salvation   (Hebrews 9:28).

> And ye know that he was manifested to take away our sins; and in him is no sin   (1 John 3:5).

> Take heed therefore unto yourselves, and to all the flock, over the which the Holy Ghost hath made you overseers, to feed the church of God, which he hath purchased with his own blood   (Acts 20:28).

> Forasmuch as ye know that ye were not redeemed with corruptible things, as silver and gold, from your vain conversation received by tradition from your fathers; but with the precious blood of Christ, as of a lamb without blemish and without spot   (1 Peter 1:18–19).

> But if we walk in the light, as he is in the light, we have
> fellowship one with another, and the blood of Jesus Christ his
> Son cleanseth us from all sin (1 John 1:7).

The substitution by Jesus in no wise limits the power of the cross.
It brings with it victory over sin. Some have misunderstood Paul's
comment that "Christ died for the ungodly" (Romans 5:6) to
indicate that Christ saved man in his sins. But a comparison of
scripture with scripture clarifies this matter and demonstrates that
God died to rescue the ungodly from his ungodliness. Those who
remain in ungodliness will perish.

> But the heavens and the earth, which are now, by the same
> word are kept in store, reserved unto fire against the day of
> judgment and perdition of ungodly men (2 Peter 3:7).

The ministry of Jesus was designed to lead men away from sin.

> Unto you first God, having raised up his Son Jesus, sent him
> to bless you, in turning away every one of you from his iniqui-
> ties (Acts 3:26).

The sacrifice of Jesus established the extent to which the love of
God would reach to wretched man in order that He might ensure
his salvation. It extended far beyond Christ's example to man; it
provided the only basis for the forgiveness of man's sins. Without
the substitutionary ministry of Jesus on Calvary, our life would be
meaningless and our hope vain. While most Evangelicals would
undoubtedly agree with this understanding, those who have accepted the moral-influence theory find themselves in direct conflict with the clearest testimony of Scripture.

On the other hand, the majority of Evangelicals have failed to
capture the importance of the second aspect of Christ's ministry.
Yet the Bible is just as clear concerning the fact that Jesus is our
complete Example, as it is concerning the substitutionary role of
Jesus. The ministry of Jesus is greatly diminished if we try to
separate His substitutionary role from His role as man's supreme
Example.

> For I have given you an example, that ye should do as I have
> done to you (John 13:15).

Of course these words were spoken in connection with the washing of the disciples' feet. It would demonstrate a particularly narrow reading of God's Word to defend the position that this alone was the area in which Christ was our Example. Peter in his well-known utterance stated:

> For even hereunto were ye called: because Christ also suffered for us, leaving us an example, that ye should follow his steps
> (1 Peter 2:21).

Many times we do not seek to examine the specific nature of the example to which Peter referred. But the next verse renounces all doubt on this point.

> Who did no sin, neither was guile found in his mouth
> (1 Peter 2:22).

Jesus was an example of obedience. Many rightly emphasize the wonderful substitutionary role of Christ's life and death, but do it to the minimizing of the exemplary aspect of His life. The Word of God teaches that Christ gave His perfect life that sinful and unworthy man might have eternal life.

> But he was wounded for our transgressions, he was bruised for our iniquities: the chastisement of our peace was upon him; and with his stripes we are healed   (Isaiah 53:5).

Yet we must not limit Christ's ministry to that of substitution; for one of the great eternal truths that arise from the selfless sacrifice of Jesus is His great example to those who are imprisoned by self-seeking motivation, which destroys the peace and fulfillment that Christ has offered to all mankind. This inevitably leads to a false concept of His life and substitution. Some claim that obedience is impossible; that by faith we must let Christ's life of perfect obedience substitute for our claimed inability to obey. Thus it is urged that we cannot possibly keep the law, nor need we keep the law, but that Christ's perfect law-keeping is a substitute for our moral violations. Thus it is claimed that God sees Christ's perfect law-keeping and imputes it to us. But there is a great difficulty with this assertion. Nowhere in the Scripture is there even the slightest support for such a concept. The Bible teaches that Christ's life of obedience is indeed a substitute for our days of disobedience from which we have repented; but never does the inspired Word declare that Christ's perfect life is a substitute for the required obedience of Christians. This understanding is a most important point, and must be reexamined by those who have permitted themselves to be deceived by the belief that God does not provide through Christ for daily victorious living. Paul points out the aim that Christ has for us.

> Always bearing about in the body the dying of the Lord Jesus,
> that the life also of Jesus might be made manifest in our body
> (2 Corinthians 4:10).

Since many now believe the devil's lie, That complete obedience in this life is impossible, they overlook the fact that there is absolutely no warrant in the Bible for their contention. Indeed, John adds his testimony to the fact that we should ever look to Christ as our Example. We would do well to review these precious promises.

> And every man that hath this hope in him purifieth himself,
> even as he is pure   (1 John 3:3).

> Little children, let no man deceive you: he that doeth righteousness is righteous, even as he is righteous   (1 John 3:7).

> He that saith he abideth in him ought himself also so to walk,
> even as he walked   (1 John 2:6).

In the above statements, John reflects the great pronouncement on the divine example given by Christ in His sermon on the mount.

> Be ye therefore perfect, even as your Father which is in heaven
> is perfect   (Matthew 5:48).

Christ's substitutionary virtues are not appropriated to those who persist in sin. It is mandatory that Christians comprehend this truth, or many will continue to believe the Devil's promise that sinning does not bar an individual from the promised eternal life. The glory of God is at stake in the victory of His children. Many will concede that Christ is our example of conduct, and that while we can never have complete victory over sin, we should aim at this ideal. But such a concept is far short of God's goal for His children. The Scripture brings us face to face with the truth that Christ is not only our Example of what we *should* be, but our example of what we *may* be when imbued with His Holy Spirit.

How plain are God's statements, when we accept the positive truth that Christ came to our earth in *our* human nature. When that is accepted as precious truth, all excuses for sin soon vanish, and we are thrown on the Rock Christ Jesus to make us in His likeness. Some Evangelicals have sought to make this scripturally backed truth of victorious Christian living of none effect, by talking in disparaging fashion of thousands of "little Christs" running around. Such mocking will only confirm the mocker in his or her unbelief. It will in no wise change the truth of God. Christ came to earth to redeem us from the *penalty* of sin and from the *power* of sin. In His substitutionary role He redeems us from the penalty of sin, and in His exemplary role He redeems man from the power of sin. It is of the greatest urgency that Evangelicals establish their understanding of the power of the gospel of Jesus Christ in their lives. What joy it is to realize that we have a Saviour who can save us to the uttermost; who is able to accomplish the restoration of the image of God in the soul. As our first act each morning we may ask Christ to take our lives and work His miracle of sustaining grace in our hearts. Let us again be reminded,

> Submit yourselves therefore to God. Resist the devil, and he will flee from you   (James 4:7).

THE DILEMMA OF
ACCEPTANCE AND ASSURANCE

Very prominent in the beliefs of Evangelicals is the claim to acceptance by God and assurance of salvation. It is understandable that those who believe in predestination will strongly support the concept of divine assurance and salvation. Their doctrine is that through the sacrifice of Christ, all are accepted who have been preordained by God to salvation. The concept that once one is saved, he can never be lost is an assurance that is often expressed by Evangelicals. Not uncommonly, Evangelicals state a specific day in which they were saved, and then declare that nothing they can do could lose them that salvation. They see salvation guaranteed through the Word of God. But surely it has been a selective use of scriptural passages such as those quoted below that has led many to believe that their salvation has been accomplished prior to the surrender of their lives fully to Christ.

> For the preaching of the cross is to them that perish foolishness; but unto us which are saved it is the power of God
> (1 Corinthians 1:18).

> For we are unto God a sweet savour of Christ, in them that are saved, and in them that perish   (2 Corinthians 2:15).

But to extract these and similar texts out of Scripture without understanding that there are conditions of salvation, is to lose the very impact of the gospel proclamation.

> By which also ye are saved, if ye keep in memory what I preached unto you, unless ye have believed in vain
> (1 Corinthians 15:2).

> For I am not ashamed of the gospel of Christ: for it is the power of God unto salvation to every one that believeth
> (Romans 1:16).

> He that believeth and is baptized shall be saved; but he that believeth not shall be damned   (Mark 16:16).

The Bible states that salvation in the fullest sense is yet future.

> Much more then, being now justified by his blood, we shall be saved from wrath through him. For if, when we were enemies, we were reconciled to God by the death of his Son, much more, being reconciled, we shall be saved by his life
> (Romans 5:9–10).

Acceptance and assurance are not apart from the commitment of God's people to continue in the faith.

> But he that shall endure unto the end, the same shall be saved
> (Matthew 24:13).

Peter perceptively enunciated this truth when he said,

> But in every nation he that feareth him, and worketh righteousness, is accepted with him   (Acts 10:35).

This verse can only be seen to mean God's sanctifying work in man. God Himself made the same declaration to Cain.

> If thou doest well, shalt thou not be accepted? and if thou doest not well, sin lieth at the door   (Genesis 4:7).

The concept that our salvation is unrelated to anything within us, so commonly held among evangelical Protestants, results from the emphasis that sanctification is at least partly the result of man's own efforts. This belief leads into many difficulties, one of which is the denial that doing righteousness results from God's work within man. When we accept that sanctification is by faith, then we can understand the beautiful truth that not only our justification, but also our sanctification is part of God's gift and of His acceptance. Furthermore we take no credit to ourselves, but praise God for all His merciful love in providing all that we need for acceptance. Paul, like Peter, reflected upon this truth of God.

> Let not then your good be evil spoken of: for the kingdom of God is not meat and drink; but righteousness, and peace, and joy in the Holy Ghost. For he that in these things serveth Christ is acceptable to God, and approved of men
> (Romans 14:16–18).

Earlier in the same letter to the Romans, Paul admonished,

> I beseech you therefore, brethren, by the mercies of God, that
> ye present your bodies a living sacrifice, holy, acceptable unto
> God, which is your reasonable service. And be not conformed
> to this world: but be ye transformed by the renewing of your
> mind, that ye may prove what is that good, and acceptable,
> and perfect, will of God   (Romans 12:1–2).

Paul was no less emphatic on this matter when he wrote to the
Corinthian believers.

> Wherefore we labour, that, whether present or absent, we may
> be accepted of him   (2 Corinthians 5:9).

Let us return to Peter who, substituting the word "elect" for
"accepted," stated that sanctification and obedience are involved
in acceptance.

> Elect according to the foreknowledge of God the Father,
> through sanctification of the Spirit, unto obedience and sprin-
> kling of the blood of Jesus Christ: Grace unto you, and peace,
> be multiplied   (1 Peter 1:2).

It is a most dangerous heresy to assume that without fully believing in Jesus we can be acceptable to Him, and that without obeying His commandments we can have the assurance of salvation.
Of course, there is nothing a Christian desires more than the
precious assurance that Jesus has accepted him as His child. The
authors no less than the readers desire such assurance. But we
must guard against presumption, a counterfeit assurance which
will blunt our realization of our lost condition. If our acceptance
into the family of heaven involves God-empowered obedience together with God's justifying gift, then "assurance" based on anything less leads to a false sense of security. It would be eternally
dangerous to encourage good men and women to claim salvation
while playing down the role of obedience. There are those who,
knowing the peril of this teaching, knowing that men and women
will be lost eternally as a consequence of accepting it, yet appear
to mute their concern, possibly in order to please the "Laodicean"
flock, or to gain or maintain a position of leadership.

> Let us draw near with a true heart in full assurance of faith,
> having our hearts sprinkled from an evil conscience, and our
> bodies washed with pure water   (Hebrews 10:22).

Here we discover that assurance is based upon faith, not presumption. We are to have our hearts sprinkled from an evil conscience and our bodies washed with pure water. This passage of Scripture does not present a description of a carnal person, but of one purified by the Holy Ghost, one who has met the conditions of salvation by the power of Christ in his life. Many evangelical Protestants have disseminated the false view that aged Christians are facing death tormented by the thought that they have, even at the sunset of their lives, no assurance of salvation. This argument is presented because some have taught that commandment-keeping plays a role in man's assurance; and these elderly persons are characterized as finding themselves so far short of the standard that they approach death with terror in their hearts rather than sweet assurance. Yet myriads of Christians, believing in the power of God to give the victory over the temptations of Satan, have serenely praised God for His perfect assurance of eternal life on their death beds. It is true that such souls see no good in themselves, but with supreme trust in Christ's perfect work for and in them, they have closed their eyes in full certainty of salvation. This peace comes because they have the purest knowledge that God has led them and guided them, in spite of their past sinful lives. Like Paul coming to the end of his earthly pilgrimage they could say,

> For I am now ready to be offered, and the time of my departure is at hand. I have fought a good fight, I have finished my course, I have kept the faith: henceforth there is laid up for me a crown of righteousness, which the Lord, the righteous judge, shall give me at that day: and not to me only, but unto all them also that love his appearing   (2 Timothy 4:6–8).

They may not have faced the executioner's block as did Paul, but as they face death it is with the full knowledge that God has strengthened their weak, frail human will and given them access to the divine strength purchased by Christ on Calvary. The authors have spent many hours with dying men and women and have been amazed at the assurance of those who have had confidence that Christ will keep them from falling and present them faultless before His Father (Jude 24).

The crucial problem is that many Christians have not given themselves wholly to allow the Lord to control their lives. As a result they are guilt-ridden and insecure, because they recognize that they cannot of themselves achieve salvation. There is a danger that to such persons, this concept of "once saved, always saved" offers hope, albeit false, for it preaches the "assurance" of salvation independent of Christ's victory in the life. Wishful thinking replaces sound biblical evidence as a basis for doctrine. Such persons accept the concept of the total depravity of man as a reason for their failure to meet God's unalterable conditions. Some "Christ-centered" sermons leave the impression that men and women can be assured of Christ's acceptance while still dabbling with sin. But such sermons offer these poor souls a counterfeit assurance. They do not bring real soul satisfaction, nor do they bestow that peace which passeth all understanding. Rather, ministers should uplift the sin-cleansing power of Christ in the life as well as His forgiveness. Here is genuine assurance. Peter, knowing he would shortly be martyred, evidenced the condition of his assurance in this way: After receiving the gift of the Holy Spirit in the life and advocating that we become partakers of the divine nature, he wrote,

> Wherefore the rather, brethren, give diligence to make your calling and election sure: for if ye do these things, ye shall never fall: for so an entrance shall be ministered unto you abundantly into the everlasting kingdom of our Lord and Saviour Jesus Christ   (2 Peter 1:10–11).

Here is assurance indeed! It is God's assurance, when we also have the merits of Christ in the life. We believe that every faithful, truth-loving, and Christ-empowered Christian has assurance. But we see the deadly danger of reliance upon false assurance. Those who attempt to claim the assurance of Christ's salvation while living in sin, are destined to the greatest anguish imaginable when they realize that they are lost from the kingdom of heaven. Nothing is more eternally hurtful than to preach to unsuspecting church members an assurance of salvation which cannot be claimed. Surely at the return of Jesus, those to whom such deadly errors have been preached will turn upon their pastors with unsurpassed savagery when they realize all too late that they have been misled so cruelly. When we recognize that our assurance is secure in Jesus, not in anything that we can do or have done, but in the fact that through His forgiving and cleansing sacrifice each one of us may gain daily strength to grow toward the kingdom of heaven, then that is assurance indeed. Never will our assurance be reflected in self-confidence, but it will be riveted upon the unfailing promises of God.

> Wherefore he is able also to save them to the uttermost that come unto God by him, seeing he ever liveth to make intercession for them   (Hebrews 7:25).

> Now unto him that is able to keep you from falling, and to present you faultless before the presence of his glory with exceeding joy   (Jude 24).

> The Lord is not slack concerning his promise, as some men count slackness; but is longsuffering to us-ward, not willing that any should perish, but that all should come to repentance   (2 Peter 3:9).

> There hath no temptation taken you but such as is common to man: but God is faithful, who will not suffer you to be tempted above that ye are able; but will with the temptation also make a way to escape, that ye may be able to bear it   (1 Corinthians 10:13).

THE DILEMMA OF
IMMEDIATE LIFE AFTER DEATH

Colin was walking through the graveyard of an ancient country church in England when he noted on the gravestone of a seventeenth-century tomb these words, "He sleepeth until Jesus comes." No more than twenty or so paces from that grave was a nineteenth-century gravestone on which was inscribed, "At home with the Lord." These represent two incompatible concepts of life after death. Clearly this Anglican church had been greatly influenced by the Reformation, for at that time many Bible-believing rectors were teaching a death sleep for the dead awaiting the Second Coming of Jesus. But obviously, as the years went by, the subsequent rectors reverted to the pre-Reformation concept of immediate life after death and the immortality of the soul. It is difficult to understand any believing Christian not recognizing the focus of the New Testament writers upon the Resurrection as the great hope of the Christian. Let us see this emphasis.

> Let not your heart be troubled: ye believe in God, believe also in me. In my Father's house are many mansions: if it were not so, I would have told you. I go to prepare a place for you. And if I go and prepare a place for you, I will come again, and receive you unto myself; that where I am, there ye may be also (John 14:1–3).

> For the Lord himself shall descend from heaven with a shout, with the voice of the archangel, and with the trump of God: and the dead in Christ shall rise first (1 Thessalonians 4:16).

> But every man in his own order: Christ the firstfruits; afterward they that are Christ's at his coming (1 Corinthians 15:23).

> So also is the resurrection of the dead. It is sown in corruption; it is raised in incorruption: it is sown in dishonour; it is raised in glory: it is sown in weakness; it is raised in power: it is sown a natural body; it is raised a spiritual body. There is a natural body, and there is a spiritual body (1 Corinthians 15:42–44).

If death were the liberation of the soul to live in eternal joy and happiness, then death would be the friend of man. Indeed, the sooner we die the better it would be. But the Bible does not treat death as a friend, but as an enemy.

> The last enemy that shall be destroyed is death
>   (1 Corinthians 15:26).

The destruction of death takes place at the time of the destruction of the wicked.

> And death and hell were cast into the lake of fire. This is the
> second death   (Revelation 20:14).

At that time we have the promise that death will never happen again in the history of mankind.

> And God shall wipe away all tears from their eyes; and there
> shall be *no more death,* neither sorrow, nor crying, neither
> shall there be any more pain: for the former things are passed
> away   (Revelation 21:4, emphasis added).

The concept of an immortal soul is rooted in paganism. The Greek pagans believed in a soul that eternally preexisted the body; and for a short period of time this good soul was, as it were, incarcerated in an evil body. That was the basis of the Greek concept that the soul was good and the body was evil. The Greeks joyously looked for the liberation of the soul from the imprisonment of the body. It was upon this basis the Greeks decided that free men could not work with their hands, but only with their mind; and that manual work was the work of slaves. So strict was Plato on this belief that he declared that the study of engineering was unfit for a free man. Aristotle, however, did sanction the study of engineering by free men, so long as engineering was not practiced by them.

But the concept of immediate life after death far antedates the Greek civilization. The Babylonian kingdom was established by Nimrod, the postdiluvian who became the founder of paganism, the elements of which can be seen in all modern pagan religions. With the abundance of evidence that we have on the issue of mortality and immortality, it would seem unlikely that any Christian could make a mistake; yet this error is deeply tenacious and widespread. The acceptance by evangelical Protestants of immediate life after death is perhaps one of the greatest of errors, and certainly opens the floodgate toward the spiritism which is rampant within many Christian circles today.

The Bible teaches that at this time only God has immortality.

> Now unto the King eternal, immortal, invisible, the only wise God, be honour and glory for ever and ever. Amen
> (1 Timothy 1:17).

> Which in his times he shall shew, who is the blessed and only Potentate, the King of kings, and Lord of lords; who only hath immortality, dwelling in the light which no man can approach unto; whom no man hath seen, nor can see: to whom be honour and power everlasting. Amen
> (1 Timothy 6:15–16).

Paul teaches that we are mortal until the return of Jesus Christ, when we will at last be clothed with immortality.

> Who will render to every man according to his deeds: to them who by patient continuance in well doing seek for glory and honour and immortality, eternal life   (Romans 2:6–7).

> For this corruptible must put on incorruption, and this mortal must put on immortality. So when this corruptible shall have put on incorruption, and this mortal shall have put on immortality, then shall be brought to pass the saying that is written, Death is swallowed up in victory   (1 Corinthians 15:53–54).

These texts are so clear and closely defined that there is absolutely no way in which the pagan concept of the immortal soul can have any credence in Christian dogma. Death is consistently treated in the Bible as a state of unconsciousness, frequently referred to as sleep.

> But I would not have you to be ignorant, brethren, concerning them which are *asleep,* that ye sorrow not, even as others which have no hope (1 Thessalonians 4:13, emphasis added).

> Then they also which are fallen *asleep* in Christ are perished. . . . But now is Christ risen from the dead, and become the firstfruits of them that *slept*
> (1 Corinthians 15:18, 20, emphasis added).

These things said he: and after that he saith unto them, Our friend Lazarus *sleepeth;* but I go, that I may awake him out of *sleep.* Then said his disciples, Lord, if he sleep, he shall do well. Howbeit Jesus spake of his death: but they thought that he had spoken of taking of rest in sleep. Then said Jesus unto them plainly, Lazarus is dead
(John 11:11–14, emphasis added).

This concept is also clearly presented in the Old Testament.

And many of them that *sleep* in the dust of the earth shall awake, some to everlasting life, and some to shame and everlasting contempt (Daniel 12:2, emphasis added).

Any idea that the dead might have any conscious awareness of what takes place after their demise is wholly denied by Scripture.

For the living know that they shall die: but the dead know not any thing, neither have they any more a reward; for the memory of them is forgotten. Also their love, and their hatred, and their envy, is now perished; neither have they any more a portion for ever in any thing that is done under the sun
(Ecclesiastes 9:5–6).

Whatsoever thy hand findeth to do, do it with thy might; for there is no work, nor device, nor knowledge, nor wisdom, in the grave, whither thou goest (Ecclesiastes 9:10).

For in death there is no remembrance of thee: in the grave who shall give thee thanks? (Psalm 6:5).

His sons come to honour, and he knoweth it not; and they are brought low, but he perceiveth it not of them (Job 14:21).

His breath goeth forth, he returneth to his earth; in that very day his thoughts perish (Psalm 146:4).

The dead praise not the LORD, neither any that go down into silence (Psalm 115:17).

If a man die, shall he live again? all the days of my appointed time will I wait, till my change come (Job 14:14).

If I wait, the grave is mine house: I have made my bed in the darkness (Job 17:13).

> I charge thee therefore before God, and the Lord Jesus Christ,
> who shall judge the quick and the dead at his appearing and
> his kingdom   (2 Timothy 4:1).

The Second Coming is the awakening of the saints from their
death sleep.

> Thy dead men shall live, together with my dead body shall
> they arise. Awake and sing, ye that dwell in dust: for thy dew
> is as the dew of herbs, and the earth shall cast out the dead
> (Isaiah 26:19).

> As for me, I will behold thy face in righteousness: I shall be
> satisfied, when I awake, with thy likeness   (Psalm 17:15).

> For the Lord himself shall descend from heaven with a shout,
> with the voice of the archangel, and with the trump of God:
> and the dead in Christ shall rise first (1 Thessalonians 4:16).

It is true that on first reflection there are texts which appear to
indicate eternal torment for the wicked. But if the wicked were in
torment eternally, sin would be in the universe for eternity; some-
thing which God will not allow. One text that has frequently been
used to support eternal burning torment is the third angel's message of Revelation 14.

> And the third angel followed them, saying with a loud voice,
> If any man worship the beast and his image, and receive his
> mark in his forehead, or in his hand, the same shall drink of
> the wine of the wrath of God, which is poured out without
> mixture into the cup of his indignation; and he shall be tor-
> mented with fire and brimstone in the presence of the holy
> angels, and in the presence of the Lamb: And the smoke of
> their torment ascendeth up for ever and ever: and they have
> no rest day nor night, who worship the beast and his image,
> and whosoever receiveth the mark of his name
> (Revelation 14:9–11).

Understood in the light of similar texts in the Bible, this passage
has to refer to the death, not the punishment, being eternal.

> Even as Sodom and Gomorrha, and the cities about them in
> like manner, giving themselves over to fornication, and going
> after strange flesh, are set forth for an example, suffering the
> vengeance of eternal fire   (Jude 7).

Clearly the fires are not still burning in Sodom and Gomorrha. The destruction of those cities has been forever. It is in such a sense that we must understand the Bible concept of "everlasting" in relationship to the destruction of the wicked. When we consider Revelation 14:9–11 in the light of 2 Thessalonians 1, we understand the picture clearly, for here it states that the wicked are punished with everlasting destruction.

> In flaming fire taking vengeance on them that know not God, and that obey not the gospel of our Lord Jesus Christ: who shall be punished with everlasting destruction from the presence of the Lord, and from the glory of his power
> (2 Thessalonians 1:8–9).

Jesus also indicated that the punishment was everlasting. That is to say, destruction and separation from God is everlasting.

> And these shall go away into everlasting punishment: but the righteous into life eternal   (Matthew 25:46).

Many texts of the Bible indicate the perishing of the wicked.

> I tell you, Nay: but, except ye repent, ye shall all likewise perish   (Luke 13:3).

> For the wages of sin is death; but the gift of God is eternal life through Jesus Christ our Lord   (Romans 6:23).

> Behold, all souls are mine; as the soul of the father, so also the soul of the son is mine: the soul that sinneth, it shall die
> (Ezekiel 18:4).

> But these, as natural brute beasts, made to be taken and destroyed, speak evil of the things that they understand not; and shall utterly perish in their own corruption   (2 Peter 2:12).

> And fear not them which kill the body, but are not able to kill the soul: but rather fear him which is able to destroy both soul and body in hell   (Matthew 10:28).

Wrongly some defenders of the immortal soul have claimed that those supporting the concept of death as sleep rely almost wholly on the Old Testament. It is implied that the Old Testament taught one way and the New Testament another, but as this chapter confirms, they speak with a single voice. Thus we must reject those claims to the contrary like the following.

> A survey of [those who believe that death is a sleep] reveals an almost total dependence on Old Testament texts to support their theory of soul sleep and annihilationism. If one brings up New Testament texts which clearly teach the contrary, they are dismissed on the basis of an assumed priority of the Old Testament as over against the New Testament. They do not see any progress from the Old Testament to the New Testament but flatten out the distinction between the Testaments. Instead of giving priority to the clarity of the New Testament, they feel safer staying with the blurred vision found in the Old Testament. We must beware of those theological positions which depend primarily on Old Testament texts
>
> (Morey, R., *Death and the Afterlife*, Minneapolis: Bethany House Publishers, 1984, p. 23).

Some have offered as "proof" of eternal life after death, the parable of the rich man and Lazarus. But even a superficial review of this parable leads one to recognize that it is not built upon a factual situation. For example, how could Lazarus be so close to the rich man burning in hell that he could touch him and put water upon his tongue? The whole parable has an entirely different purpose, seeking to explain to the Pharisees that riches are not a sign of the approbation of God; and that often paupers whom they despised would find their way into the kingdom of heaven if they were faithful to God.

In the light of the Bible understanding that death is an unconscious state, it is wholly understandable why the New Testament writers are so riveted upon the Second Coming, and why it was the all-consuming passion of their preaching. Surely the return of Jesus is the blessed hope of all Christians.

> Looking for that blessed hope, and the glorious appearing of the great God and our Saviour Jesus Christ   (Titus 2:13).

Of course, at the Resurrection, those who have died will not have any consciousness of the passage of time, and the return of Jesus will seem just as immediate for Abel, the first human to die, as for the last to have died. The concept is reasonable, and as we look for the return of Jesus, it strengthens our heart and mind against any of the pagan practices that are associated with such issues as spiritism, reincarnation, necromancy, seances, and the like.

There is no question that just before the return of Jesus, Satan will exploit the widespread belief in immediate life after death as a basis to deceive men and women and capture them for eternal destruction. Evangelical Protestants have an urgent need to wholly reevaluate this issue of the state of man in death. If they do not, they will be in perilous danger of being deceived by spiritist impersonations of Satan and his wicked angels.

> And no marvel; for Satan himself is transformed into an angel of light   (2 Corinthians 11:14).

> And I saw three unclean spirits like frogs come out of the mouth of the dragon, and out of the mouth of the beast, and out of the mouth of the false prophet. For they are the spirits of devils, working miracles, which go forth unto the kings of the earth and of the whole world, to gather them to the battle of that great day of God Almighty   (Revelation 16:13–14).

> Now the Spirit speaketh expressly, that in the latter times some shall depart from the faith, giving heed to seducing spirits, and doctrines of devils   (1 Timothy 4:1).

The biblical understanding of man's state in death will protect God's people from the most compelling deceptions that Satan and his angels will bring against them just before the return of Jesus.

THE DILEMMA OF
THE END-TIME JUDGMENT

While Evangelicals frequently make much of the white-throne judgment, it still is a particularly difficult concept to understand the purpose of this end-time judgment in the light of belief in immediate life after death. If at death the soul has gone either to heaven or to hell, then the life has been already judged. But as we have seen, Scripture testifies against this pagan doctrine.

Scripture is explicit on this end-time judgment. Paul spoke of it as he talked to the Athenians on Mars Hill.

> And the times of this ignorance God winked at; but now commandeth all men every where to repent: because he hath appointed a day, in the which he will judge the world in righteousness by that man whom he hath ordained; whereof he hath given assurance unto all men, in that he hath raised him from the dead   (Acts 17:30–31).

Paul unquestionably believed the judgment was future to his time.

> And as he reasoned of righteousness, temperance, and judgment to come, Felix trembled, and answered, Go thy way for this time; when I have a convenient season, I will call for thee   (Acts 24:25).

Judgment, according to the Scriptures, involves all humanity.

> I said in mine heart, God shall judge the righteous and the wicked: for there is a time there for every purpose and for every work   (Ecclesiastes 3:17).

> For we must all appear before the judgment seat of Christ; that every one may receive the things done in his body, according to that he hath done, whether it be good or bad   (2 Corinthians 5:10).

The deeds of man do not save him, but nevertheless, we are judged by our deeds.

> For God shall bring every work into judgment, with every secret thing, whether it be good, or whether it be evil   (Ecclesiastes 12:14).

For I was an hungred, and ye gave me meat: I was thirsty,
and ye gave me drink: I was a stranger, and ye took me in:
naked, and ye clothed me: I was sick, and ye visited me: I was
in prison, and ye came unto me. Then shall the righteous
answer him, saying, Lord, when saw we thee an hungred, and
fed thee? or thirsty, and gave thee drink? When saw we thee a
stranger, and took thee in? or naked, and clothed thee? Or
when saw we thee sick, or in prison, and came unto thee?
And the King shall answer and say unto them, Verily I say
unto you, Inasmuch as ye have done it unto one of the least of
these my brethren, ye have done it unto me. Then shall he say
also unto them on the left hand, Depart from me, ye cursed,
into everlasting fire, prepared for the devil and his angels: for
I was an hungred, and ye gave me no meat: I was thirsty, and
ye gave me no drink: I was a stranger, and ye took me not in:
naked, and ye clothed me not: sick, and in prison, and ye
visited me not. Then shall they also answer him, saying, Lord,
when saw we thee an hungred, or athirst, or a stranger, or
naked, or sick, or in prison, and did not minister unto thee?
Then shall he answer them, saying, Verily I say unto you,
Inasmuch as ye did it not to one of the least of these, ye did it
not to me   (Matthew 25:35–45).

This end-time judgment is defined in both the Old and the New
Testaments. In the prophetic message of Daniel chapter seven we
find a judgment just before the end of human history. This judgment clearly takes place at a set period of time, and not at the
death of each person.

I beheld till the thrones were cast down, and the Ancient of
days did sit, whose garment was white as snow, and the hair
of his head like the pure wool: his throne was like the fiery
flame, and his wheels as burning fire. A fiery stream issued
and came forth from before him: thousand thousands ministered unto him, and ten thousand times ten thousand stood
before him: the judgment was set, and the books were opened.
I beheld then because of the voice of the great words which
the horn spake: I beheld even till the beast was slain, and his
body destroyed, and given to the burning flame. As concerning the rest of the beasts, they had their dominion taken away:
yet their lives were prolonged for a season and time. I saw in
the night visions, and, behold, one like the Son of man came

with the clouds of heaven, and came to the Ancient of days, and they brought him near before him. And there was given him dominion, and glory, and a kingdom, that all people, nations, and languages, should serve him: his dominion is an everlasting dominion, which shall not pass away, and his kingdom that which shall not be destroyed   (Daniel 7:9–14).

But the judgment shall sit, and they shall take away his dominion, to consume and to destroy it unto the end. And the kingdom and dominion, and the greatness of the kingdom under the whole heaven, shall be given to the people of the saints of the most High, whose kingdom is an everlasting kingdom, and all dominions shall serve and obey him
(Daniel 7:26–27).

Records of heaven have been kept with unerring accuracy, reflecting the life of every human being, and it is from these records that judgment is made.

And I saw the dead, small and great, stand before God; and the books were opened: and another book was opened, which is the book of life: and the dead were judged out of those things which were written in the books, according to their works   (Revelation 20:12).

In this judgment some, whose names have been written in the book of life, are tragically blotted out because sometime during their lives they have turned away from their commitment to God. This fact is again incontrovertible evidence against the error of "once saved, always saved."

He that overcometh, the same shall be clothed in white raiment; and I will not blot out his name out of the book of life, but I will confess his name before my Father, and before his angels   (Revelation 3:5).

Whosoever therefore shall confess me before men, him will I confess also before my Father which is in heaven. But whosoever shall deny me before men, him will I also deny before my Father which is in heaven   (Matthew 10:32–33).

Whosoever therefore shall be ashamed of me and of my words in this adulterous and sinful generation; of him also shall the Son of man be ashamed, when he cometh in the glory of his Father with the holy angels   (Mark 8:38).

On the other hand, it is at this time that the sins of God's faithful people are blotted out from the records of heaven.

> Repent ye therefore, and be converted, that your sins may be blotted out, when the times of refreshing shall come from the presence of the Lord   (Acts 3:19).

To fully understand this end-time judgment, it is necessary to understand all the great judgments of God, each of which is essential to God's plan to restore perfect harmony in the universe in a way that sin will never rise again throughout the eons of eternity. It was the first "judgment" that necessitated the subsequent four judgments required in God's restoration plan.

(1) *Judgment in Eden:* When man sinned, violating God's holy law, death was pronounced upon the whole human race, for:

> The wages of sin is death   (Romans 6:23).

> For all have sinned, and come short of the glory of God   (Romans 3:23).

In this one act of disobedience man judged himself unworthy of eternal life, and separated himself from God.

> Therefore as by the offence of one judgment came upon all men to condemnation; even so by the righteousness of one the free gift came upon all men unto justification of life   (Romans 5:18).

Accepting Satan's lie that man can disobey God and yet live eternally, man made a judgment for Satan and against God. Adam and Eve had the choice of accepting the Word of the One who is the Truth (Deuteronomy 32:4); the One who cannot lie (Titus 1:2); or accepting the word of the one who is the father of lies (John 8:44). Adam and Eve unaccountably made the wrong choice. Thus man brought the inevitable judgment of God against him. But before we condemn Adam and Eve for their choice, we must recognize that every human being ever since has had to make the same decision and tragically, all have chosen at some time during their lives to follow the deceptions of Satan.

(2) *Judgment at the Cross:* Because the judgment at Eden left man helpless and without hope, God provided the blood sacrifice of His own beloved Son, thus providing hope for the doomed race. Satan had declared God to be unjust and arbitrary, but the sacrifice of Jesus removed from the universe all doubt concerning the character of God. At the cross, Satan's lies were laid bare for all to see. At the cross, the righteous character of God was fully vindicated. At the cross, the true rightful ownership of the world was determined. At the cross, the depth of the love of God was totally revealed to mankind. In contrast to the failure of the first Adam in Eden, the second Adam made a judgment for God and against Satan.

> Now is the judgment of this world: now shall the prince of this world be cast out. And I, if I be lifted up from the earth, will draw all men unto me   (John 12:31–32).

Thus man was reconciled to God.

> For if, when we were enemies, we were reconciled to God by the death of his Son, much more, being reconciled, we shall be saved by his life   (Romans 5:10).

> Even so by the righteousness of the one the free gift came upon all men unto justification of life   (Romans 5:18).

(3) *The End-Time Judgment:* Before the return of Jesus He makes a judgment *for* his people and *against* those who have falsely claimed to be His followers. Pointing to the time just prior to the return of Jesus, Daniel says:

> And at that time shall Michael stand up, the great prince which standeth for the children of thy people: and there shall be a time of trouble, such as never was since there was a nation even to that same time: and at that time thy people shall be delivered, every one that shall be found written in the book   (Daniel 12:1).

This judgment provides assurance to the inhabitants of the universe that none who would perpetuate sin will inhabit heaven, and that no one surrendered to the will of Christ will be lost.

(4) *Judgment of the Wicked:* John further depicts a judgment scene in heaven in which the saints participate. It takes place during the thousand years when the saints reign with Christ.

> And I saw thrones, and they sat upon them, and judgment was given unto them: and I saw the souls of them that were beheaded for the witness of Jesus, and for the word of God, and which had not worshipped the beast, neither his image, neither had received his mark upon their foreheads, or in their hands; and they lived and reigned with Christ a thousand years   (Revelation 20:4).

While John does not specify the identities of those who are being judged by the saints, other scripture indicates that this judgment refers to both the judgment of the wicked of earth, and the fallen angels. Paul declares:

> Do ye not know that the saints shall judge the world? and if the world shall be judged by you, are ye unworthy to judge the smallest matters? Know ye not that we shall judge angels? how much more things that pertain to this life?
> (1 Corinthians 6:2–3).

Therefore the names of all created beings who have not been redeemed will be reviewed by the saints prior to their eternal destruction. This in no way indicates that God is uncertain of the justice of His judgment; but God allows redeemed men to understand fully His absolute justice as a righteous judge.

(5) *The Judgment of Destruction:* The final judgment of God is an executive judgment. In this judgment the unfaithful of heaven and earth are eternally destroyed, so that the canker of sin can be eliminated from the universe. In this judgment, not only will the wicked be eternally destroyed and sin forever expunged from the universe, but the earth, now fearfully marred by sin, will be cleansed by fire so that a new and perfect earth can be recreated for the home of the saints. Peter talks of this executive judgment when he says that God reserves "the unjust unto the day of judgment to be punished" (2 Peter 2:9).

In this judgment the rebellious angels also are destroyed.

For if God spared not the angels that sinned, but cast them down to hell, and delivered them into chains of darkness, to be reserved unto judgment   (2 Peter 2:4).

And the angels which kept not their first estate, but left their own habitation, he hath reserved in everlasting chains under darkness unto the judgment of the great day   (Jude 6).

It was certainly this judgment to which Jesus pointed when He said:

Verily I say unto you, It shall be more tolerable for the land of Sodom and Gomorrha in the day of judgment, than for that city   (Matthew 10:15).

Woe unto thee, Chorazin! woe unto thee, Bethsaida! for if the mighty works, which were done in you, had been done in Tyre and Sidon, they would have repented long ago in sackcloth and ashes. But I say unto you, It shall be more tolerable for Tyre and Sidon at the day of judgment, than for you. And thou, Capernaum, which art exalted unto heaven, shalt be brought down to hell: for if the mighty works, which have been done in thee, had been done in Sodom, it would have remained until this day. But I say unto you, That it shall be more tolerable for the land of Sodom in the day of judgment, than for thee   (Matthew 11:21–24).

The judgment of the righteous, sometimes called the investigative judgment, needs to be separated from the other judgments in order to more fully understand Christ's ministry in the heavenly sanctuary prior to His Second Coming. Frequently the investigative judgment is referred to as the pre-Advent judgment. This term can be misleading and confusing. Some who use the term "pre-Advent judgment" apply it to the judgment of the world at the cross. Others believe that the pre-Advent judgment began when Christ entered heaven upon His ascension. It is impossible that this judgment of the righteous could have commenced at either of these times. Daniel chapter seven certainly precludes such an interpretation. The judgment spoken of there is prophetic of the last days, and could not refer to the cross nor to an event which began at Christ's ascension. It points to judgment subsequent to the rise of the little-horn power. Furthermore, because of the end-time setting of Daniel 7:9-14, this judgment must necessarily take place near the end of time. Paul also referred to this judgment well beyond the time in which he lived:

> And the times of this ignorance God winked at; but now commandeth all men every where to repent: because he hath appointed a day, in the which he will judge the world in righteousness by that man whom he hath ordained; whereof he hath given assurance unto all men, in that he hath raised him from the dead   (Acts 17:30–31).

> In the day when God shall judge the secrets of men by Jesus Christ according to my gospel   (Romans 2:16).

> For we must all appear before the judgment seat of Christ; that every one may receive the things done in his body, according to that he hath done, whether it be good or bad
> (2 Corinthians 5:10).

Further, Paul looked for a judgment in the future when he addressed Felix.

> And as he reasoned of righteousness, temperance, and judgment to come, Felix trembled, and answered, Go thy way for this time; when I have a convenient season, I will call for thee
> (Acts 24:25).

James also pointed his readers to a future judgment:

> So speak ye, and so do, as they that shall be judged by the law of liberty   (James 2:12).

It is this investigative judgment to which Daniel refers in the seventh chapter of his prophetic book. After dealing briefly with the history of the Babylonian, Medo-Persian, Grecian and Roman empires (Daniel 7:1–7), he depicts the little-horn power which was identified by the sixteenth-century Reformers as the Papal Church which arose out of the ashes of pagan Rome (Daniel 7:8).[1] Then Daniel portrays the great judgment scene where the books of heavenly record are reviewed.

---

[1] See chapter 21, "The Dilemma of the Antichrist."

> I beheld till the thrones were cast down, and the Ancient of days did sit, whose garment was white as snow, and the hair of his head like the pure wool: his throne was like the fiery flame, and his wheels as burning fire. A fiery stream issued and came forth from before him: thousand thousands ministered unto him, and ten thousand times ten thousand stood before him: the judgment was set, and the books were opened (Daniel 7:9–10).

Daniel is here describing the end-time judgment prior to the destruction of the little-horn power.

> I beheld then because of the voice of the great words which the horn spake: I beheld even till the beast was slain, and his body destroyed, and given to the burning flame (Daniel 7:11).

Further confirmation that this judgment is just prior to Christ's return is provided by Daniel.

> I saw in the night visions, and, behold, one like the Son of man came with the clouds of heaven, and came to the Ancient of days, and they brought him near before him. And there was given him dominion, and glory, and a kingdom, that all people, nations, and languages, should serve him: his dominion is an everlasting dominion, which shall not pass away, and his kingdom that which shall not be destroyed (Daniel 7:13–14).

In Revelation chapter 14, the context pinpoints the fact that the end-time judgment of verse seven is for the righteous.

> And I saw another angel fly in the midst of heaven, having the everlasting gospel to preach unto them that dwell on the earth, and to every nation, and kindred, and tongue, and people, saying with a loud voice, Fear God, and give glory to him; for the hour of his judgment is come: and worship him that made heaven, and earth, and the sea, and the fountains of waters (Revelation 14:6–7).

This message was not given with power and understanding until the nineteenth century, and is given within the framework of the call for the separation of God's people from Babylon and the presentation of the everlasting gospel to "every nation, kindred, tongue, and people." This message points to an investigative judgment which precedes the coming of Christ. Ezekiel explicitly described the final judgment, saying:

> And to the others he said in mine hearing, Go ye after him through the city, and smite: let not your eye spare, neither have ye pity: slay utterly old and young, both maids, and little children, and women: but come not near any man upon whom is the mark; and begin at my sanctuary. Then they began at the ancient men which were before the house (Ezekiel 9:5–6).

Some have held to a different interpretation of Daniel's prophecy. They point to the context of Daniel 7:10 as evidence that it is the little-horn power that is judged. That is true, and consistent with the investigative judgment. The little-horn power at the end of time is not an atheistic power, but one which claims to be chosen of God. The investigative judgment reviews not only the little-horn power, but all those who have claimed allegiance to God. However, this judgment is not limited to the little-horn power. Daniel chapters seven, eight and twelve are parallel chapters. Daniel indicates that it is in the judgment that Michael (Christ)[2] stands up for His people.

> And at that time shall Michael stand up, the great prince which standeth for the children of thy people: and there shall be a time of trouble, such as never was since there was a nation even to that same time: and at that time thy people shall be delivered, every one that shall be found written in the book   (Daniel 12:1).

Thus in the investigative judgment, those following the little-horn power who have made false claims to be the people of God will be revealed. But the true children of God will be revealed also. The judgment is in favor of the faithful of all ages. This judgment holds the richest assurance to God's people as our Lord stands up for His children. The all-loving and just character of God is also displayed before the entire universe throughout this judgment. God's Word assures us that in the judgment His name will be vindicated. In his great prayer of repentance, David cried out:

---

[2] Evidence that Michael is another of Christ's names can be derived from the following texts: Jude 9; 1 Thessalonians 4:16.

> Against thee, thee only, have I sinned, and done this evil in
> thy sight: that thou mightest be justified when thou speakest,
> and be clear when thou judgest   (Psalm 51:4).

Seizing upon this prophetic statement, Paul stated:

> God forbid: yea, let God be true, but every man a liar; as it is
> written, That thou mightest be justified in thy sayings, and
> mightest overcome when thou art judged   (Romans 3:4).

Thus the investigative judgment at the end of time is not alone to
judge man, but to demonstrate the unquestionable purity and righteousness of God's character. It is true that on Calvary, God's
character was fully vindicated, when He showed the infinite love
that was demonstrated in the sacrifice of Jesus. In the judgment
He demonstrates that all are saved that have responded to the
matchless love of heaven. The end-time judgment not only vindi-
cates God, but also His people. Those whose names are written in
the Lamb's Book of Life will not come into condemnation, for
Jesus said:

> Verily, verily, I say unto you, He that heareth my word, and
> believeth on him that sent me, hath everlasting life, and shall
> not come into condemnation; but is passed from death unto
> life   (John 5:24).

The three angels' messages of Revelation 14:6–12, like the message of Daniel 7:9–10, bring into condemnation the followers of a
false apostate message. These people have professed to be followers of the true God, while following the deceptions of Satan. It is
in the first of these messages that the judgment is introduced.

> Saying with a loud voice, Fear God, and give glory to him;
> for the hour of his judgment is come: and worship him that
> made heaven, and earth, and the sea, and the fountains of
> waters   (Revelation 14:7).

It is not difficult to understand why Evangelicals have found
grave difficulty in understanding the fullness of this end-time judgment. It is because they have failed to cast off the pagan concepts
of the immortal soul which overcame Catholicism in the early
centuries of the Christian era. If immediate life after death were a
soundly-based Bible principle, then there would be no need for an
end-time judgment.

It is readily acknowledged that God Himself does not need an end-time judgment. He has known from eternity by His fore-knowledge who will be saved, and who will be lost. But that is not the case with the angels. They do not have infinite knowledge, and God in His tender mercy does not save one person eternally until the angels have had the opportunity to review the records. That is fulfilled during this end-time judgment. It is evident that the myriads before the throne are angels participating in this judgment.

> I beheld till the thrones were cast down, and the Ancient of days did sit, whose garment was white as snow, and the hair of his head like the pure wool: his throne was like the fiery flame, and his wheels as burning fire. A fiery stream issued and came forth from before him: thousand thousands ministered unto him, and ten thousand times ten thousand stood before him: the judgment was set, and the books were opened
> (Daniel 7:9–10).

That these myriads ministering to Christ in His judgment are angels, is certified by John.

> And I beheld, and I heard the voice of many angels round about the throne and the beasts and the elders: and the number of them was ten thousand times ten thousand, and thousands of thousands
> (Revelation 5:11).

It is after the angels have reviewed the records that every human being that has been faithful to Christ will be redeemed into the kingdom of heaven. But not one soul, angelic or human, is destroyed eternally at this time, for there is one group who will inhabit eternity who have not had the opportunity of reviewing the records. This group comprises the redeemed saints. During the millennium they will be sitting in judgment reviewing the records of the lost.

> And I saw thrones, and they sat upon them, and judgment was given unto them: and I saw the souls of them that were beheaded for the witness of Jesus, and for the word of God, and which had not worshipped the beast, neither his image, neither had received his mark upon their foreheads, or in their hands; and they lived and reigned with Christ a thousand years
> (Revelation 20:4).

Do ye not know that the saints shall judge the world? and if the world shall be judged by you, are ye unworthy to judge the smallest matters? know ye not that we shall judge angels? how much more things that pertain to this life?

(1 Corinthians 6:2–3).

God leaves no doubt as to His justice and mercy. Before the destruction of the wicked, all God's created beings will have reviewed the records of the lost, and acknowledged the perfect justice of God. It is not that the heavenly angels nor the redeemed saints will find any errors in the justice of God, but God, determined to secure eternity, opens before the angels and man the opportunity to understand all that has been done for the salvation of the human race. Thus it is that the Scripture proclaims that affliction shall not rise a second time.

What do ye imagine against the LORD? he will make an utter end: affliction shall not rise up the second time (Nahum 1:9).

An understanding of the end-time judgment provides a wonderful understanding of the great love and mercy of God in the salvation of His people, consistent with the love and mercy demonstrated on Calvary. In addition, it demonstrates the extent to which our God will go to leave no doubt whatsoever concerning His love and absolute justice throughout the entire universe.

THE DILEMMA OF
CHRIST, OUR HEAVENLY HIGH PRIEST

With such a strong emphasis upon the sacrifice of Jesus on Calvary, and its centrality to human salvation, it is surprising that most Evangelicals have little understanding of the High-Priestly ministry of Jesus Christ. The book of Hebrews, particularly, expounds in great detail the ministration of Christ in the heavenly sanctuary. In this book we discover many aspects of Christ's heavenly-sanctuary ministry that enhance our knowledge of the principles of salvation. Other biblical writers also elucidate Christ's High-Priestly ministry.

(1) Christ is our sacrifice.

> For then must he often have suffered since the foundation of the world: but now once in the end of the world hath he appeared to put away sin by the sacrifice of himself
> (Hebrews 9:26).

> But this man, after he had offered one sacrifice for sins for ever, sat down on the right hand of God (Hebrews 10:12).

> Purge out therefore the old leaven, that ye may be a new lump, as ye are unleavened. For even Christ our passover is sacrificed for us (1 Corinthians 5:7).

(2) He is our High Priest.

> Wherefore, holy brethren, partakers of the heavenly calling, consider the Apostle and High Priest of our profession, Christ Jesus (Hebrews 3:1).

> For such an high priest became us, who is holy, harmless, undefiled, separate from sinners, and made higher than the heavens (Hebrews 7:26).

> But Christ being come an high priest of good things to come, by a greater and more perfect tabernacle, not made with hands, that is to say, not of this building (Hebrews 9:11).

(3) He is our Advocate.

My little children, these things write I unto you, that ye sin not. And if any man sin, we have an advocate with the Father, Jesus Christ the righteous (1 John 2:1).

(4) He is our Mediator.

For there is one God, and one mediator between God and men, the man Christ Jesus (1 Timothy 2:5).

Wherefore then serveth the law? It was added because of transgressions, till the seed should come to whom the promise was made; and it was ordained by angels in the hand of a mediator. Now a mediator is not a mediator of one, but God is one (Galatians 3:19–20).

And for this cause he is the mediator of the new testament, that by means of death, for the redemption of the transgressions that were under the first testament, they which are called might receive the promise of eternal inheritance (Hebrews 9:15).

But now hath he obtained a more excellent ministry, by how much also he is the mediator of a better covenant, which was established upon better promises (Hebrews 8:6).

And to Jesus the mediator of the new covenant, and to the blood of sprinkling, that speaketh better things than that of Abel (Hebrews 12:24).

(5) He is our Intercessor.

Therefore will I divide him a portion with the great, and he shall divide the spoil with the strong; because he hath poured out his soul unto death: and he was numbered with the transgressors; and he bare the sin of many, and made intercession for the transgressors (Isaiah 53:12).

Wherefore he is able also to save them to the uttermost that come unto God by him, seeing he ever liveth to make intercession for them (Hebrews 7:25).

(6) He is our Judge.

I charge thee therefore before God, and the Lord Jesus Christ, who shall judge the quick and the dead at his appearing and his kingdom (2 Timothy 4:1).

> Henceforth there is laid up for me a crown of righteousness,
> which the Lord, the righteous judge, shall give me at that day:
> and not to me only, but unto all them also that love his
> appearing   (2 Timothy 4:8).

> For the Father judgeth no man, but hath committed all judg-
> ment unto the Son   (John 5:22).

It will be noted that at least six terms are used in the Scriptures to
define the High-Priestly ministration of Christ: Sacrifice, Advocate, Mediator, Intercessor, High Priest and Judge. The ministry
therefore is worthy of much deeper and insightful study by
Evangelicals, so that this aspect of Christ's ministry for the salvation of mankind is better understood. The High-Priestly ministry
of Christ is essential to rounding off our concepts of the salvation
acts of God for the human race.

It will be recalled that the tabernacle in the wilderness and the
temple in Jerusalem were symbols and types of the heavenly sanctuary, and the priesthood was a type of Christ's ministry. Thus
the Word of God to Moses was as follows:

> And let them make me a sanctuary; that I may dwell among
> them. According to all that I shew thee, after the pattern of
> the tabernacle, and the pattern of all the instruments thereof,
> even so shall ye make it   (Exodus 25:8–9).

Exodus chapters 25 through 27 provide precise details of the
earthly tabernacle. In Exodus chapter 28, the details of the high
priest's garb and ministry are outlined. For century after century
the Jews followed these instructions. However, these earthly services were to point to the heavenly High Priest who now ministers
in the heavenly sanctuary. That the earthly sanctuary was but a
type of the heavenly, and that the ministry of the high priest is but
a type of the heavenly ministry of Jesus Christ is declared in the
book of Hebrews.

> Now of the things which we have spoken this is the sum: We
> have such an high priest, who is set on the right hand of the
> throne of the Majesty in the heavens; a minister of the sanctu-
> ary, and of the true tabernacle, which the Lord pitched, and
> not man. For every high priest is ordained to offer gifts and
> sacrifices: wherefore it is of necessity that this man have
> somewhat also to offer. For if he were on earth, he should not

be a priest, seeing that there are priests that offer gifts according to the law: who serve unto the example and shadow of heavenly things, as Moses was admonished of God when he was about to make the tabernacle: for, See, saith he, that thou make all things according to the pattern shewed to thee in the mount   (Hebrews 8:1–5).

The sanctuary message and the High-Priestly ministry of Christ is much more important to us than was the ministry of the earthly sanctuary by earthly priests in the time of the psalmist. Yet some of the same lessons the psalmist learned can be a rich blessing in our understanding of salvation today. In the seventy-third Psalm, David expresses his frustration at what appeared to be the prosperity of the wicked, and expresses his envy of them, but it was when he evaluated the prosperity of the wicked in the light of the sanctuary that he received a new and better understanding.

Until I went into the sanctuary of God; then understood I their end. Surely thou didst set them in slippery places: thou castedst them down into destruction. How are they brought into desolation, as in a moment! they are utterly consumed with terrors   (Psalm 73:17–19).

The earthly sanctuary ministries were divided into the daily and the yearly services. The daily services included the evening and morning sacrifices and other offerings which were used for many different purposes. (1) The thank offering (Genesis 8:20); (2) at the consecration of the priests (Exodus 29:15–28); (3) for a ceremonial cleansing after a physical ailment (Leviticus 15:1–15); (4) for when a leper was healed of his leprosy (Leviticus 14:1–32); (5) for the cleansing of a woman after childbirth (Leviticus 12:1–8). Sin offerings were sacrifices made for ignorant or unpremeditated sins.

But the soul that doeth ought presumptuously, whether he be born in the land, or a stranger, the same reproacheth the LORD; and that soul shall be cut off from among his people. Because he hath despised the word of the LORD, and hath broken his commandment, that soul shall utterly be cut off; his iniquity shall be upon him   (Numbers 15:30–31).

> Speak unto the children of Israel, saying, If a soul shall sin through ignorance against any of the commandments of the LORD concerning things which ought not to be done, and shall do against any of them: if the priest that is anointed do sin according to the sin of the people; then let him bring for his sin, which he hath sinned, a young bullock without blemish unto the LORD for a sin offering (Leviticus 4:2–3).

The trespass offering was especially designed for sins against fellow humans or in those instances where God had been deprived of that due to Him. The offering was for sins ignorantly committed, but it appears, on some occasions, to have been for deliberate sin against one's fellow man. The trespass sacrifice was offered for dishonesty involving property or person. Complete restitution required full restoration, plus a twenty-percent additional amount which was required before the trespass offering could be made.

> If a soul commit a trespass, and sin through ignorance, in the holy things of the LORD; then he shall bring for his trespass unto the LORD a ram without blemish out of the flocks, with thy estimation by shekels of silver, after the shekel of the sanctuary, for a trespass offering: and he shall make amends for the harm that he hath done in the holy thing, and shall add the fifth part thereto, and give it unto the priest: and the priest shall make an atonement for him with the ram of the trespass offering, and it shall be forgiven him
>
> (Leviticus 5:15–16).

The peace offering centered upon man's relationship with God. The most common peace offering was a thank offering. God allowed less than perfect offerings for a freewill offering, but when the peace offerings sealed a vow with God, the animal had to be without spot, for it represented the perfect Son of God.

> Either a bullock or a lamb that hath any thing superfluous or lacking in his parts, that mayest thou offer for a freewill offering; but for a vow it shall not be accepted
>
> (Leviticus 22:23).

The meat offering was an offering of meal or flour as a recognition of man's dependence upon God for all his physical sustenance.

> And if thy oblation be a meat offering baken in the fryingpan, it shall be made of fine flour with oil   (Leviticus 2:7).

> And every oblation of thy meat offering shalt thou season with salt; neither shalt thou suffer the salt of the covenant of thy God to be lacking from thy meat offering: with all thine offerings thou shalt offer salt   (Leviticus 2:13).

> No meat offering, which ye shall bring unto the LORD, shall be made with leaven: for ye shall burn no leaven, nor any honey, in any offering of the LORD made by fire
> (Leviticus 2:11).

The yearly services occurred in the spring, summer and autumn. The services centered around first the Passover, which commenced on the fourteenth day of the first month (Abib) of the Jewish calendar, corresponding to late March or April. The Passover was first celebrated immediately prior to God's deliverance of His people from Egypt. The term Passover refers to the fact that just before the departure of the Israelites from Egypt, the destroying angel passed over the homes where the blood of the pascal lamb was painted on the doorpost, thus insuring that the firstborn son would not be destroyed. This service prefigured the fact that Christ would be slain for the deliverance of God's people from sin and death.

Associated with the Passover were the Feast of Unleavened Bread and the Feast of Firstfruits. The Feast of Pentecost was held fifty days after the Feast of Firstfruits, to signify the end of the harvest of the winter crops. Thus the feast was held early in summer.

> Even unto the morrow after the seventh sabbath shall ye number fifty days; and ye shall offer a new meat offering unto the LORD   (Leviticus 23:16).

The Passover was fulfilled with the death of Jesus, who became the risen Firstfruits.

> But now is Christ risen from the dead, and become the firstfruits of them that slept   (1 Corinthians 15:20).

So also the antitype of the Feast of Pentecost was fulfilled when the disciples received the outpouring of the Holy Spirit in their lives.

> And when the day of Pentecost was fully come, they were all
> with one accord in one place. . . . And they were all filled
> with the Holy Ghost, and began to speak with other tongues,
> as the Spirit gave them utterance   (Acts 2:1, 4).

The most solemn of all the Jewish feasts was the Day of Atonement in early autumn, either in September or October. With the
Day of Atonement came the Feast of Trumpets and the Feast of
Tabernacles. The Day of Atonement was another symbol of the
sacrifice of Christ, but it also represented the atonement made by
Christ, the heavenly High Priest, at the end of time. The Day of
Atonement was celebrated once a year. During the year, as it
were, the sins of the people were in symbol placed upon the
sanctuary; and the sanctuary was cleansed of these sins on the
Day of Atonement. It was a sacred time, fully explained in Leviticus
chapter sixteen. The people of the congregation were required to
have confessed all sins before this sacred day.

> And this shall be a statute for ever unto you: that in the
> seventh month, on the tenth day of the month, ye shall afflict
> your souls, and do no work at all, whether it be one of your
> own country, or a stranger that sojourneth among you: for on
> that day shall the priest make an atonement for you, to cleanse
> you, that ye may be clean from all your sins before the LORD
>   (Leviticus 16:29–30).

It was a time when the sins of the people were cleansed or blotted
out. Peter spoke of this time during the Pentecost experience.

> Repent ye therefore, and be converted, that your sins may be
> blotted out, when the times of refreshing shall come from the
> presence of the Lord   (Acts 3:19).

This text refers to the pouring out of God's Spirit at the end of
time upon His faithful people, as prophesied by the prophet Joel.

> And it shall come to pass afterward, that I will pour out my
> spirit upon all flesh; and your sons and your daughters shall
> prophesy, your old men shall dream dreams, your young men
> shall see visions: and also upon the servants and upon the
> handmaids in those days will I pour out my spirit. And I will
> shew wonders in the heavens and in the earth, blood, and fire,

and pillars of smoke. The sun shall be turned into darkness, and the moon into blood, before the great and the terrible day of the LORD come   (Joel 2:28–31).

Evangelicals proclaim that the cross is the center of faith, and they are correct in doing so. However, the sacrifices, without the priestly ministry that was indivisibly linked with the sacrifices, would have been incomplete. In Leviticus chapter sixteen, the term *atonement* is used thirteen times. Every aspect of the sacrifice and High-Priestly ministry is referred to as part of the "atonement." While it is true that Christ's sacrificial atonement was complete on the cross, it is erroneous to conclude that Christ's atonement was completed on the cross. The atonement also includes the High-Priestly ministry of Jesus. The high priest ministered the blood of the sacrifice for the forgiveness of sin (justification) and for character cleansing (sanctification).

Paul points out that Jesus was a priest of an entirely higher order than the order of the Levitical priest.

As he saith also in another place, Thou art a priest for ever after the order of Melchisedec. . . . Called of God an high priest after the order of Melchisedec   (Hebrews 5:6, 10).

Jesus was the fulfillment of the prophecy of Psalm 110:4.

The LORD hath sworn, and will not repent, Thou art a priest for ever after the order of Melchizedek   (Psalm 110:4).

In Hebrews is provided the explanation of the reason that the Melchidesec priesthood is superior to the Levitical priesthood.

(For those priests were made without an oath; but this with an oath by him that said unto him, The Lord sware and will not repent, Thou art a priest for ever after the order of Melchisedec:) By so much was Jesus made a surety of a better testament. And they truly were many priests, because they were not suffered to continue by reason of death: but this man, because he continueth ever, hath an unchangeable priesthood. Wherefore he is able also to save them to the uttermost that come unto God by him, seeing he ever liveth to make intercession for them. For such an high priest became us, who is holy, harmless, undefiled, separate from sinners, and made higher than the heavens; who needeth not daily, as those high priests, to offer up sacrifice, first for his own sins, and then for the

people's: for this he did once, when he offered up himself.
For the law maketh men high priests which have infirmity;
but the word of the oath, which was since the law, maketh the
Son, who is consecrated for evermore.   (Hebrews 7:21–28).

Paul further links the sacrifice of Christ with His High-Priestly
ministry and its relationship to our salvation.

But Christ being come an high priest of good things to come,
by a greater and more perfect tabernacle, not made with hands,
that is to say, not of this building; neither by the blood of
goats and calves, but by his own blood he entered in once into
the holy place, having obtained eternal redemption for us. For
if the blood of bulls and of goats, and the ashes of an heifer
sprinkling the unclean, sanctifieth to the purifying of the flesh:
how much more shall the blood of Christ, who through the
eternal Spirit offered himself without spot to God, purge your
conscience from dead works to serve the living God?
                                          (Hebrews 9:11–14).

His ministry is wonderfully detailed in the same chapter.

It was therefore necessary that the patterns of things in the
heavens should be purified with these; but the heavenly things
themselves with better sacrifices than these. For Christ is not
entered into the holy places made with hands, which are the
figures of the true; but into heaven itself, now to appear in the
presence of God for us   (Hebrews 9:23–24).

In the type, the atonement was not completed until the blood was
ministered on and before the mercy seat.

And there shall be no man in the tabernacle of the congregation when he goeth in to make an atonement in the holy
place, until he come out, and have made an atonement for
himself, and for his household, and for all the congregation of
Israel   (Leviticus 16:17).

So Christ is ministering His blood for penitent sinners today. The
atonement accomplished on the cross is completed in the heavenly
sanctuary above. This understanding of the High-Priestly ministry
of Christ completes the total concept of the salvation of God and
exactly parallels the Old Testament types which were no longer
necessary once Jesus, our Passover, had died for us. Everything
that Jesus did and is doing is essential for our salvation. If He had

not been born a babe in Bethlehem, we could not be saved. If he had not lived a perfect life upon the earth, we could not be saved. If he had not died the death of reconciliation, we could not be saved. If he had not been resurrected from the dead, we could not be saved. If He had not ascended to His Father in heaven, we could not be saved. If he were not now our ministering High Priest, we could not be saved. If He did not return to take home His faithful people, we could not be saved.

The understanding of the High-Priestly ministry of Christ in the heavenly sanctuary above gives us a much clearer picture of the total commitment of God through Jesus for the salvation of men and women. It helps us to understand the justification of God's people. It helps us to understand sanctification and the eradication of sin from God's people. It helps us to understand the time gap between Christ's death and His Second Coming.

Most Evangelicals have tended to minimize this critical part of the salvation acts of God. Yet as we read through the Old Testament and into the New Testament we discover that the sanctuary service is intimately linked with the sacrificial services which preshadowed both the death and the ministry of Jesus Christ. Just as the priest of Old Testament times sprinkled the blood of sacrifices before and in the sanctuary built on earth, so Christ in the heavenly sanctuary is sprinkling the blood of His sacrifice for the forgiveness and cleansing of the human race, preparing them for the eternal home. As Paul described this heavenly ministration, so John in vision saw the temple in heaven.

> And the temple of God was opened in heaven, and there was seen in his temple the ark of his testament: and there were lightnings, and voices, and thunderings, and an earthquake, and great hail   (Revelation 11:19).

> And after that I looked, and, behold, the temple of the tabernacle of the testimony in heaven was opened (Revelation 15:5).

In the scope of this book we do not have space to enlarge upon the fullness of the sanctuary message. The authors have written a book, *The Sacrificial Priest*,[1] which deals comprehensively with

---

[1] Standish, Colin & Russell, *The Sacrificial Priest*, Hartland Publications, Box 1, Rapidan, VA 22733.

the wonderful High-Priestly ministry of Christ. This book would be of considerable help to Evangelicals interested in a much greater understanding of the ministry of Christ prior to His Second Coming.

THE DILEMMA OF
THE ANTICHRIST

The powerful impact that the Reformers made in identifying the Roman Catholic Church as the antichrist can scarcely be imagined today. As millions of Christians joined the Reform movement, the Roman Church attempted to use methodology that had proven successful for more than a thousand years, in order to eliminate those whom it designated as heretics. With the exception of isolated communities of faithful Christians (often hidden in the natural fortresses of the earth), the Church had been remarkably successful in its persecution. This success had been achieved by the strong arm of the state, which ruthlessly eliminated millions of those who would not bow to the Church's authority. Historians have not agreed upon the number of people who were tortured and martyred for their efforts to uphold pure Bible truth, but estimates range from fifty to one hundred-twenty million. These men, women and children lost their lives during the period of papal domination. Almost all of this was done at the hand of secular governments which subserved the desires of the Papacy.

The period of the sixteenth century proved different. Sickened by the excesses and corruptions of the Papacy, many monarchs and rulers embraced the Protestant proclamation and were no longer vassals of the Papacy, obeying its every command. Thus in a number of European countries the arm of flesh was not available to carry out the Roman Church's dictates. The situation naturally alarmed the Roman Catholic Church. The Papacy was not accustomed to these circumstances. Therefore it discerned that a new methodology had to be devised to counter the rapid spread of the Reformation which was engulfing Europe.

Looking back for understanding of this development, we must go to the fourteenth century. Ecclesiastical turmoil was everywhere. The new pope, Urban VI, returned the seat of the Papacy to Rome after seventy years of exile in Avignon, France. But many of the cardinals rebelled against Urban's strict discipline. They returned to Avignon and crowned the bishop of Geneva, Robert of Canbray, as Pope Clement VII. Now there were two popes. The year was 1378. For thirty-one years both Rome and Avignon continued to elect popes, each claiming to be the vicar of Christ, each claiming to be the infallible successor of Peter, each claiming that the other was the antichrist. In England a powerful priest, the rector of Lutterworth, John Wycliffe, agreed with both of them:

> The fiend no longer reigns in one, but in two priests that men may the more easily overcome them both in Christ's name.
>
> Now is antichrist divided and one pope fights against the other (Emma H. Adams, *John Wycliffe*, Pacific Publishing Association, Oakland, 1890).

Wycliffe's stand against papal taxation would have led him to the stake if it were not for the powerful friendship of English peers and even the royal court.

However two great Bohemian Reformers, John Huss and Jerome of Prague, were burned at the stake four decades later for their stand against the Papacy. They had been greatly influenced by Wycliffe. Identification of the Papacy as the antichrist became the constant theme of the Protestant Reformation. Martin Luther believed that the Papacy, not an individual pope, is the antichrist. This sentiment was shared by Zwingli, Calvin, Knox, and other Reformers. The following are comments of just a few of the Reformers; the consensus of the views is striking:

(1) Martin Luther:

> There sits the man, of whom the apostle wrote (2 Thessalonians 2:3–4), that will oppose and exalt himself above all that is called God. That man of sin to be revealed, the son of perdition . . . He suppresses the law of God and exalts his commandments above the commandments of God (LeRoy Froom, *The Prophetic Faith of Our Fathers*, Volume 2, page 281).
>
> We here are of the conviction that the Papacy is the seat of the true and real antichrist (ibid, 256).

(2) John Calvin:

> I deny him to be the vicar of Christ. . . . He is an antichrist—I deny him to be the head of the Church (*John Calvin Tracts*, Volume 1, pages 219, 220).

(3) John Knox:

> That tyranny which the pope himself has for so many ages exercised over the church, the very antichrist and son of perdition, of whom Paul speaks   (*The Zurich Letters,* page 199).

(4) Philip Melanchthon:

> It is most manifest, and true without any doubt, that the Roman pontiff, with his whole order and kingdom, is very antichrist. . . . Likewise, in 2 Thessalonians 2, Paul clearly says that the man of sin will reign in the church by showing himself above the worship of God   (LeRoy Froom, *The Prophetic Faith of Our Fathers,* Volume 2, page 296–299).

(5) Sir Isaac Newton:

> But it [the Papacy] was a kingdom of a different kind than the other kingdoms (referred to in Daniel 7:7–8) . . . and such a seer, prophet, and king is the church of Rome [referring to the little horn of Daniel 7]
> (Sir Isaac Newton, *Observations of the Prophecies,* page 75).

(6) John Wesley:

> Romanish papacy, he is, in an emphatical sense, the man of sin
> (John Wesley, *Antichrist and His Ten Kingdoms,* page 110).

(7) Samuel Lee (a seventeenth-century Rhode Island minister):

> It is agreed among all main lines of the English Church that the Roman pontiff is the antichrist
> (Samuel Lee, *The Cutting Off of Antichrist,* page 1).

The statement from the *Westminster Confession of Faith* of the Church of England, which was also adopted by the Presbyterians, is significant:

> There is no other head of the church but the Lord Jesus Christ, nor can the pope of Rome in any sense be head thereof, but is that antichrist, that man of sin and son of perdition that exalteth himself in the church against Christ and all that is called God   (*The Westminster Confession of Faith,* Section 6, Chapter 24).

The Helvetic Convention of Switzerland mentions the Papacy as the predicted antichrist. The Lutheran statement contained in the Smalcald Articles refers to the pope as the very antichrist who exalts himself and opposes Christ. The 1680 New England Confession of Faith states that Jesus Christ is the head of the church, and not the pope of Rome, who is identified as the antichrist and the son of perdition.

The identification of the Papacy as the antichrist was the focal point of the Reformation.

These ideas became the dynamic force which drove Luther [and the other Reformers] on in his contest with the Papacy (*Encyclopedia Brittanica,* 1962 edition, Volume 2, page 61).

After the initial thrust of the Reformation, the identification of the Papacy as the antichrist became less common. However, it was still strong among Protestants of almost all denominations until about the end of the nineteenth century. Today, in the environment created by the Ecumenical movement, it has certainly become most unpopular to identify the Papacy as the antichrist. Some Evangelical Christians prefer to ignore the issue, believing it to be of little importance in today's modern society.

The concept of the antichrist goes back in history to the time of the sixth century B.C. when Daniel prophesied about the apostate power that he called the "little horn" (Daniel 7:8–11, 24–26; 8:9–12, 23–25). Jews living in the period before the birth of Christ often referred to the coming of the anti-Messiah. Some of the Maccabees, a powerful Jewish sect of the inter-Testamental period, were convinced that the little horn (the anti-Messiah) was fulfilled when a Seleucid king, Antiochus Epiphanes, desecrated the temple in Jerusalem during the second century B.C., necessitating the rededication of the sanctuary. Some Christians thought the emperor Nero (died A.D. 68), who ruthlessly slaughtered many of the Christians in Rome, might have been the fulfillment of Daniel's prophecy. But the apostle John clarified the matter when he indicated that neither Antiochus Epiphanes nor Nero could fulfill the specification of the antichrist. Writing about the end of the first century after Christ, John identified the antichrist, not as one person, but as many people, some of whom were present in his day.

> Little children, it is the last time: and as ye have heard that
> antichrist shall come, even now are there many antichrists;
> whereby we know that it is the last time   (1 John 2:18).

It surprises many people to learn that the antichrist is mentioned
by name only four times in the Bible, and then only by the apostle
John (1 John 2:18, 22; 4:3; 2 John 7). But it has not dampened the
enthusiasm of Christians who know that the antichrist is the most
crucial enemy of truth, salvation, the cross and of Christ Himself.
There has been no shortage of effort to provide a contemporary
identification of the antichrist. During the dreadful years of the
second World War, some identified Adolf Hitler as the antichrist.
Others have identified the great Muslim power, and more recently
atheistic communism, as antichrist. While the term *antichrist* is
sparingly used in the Scriptures, the apostate power is widely
described in the Bible. Paul uses the terms, "the man of sin," and
"the son of perdition." He pinpoints the appearance of antichrist
as occurring prior to the Second Coming of Christ.

> Let no man deceive you by any means: for that day shall not
> come, except there come a falling away first, and that man of
> sin be revealed, the son of perdition; who opposeth and exalteth
> himself above all that is called God, or that is worshipped; so
> that he as God sitteth in the temple of God, shewing himself
> that he is God   (2 Thessalonians 2:3–4).

In Revelation, John uses different symbols to identify the antichrist,
including the beast, Babylon and the impure woman.

> And the beast which I saw was like unto a leopard, and his
> feet were as the feet of a bear, and his mouth as the mouth of
> a lion: and the dragon gave him his power, and his seat, and
> great authority   (Revelation 13:2).

> And the great city was divided into three parts, and the cities
> of the nations fell: and great Babylon came in remembrance
> before God, to give unto her the cup of the wine of the fierce-
> ness of his wrath   (Revelation 16:19).

> So he carried me away in the spirit into the wilderness: and I
> saw a woman sit upon a scarlet coloured beast, full of names
> of blasphemy, having seven heads and ten horns. And the
> woman was arrayed in purple and scarlet colour, and decked
> with gold and precious stones and pearls, having a golden cup

in her hand full of abominations and filthiness of her fornication: And upon her forehead was a name written, MYSTERY, BABYLON THE GREAT, THE MOTHER OF HARLOTS AND ABOMINATIONS OF THE EARTH

(Revelation 17:3–5).

As stated earlier, the Old Testament prophet Daniel described the antichrist power with the symbol of the little horn.

And he shall speak great words against the most High, and shall wear out the saints of the most High, and think to change times and laws: and they shall be given into his hand until a time and times and the dividing of time (Daniel 7:25).

The centuries-old question remains: Who or what is the antichrist? Is it one individual, or is it a succession of individuals, a nation or a power? Has the antichrist come? Is he here now or will he appear in the future? Many within Evangelical Protestantism look for a satanic individual who appears just prior to the end of the world who will sit in the rebuilt temple in Jerusalem blaspheming and desecrating it and ruthlessly persecuting. But such a description defies the whole Evangelical understanding of the Reformation. In his book, *The Church of Rome, The Apostasy*, Presbyterian Board of Publication, 1841, William Cuninghame specifically identified the Papacy as the man of sin and the antichrist. He pointed to the Roman Catholic church as guilty of idolatry, Mary reverence, image worship and Satan worship (page 105). He also pointed out numerous instances of blasphemy by the Church (pages 199, 120). He identified the call to come out of Babylon (Revelation 18:4–5) as a call out of the Roman Catholic Church (pages 155–160).

In 1846, in his book, *Christ and Antichrist,*[1] the former pastor of the Norfolk, Virginia, Presbyterian Church, Samuel J. Cassels, presented one of the most comprehensive reviews that identified the Papacy as the antichrist. This book was thoroughly endorsed by Presbyterian, Episcopalian, Methodist and Baptist leaders of the day. Yet by the end of the nineteenth century, identification of the Papacy as the antichrist had been undermined.

---

[1] Available from Hartland Publications, Box 1, Rapidan, VA 22733.

In his book, *Christianity and Anti-Christianity in Their Final Conflict,* Samuel Andrews identified the beast that is described in Revelation 13 as a cruel and oppressing secular state. He did not identify it as the Papacy, as Protestants prior to the twentieth century had consistently identified it. By the earlier part of the twentieth century, the futuristic interpretation of prophecy had received almost universal acceptance among Protestants; yet there were still a few Protestants who correctly identified the Papacy as the antichrist. Fred J. Peters in his work, *The Present Antichrist,* (1920) was one of these. He cited the Waldensians, Huss, Jerome, Luther, Calvin, Sir Isaac Newton, Latimer, Bunyan, Moody and Spurgeon as dedicated Christians who were agreed that the man of sin is the antichrist pope. Peters correctly identified the seventy-week prophecy of Daniel 9 as the 490 years left to the Jews to be God's chosen people, a period of time which ended in A.D. 34.

It is because of the failure to identify the Papacy as the antichrist of biblical prophecy, that conservative Protestants have dared to join hands with conservative Catholics in an alliance that would have filled the Reformers with the utmost grief.

> In what's being called a historic declaration, evangelicals including Pat Robertson and Charles Colson joined with conservative Roman Catholic leaders Tuesday in upholding the ties of faith that bind the nation's largest and most politically active religious groups.
>
> They urged Catholics and evangelicals to increase their efforts against abortion and pornography and to lobby for value-laden education, but to no longer hold each other at theological arm's length and to stop aggressive proselytization of each other's flocks.
>
> Addressing a major source of tension between Catholics and evangelicals in the United States, Eastern Europe and South America, the declaration says "it is neither theologically legitimate nor a prudent use of resources" to proselytize among active members of another Christian community
> (*The San Bernardino Sun,* March 30, 1994, p A2).

The Roman Catholic Church was determined to dispel the indisputable scriptural evidence that identified the Papacy as the antichrist power. They claim that the antichrist is an individual who will appear only at the end of time and will cause havoc in the Christian church for a literal period of three-and-a-half years.

Today this Jesuit-devised futurist view predominates in mainstream Protestantism. In his book, *His Apocalypse* (1924), John Quincy Adams presents the futurist's concept of the satanic power that will appear at the end of time. This false concept was also supported by F. M. Messenger in his book, *The Coming Superman* (1928). More recently the futurist view was supported by Herman Hoyt in his book *The End Time*, Moody Press, (1969). Yet John's description of the antichrist excluded the possibility that it be one individual.

It has taken time, but the Jesuits have done an effective work. In the Council of Trent (1545–1563), one of the great burdens of the Roman Catholic bishops was to destroy the influence of the Protestant identification of the Papacy as the antichrist. Eventually the task was given to the newly formed elite intelligentsia, the Jesuits. In 1585 Francisco Ribera contrived his futurist interpretation of prophecy. His thesis was that the antichrist is a future personage who at the end of time will challenge the power of Christ, and with great persecution suppress God's people.

The early part of the nineteenth century saw the rise of the Anglo-Catholic movement within the Church of England. The Oxford professors S. R. Maitland, James Todd and William Burgh imbibed and taught the futurist concept of Ribera, in order to muffle the alarmed protest of faithful evangelical Anglicans against the suggestions of reunification with Rome. The pioneers of the Protestant Reformation were not simply following a concept of retaliation when they identified the Roman Catholic Church as the great antichrist power of prophecy. They were correctly discerning the inspired words of Holy Scripture. Here are some reasons why the identification of the antichrist is so important to God's end time people:

(1) That we not be deceived by the great efforts to unite the world under the banner of this antichrist power (Revelation 13:8).

(2) That we take seriously the challenge of Revelation 18:4–5 to call God's people out of apostasy into the fullness of the truth of God. True evangelical Protestants do not make this identification out of bigotry or hatred. Instead they do it out of love for lost humanity. An integral part of the proclamation of the gospel commission necessitates that men and women be led to the salvation that will free them from the bondage and deception of sin. Today, as at no other time in history, the identification of the antichrist and the invitation to call men and women out of Babylon must be made.

(3) Both the second and third angels' messages of Revelation 14:8–12 focus upon the fall and destruction of this power and all who serve it. Its identification is necessary to warn the world. The delinquency of evangelical Protestantism over the last decades to correctly identify the antichrist must be reversed, if they are to contribute to the work that is necessary in warning men and women before the return of Jesus. God demands that the warning against the papal antichrist and his work be given. It will take a complete revision of the present presuppositions of evangelical Protestantism, but it will bring them back into line with the original evangelical identifications made by Luther and others of the sixteenth-century Reformers.

THE DILEMMA OF
THE SECRET RAPTURE

The secret rapture is one of the greatest doctrinal anomalies preached by Evangelicals. Evangelical Protestantism is riveted in the events of the sixteenth-century Reformation. Yet it is the nineteenth-century aberration of the secret rapture that holds such a central position in the prophetic understandings of present-day evangelical Protestantism. The secret rapture was not taught prior to 1812.

This belief states that the church (those who are the elect) are secretly taken to heaven before the tribulation but that later, now said to be seven years later, after the reign of the antichrist, these saints will return with Jesus to set up His kingdom. This doctrine is not taught by the apostles, it was never envisaged by the early church fathers of Christianity, and it has not been found in Protestantism until the early nineteenth century. It is a doctrine which has its foundations in Catholic theology, a doctrine which has wholly refocused the Protestant concepts of the antichrist. It is a doctrine that has confused the whole understanding of the end-time events just before the return of Jesus Christ.

The first to present of this doctrine was Manuel de Lacunza y Dias, a Chilean Jesuit of Spanish descent, born in 1731, who died in 1801. He wrote under the pseudonym of Rabbi Juan Josafat Ben-Ezra, claiming to be a converted Jew. His book *The Coming of Messiah in Glory and Majesty* was first published posthumously in Spain in 1812. Later it was translated into English by the powerful Scottish preacher, Edward Irving, in 1827. By this time, Irving was a most popular preacher in London. Unquestionably, Irving popularized the secret rapture concept and it was further enhanced by the claimed visions of a fifteen-year-old Scottish lass from Glasgow, Margaret McDonald, who, in 1830, claimed to have visions that confirmed the secret-rapture belief.

John Nelson Darby, the founder of the Plymouth Brethren faith, a former Anglican priest, further popularized this doctrine. He early had read Irving's translation of Lacunza's book and also had spent time with Margaret McDonald. He was later to bring this doctrine to the United States and, probably more than any single person, was responsible for the popularization of it among American Christians in the latter part of the nineteenth century. However, it was the Scofield Reference Bible, published in 1909 by Oxford University Press, that was the chief medium which led to the notion of the pre-tribulation secret rapture permeating the conservative Protestant churches. Scofield's Bible was spread like the leaves of autumn by colporteurs around the United States, especially in the Bible belt of the South, where its influence was such that it has been conceded that the Scofield Bible has done more to shape the theology of Protestantism than any seminary, or perhaps all seminaries combined.

This doctrine supports the more recent beliefs of most Protestantism, that the antichrist is a single individual reigning seven years at the end of time in the rebuilt temple in Jerusalem where, especially over the last three-and-one-half years, he will fearfully persecute the Jews together with post-tribulation Christians. After that it is proposed that the Lord returns with those saints whom He has secretly raptured seven years before, to destroy the antichrist and the unfaithful and to set up His millennial kingdom. But such a doctrine, first appearing approximately 1800 years after the death of Jesus, and 300 years after the Protestant Reformation, must be carefully examined.

It is an extraordinarily surprising matter that such a doctrine, which has no valid support in the writings of the apostles nor in the teachings of Jesus, and has no historical basis in the writings of the Church Fathers nor of the Reformers, could have such powerful and widespread influence over evangelical Protestantism today. The acceptance of the doctrine of the secret rapture is plain evidence that many Protestants have moved away from Bible-based truth to fables, as prophesied by Paul (2 Timothy 4:4). We note that some Evangelicals do not believe this doctrine, being very suspicious of its Jesuit origin and of its lack of strong biblical support.

As noted in chapter 21, the Reformers unitedly identified the Roman Catholic Church as the antichrist of Bible prophecy. It was also noted in that chapter that it was the Jesuits who determinedly sought for a solution that would take the heat and focus off the identification of the Roman Catholic Church as the antichrist. It is not surprising then, that the writings of a later

Jesuit, Lacunza, which formulated the further deception of the rapture, would be consonant with those of an earlier Jesuit, Francisco Ribera, who first proposed futurism to interpret prophecies regarding the antichrist. But once again, it is the Protestant churches that have become engrossed in this doctrine. So convinced are some that the secret rapture will take place in the immediate future that they have distributed cards that would be found after this alleged rapture had taken place so that people would understand it. One such card reads:

> TO WHOM IT MAY CONCERN: This household is looking for the imminent return of the Lord.
>
> When it occurs—as it surely will—that in a day, in a night, or in an hour, it is discovered that millions of people are missing and that this home is found empty, then know that there has taken place that of which the apostle Paul wrote in 1 Thessalonians 4:14–17. It will mean that Christ has called out of this world all the saved, of which we were of this household. Don't search for us. We will be back in seven years, when Christ comes with all His saints to destroy antichrist, who will come with lying wonders. Don't be deceived by antichrist, and don't let antichrist put his mark on your forehead or in your hand. Read carefully these passages of Scripture and pray and understand: Read Revelation 13 and the chapters following. Also Daniel's prophecy.

It is surprising that the very texts used in this passage speak nothing of a secret rapture, but rather of a worldwide-visible return of Jesus Christ.

> 14 For if we believe that Jesus died and rose again, even so them also which sleep in Jesus will God bring with him. 15 For this we say unto you by the word of the Lord, that we which are alive and remain unto the coming of the Lord shall not prevent them which are asleep. 16 For the Lord himself shall descend from heaven with a shout, with the voice of the archangel, and with the trump of God: and the dead in Christ shall rise first: 17 Then we which are alive and remain shall be caught up together with them in the clouds, to meet the Lord in the air: and so shall we ever be with the Lord
> (1 Thessalonians 4:14–17).

It will be noted in this passage that nothing is said about two phases of the redemption of the faithful. It will be noted in verse 16 that this is a visible, audible return. At this time all the dead in Christ rise. Verse 17 decisively states that all will be gathered together to meet the Lord in the air and that from that moment we will ever be with Jesus. That is consistent with many other passages of Scripture. On the occasion of Christ's ascension to heaven, the disciples were comforted with these words:

> Ye men of Galilee, why stand ye gazing up into heaven? this same Jesus, which is taken up from you into heaven, shall so come in like manner as ye have seen him go into heaven
> (Acts 1:11).

Jesus' ascension to heaven was visible, seen by His disciples. We are assured that He will come in like manner the second time. The psalmist stated:

> Our God shall come, and shall not keep silence: a fire shall devour before him, and it shall be very tempestuous round about him   (Psalm 50:3).

John the Revelator expressed plainly that everyone would see Him at His coming.

> Behold, he cometh with clouds; and every eye shall see him, and they also which pierced him: and all kindreds of the earth shall wail because of him. Even so, Amen   (Revelation 1:7).

Jesus gave not the slightest hint that He would come in other than an entirely visible way.

> For as the lightning cometh out of the east, and shineth even unto the west; so shall also the coming of the Son of man be. . . . And then shall appear the sign of the Son of man in heaven: and then shall all the tribes of the earth mourn, and they shall see the Son of man coming in the clouds of heaven with power and great glory. And he shall send his angels with a great sound of a trumpet, and they shall gather together his elect from the four winds, from one end of heaven to the other
> (Matthew 24:27, 30–31).

The Second Coming will be very much seen and heard by all. This truth is confirmed many times by various Bible writers. Indeed, the word translated "voice" in 1 Thessalonians 4:16 is from the Greek word *phone,* a word that is well known to us today as it has been incorporated into words like *telephone.* Elsewhere Paul describes the fact that it will be a coming that will be heard by the inhabitants of the world.

> In a moment, in the twinkling of an eye, at the last trump: for the trumpet shall sound, and the dead shall be raised incorruptible, and we shall be changed   (1 Corinthians 15:52).

Paul, Peter, and John have confirmed that Christ will appear when the faithful are redeemed to Himself.

> When Christ, who is our life, shall appear, then shall ye also appear with him in glory   (Colossians 3:4).

> That thou keep this commandment without spot, unrebukeable, until the appearing of our Lord Jesus Christ (1 Timothy 6:14).

> And when the chief Shepherd shall appear, ye shall receive a crown of glory that fadeth not away   (1 Peter 5:4).

> And now, little children, abide in him; that, when he shall appear, we may have confidence, and not be ashamed before him at his coming   (1 John 2:28).

> Beloved, now are we the sons of God, and it doth not yet appear what we shall be: but we know that, when he shall appear, we shall be like him; for we shall see him as he is
> (1 John 3:2).

Much of the secret rapture thinking is based upon the false concept of a millennium where Jesus reigns with His people on this planet; but the millennial reign is in heaven (see chapter 23). Another clear testimony that the return of Jesus is not secret, is to be found in Paul's second epistle to the Thessalonians.

> And then shall that Wicked be revealed, whom the Lord shall consume with the spirit of his mouth, and shall destroy with the brightness of his coming   (2 Thessalonians 2:8).

Since this passage unmistakably refers to the antichrist, it is obvious that that power will not appear *after* Christ's coming, but before it.

When Christ comes, the wicked will be terrified.

And the heaven departed as a scroll when it is rolled together; and every mountain and island were moved out of their places. And the kings of the earth, and the great men, and the rich men, and the chief captains, and the mighty men, and every bondman, and every free man, hid themselves in the dens and in the rocks of the mountains; and said to the mountains and rocks, Fall on us, and hide us from the face of him that sitteth on the throne, and from the wrath of the Lamb: For the great day of his wrath is come; and who shall be able to stand?
(Revelation 6:14–17).

With universal events of such cataclysmic proportions occurring, the TO WHOM IT MAY CONCERN card quoted earlier would seem to be irrelevant. No one will be calmly searching for missing persons. The terror of the lost will be such that they will think only of themselves.

Jesus Himself warned against any claims that He had come in secret.

Wherefore if they shall say unto you, Behold, he is in the desert; go not forth: behold, he is in the secret chambers; believe it not. For as the lightning cometh out of the east, and shineth even unto the west; so shall also the coming of the Son of man be (Matthew 24:26–27).

In a vain attempt to support the false theory of the secret rapture, a number of texts have been presented. For example:

Then shall two be in the field; the one shall be taken, and the other left. Two women shall be grinding at the mill; the one shall be taken, and the other left (Matthew 24:40–41).

First of all it must be understood that this passage says nothing about a secret rapture. True, it speaks of the Second Coming of Jesus. But it will be noted that it is in the context of comparing the Second Coming of Jesus to the destruction at the time of the flood.

But as the days of Noe were, so shall also the coming of the Son of man be. For as in the days that were before the flood they were eating and drinking, marrying and giving in marriage, until the day that Noe entered into the ark, and knew not until the flood came, and took them all away; so shall also the coming of the Son of man be (Matthew 24:37–39).

Sudden was the destruction that came upon the wicked at the time of the flood, and sudden the destruction that comes upon the unfaithful at the Second Coming of Jesus. This scripture teaches that some will be saved and some will be lost. It is not addressing the visibility or invisibility of the return of Jesus Christ. Further, in verse 39, it was the ones *taken* who were destroyed, not the ones left. This fact no doubt also applies to verse 40. Only upon a false presupposition could this verse be applied to the secret rapture. The other area that has often been used in an attempt to support the rapture has hinged upon several statements in Scripture which say that Christ is coming with His saints. Here are two examples:

> To the end he may stablish your hearts unblameable in holiness before God, even our Father, at the coming of our Lord Jesus Christ with all his saints (1 Thessalonians 3:13).

> And Enoch also, the seventh from Adam, prophesied of these, saying, Behold, the Lord cometh with ten thousands of his saints (Jude 14).

But that these saints are references to the angels who come with Him, who are also His saints, is made plain by Jesus.

> For the Son of man shall come in the glory of his Father with his angels; and then he shall reward every man according to his works (Matthew 16:27).

This prophecy is confirmed by the prophet Daniel.

> I saw in the night visions, and, behold, one like the Son of man came with the clouds of heaven, and came to the Ancient of days, and they brought him near before him (Daniel 7:13).

Here the clouds of heaven also refer to the angels.

> And Jesus said, I am: and ye shall see the Son of man sitting on the right hand of power, and coming in the clouds of heaven (Mark 14:62).

> Behold, he cometh with clouds; and every eye shall see him, and they also which pierced him: and all kindreds of the earth shall wail because of him. Even so, Amen (Revelation 1:7).

And then shall they see the Son of man coming in the clouds
with great power and glory   (Mark 13:26).

Hereafter shall ye see the Son of man sitting on the right hand
of power, and coming in the clouds of heaven (Matthew 26:64).

Another issue to be addressed is that of the seven-year period of
the reign of the antichrist. Lacunza postulates a time of forty-five
days between the secret rapture and the visible Second Coming of
Jesus. This supposition was taken from Daniel 12:11–12:

And from the time that the daily sacrifice shall be taken
away, and the abomination that maketh desolate set up, there
shall be a thousand two hundred and ninety days. Blessed is
he that waiteth, and cometh to the thousand three hundred
and five and thirty days   (Daniel 12:11–12).

Forty-five days is the period between the end of the one-thousand-
two-hundred-and-ninety-day period and the one-thousand-three-
hundred-and-five-and-thirty-day period. However, later refinement
of the rapture theory went back to the prophecy of Daniel chapter
9 in which a seventy-week period is presented.

This seventy-week period (490 literal days equalling 490 prophetic years) commenced in 457 B.C. with the decree of King
Artaxerxes of Persia to restore the sovereignty of Judah. It ended
in A.D. 34 with the stoning of Stephen, which signalled the taking
of the gospel to the Gentiles, thus ending the special favor of God
upon the Jewish nation.

Seventy weeks are determined upon thy people and upon thy
holy city, to finish the transgression, and to make an end of
sins, and to make reconciliation for iniquity, and to bring in
everlasting righteousness, and to seal up the vision and prophecy, and to anoint the most Holy. Know therefore and understand, that from the going forth of the commandment to restore and to build Jerusalem unto the Messiah the Prince shall
be seven weeks, and threescore and two weeks: the street shall
be built again, and the wall, even in troublous times. And
after threescore and two weeks shall Messiah be cut off, but
not for himself: and the people of the prince that shall come
shall destroy the city and the sanctuary; and the end thereof
shall be with a flood, and unto the end of the war desolations
are determined. And he shall confirm the covenant with many

> for one week: and in the midst of the week he shall cause the sacrifice and the oblation to cease, and for the overspreading of abominations he shall make it desolate, even until the consummation, and that determined shall be poured upon the desolate   (Daniel 9:24–27).

While a thorough exposition of this passage of Scripture is outside the scope of this book, nevertheless it is important to recognize that earlier understandings of this passage kept the seventy weeks together. The final, seventieth week was seen as the period of time from the beginning of Christ's ministry in A.D. 27 through His death three and one-half years later in the spring of A.D. 31, to the stoning of Stephen in the fall of A.D. 34, which signalled the close of Israel's probation as God's special people, and led to the gospel being taken to the world at large.

The idea of taking the seventieth week and presenting it separately from the other sixty-nine weeks of this prophecy has created a tremendous dilemma. It is sometimes called the gap theory—a gap of about two thousand years between the fulfillment of the first sixty-nine weeks and then the beginning and fulfillment of the seventieth week. The gap cannot be sustained contextually. That seventieth week has nothing to do with the Second Coming of Jesus, but is clearly directed toward the first advent of Jesus Christ.

Thus the evangelical Protestants have the responsibility of reexamining the presuppositions that underlie the secret rapture theory. It is not a message that can be found in the Word of God; indeed the Second Coming is a single event, not a two-part event where the special elect are redeemed by secret rapture while the rest go through the tribulation and are saved seven years later when the Lord returns. The glorious news is that Jesus is coming back soon, and at that time every eye shall see Him and every ear shall hear His voice. The faithful of all ages will be resurrected from the dead to meet the living saints and to be gathered with Christ, returning for a thousand years to heaven during which time they will judge fallen men and fallen angels.

> And I saw thrones, and they sat upon them, and judgment was given unto them: and I saw the souls of them that were beheaded for the witness of Jesus, and for the word of God,

and which had not worshipped the beast, neither his image, neither had received his mark upon their foreheads, or in their hands; and they lived and reigned with Christ a thousand years   (Revelation 20:4).

Do ye not know that the saints shall judge the world? and if the world shall be judged by you, are ye unworthy to judge the smallest matters? Know ye not that we shall judge angels? how much more things that pertain to this life?
                                    (1 Corinthians 6:2–3).

God in His great mercy is securing the universe against the possibility of rebellion ever rising up a second time. Every saint will be satisfied that God has been just and that all who can be saved have been saved. At the end of this time, the saints with Christ will descend in the New Jerusalem to the earth. Satan will rally the forces of those that have been raised in the second resurrection, the lost of all ages, in a last desperate effort to destroy God's people. As they come against the New Jerusalem, fire comes down from God out of heaven and destroys them.

And they went up on the breadth of the earth, and compassed the camp of the saints about, and the beloved city: and fire came down from God out of heaven, and devoured them
                                    (Revelation 20:9).

At this time God recreates the earth in its Edenic beauty, and this new earth becomes the home of the saved.

For, behold, I create new heavens and a new earth: and the former shall not be remembered, nor come into mind
                                    (Isaiah 65:17).

Inherent within the secret rapture doctrine is the concept of the second chance; that is, for those not spiritually ready for Christ's return there is a further extension of seven years' probationary time to accept the saving grace of Christ. But now is man's second chance. His first opportunity was lost in Eden. The concept of the secret rapture may deceive some, who are not now preparing for God's kingdom, that there will be another opportunity for salvation. This deception is deadly.

THE DILEMMA OF
THE MILLENNIUM

T he issue of the millennium has been the basis of controversy between various strands of Evangelical Protestantism. Some have held to the post-millennial view that Christ
will come at the end of the millennium. Today the majority hold to
some form of pre-millenialism, that is, that the return of Jesus
comes prior to the commencement of the millennium. However the
whole concept of the millennium has been greatly influenced by
the prevalence of the acceptance of the rapture doctrine by a large
number of Evangelicals. These Evangelicals see the millennium as
a time when peace will reign on earth and Christ will be King
over the planet.

As we come toward the beginning of the third millennium of
the Christian era, there has been a great increase in the expectancy of the return of Jesus. In spite of the evidence of greater
perplexity and the increase in iniquity of all kinds, there are many
still predicting a wonderful millennium of peace and harmony
soon to be experienced as Christ reigns upon the earth. Others
hold to this same optimistic view without necessarily believing
that Christ will be on the earth. The Rapturists believe that the
church will be raptured before the tribulation, just prior to the
millennium. The rest of the world will get yet a further opportunity to accept Christ as their Lord and Saviour. Still others believe that during the millennium the redeemed saints will be in
heaven. We need to go to the Word of God to determine the
correct solution.

The Bible declares that the saints live and reign with Christ
during the millennium.

> And I saw thrones, and they sat upon them, and judgment
> was given unto them: and I saw the souls of them that were
> beheaded for the witness of Jesus, and for the word of God,
> and which had not worshipped the beast, neither his image,
> neither had received his mark upon their foreheads, or in
> their hands; and they lived and reigned with Christ a thou-
> sand years   (Revelation 20:4).

John the Revelator explicitly stated that there would be two resurrections, one which he calls the resurrection of life for the just, and the other the resurrection of damnation for those who are evil.

> Blessed and holy is he that hath part in the first resurrection: on such the second death hath no power, but they shall be priests of God and of Christ, and shall reign with him a thousand years   (Revelation 20:6).

Jesus Himself declared that when He comes, it is to take His people home with Him to heaven.

> Let not your heart be troubled: ye believe in God, believe also in me. In my Father's house are many mansions: if it were not so, I would have told you. I go to prepare a place for you. And if I go and prepare a place for you, I will come again, and receive you unto myself; that where I am, there ye may be also   (John 14:1–3).

Paul and John indicate that the faithful are taken to heaven when Jesus returns.

> After this I beheld, and, lo, a great multitude, which no man could number, of all nations, and kindreds, and people, and tongues, stood before the throne, and before the Lamb, clothed with white robes, and palms in their hands   (Revelation 7:9).

> For the Lord himself shall descend from heaven with a shout, with the voice of the archangel, and with the trump of God: and the dead in Christ shall rise first: then we which are alive and remain shall be caught up together with them in the clouds, to meet the Lord in the air: and so shall we ever be with the Lord. Wherefore comfort one another with these words   (1 Thessalonians 4:16–18).

Jesus also disclosed what would happen to the wicked when He returns to take His faithful people home to live with Him.

> And as it was in the days of Noe, so shall it be also in the days of the Son of man. They did eat, they drank, they married wives, they were given in marriage, until the day that Noe entered into the ark, and the flood came, and destroyed them all. Likewise also as it was in the days of Lot; they did eat, they drank, they bought, they sold, they planted, they

builded; but the same day that Lot went out of Sodom it rained fire and brimstone from heaven, and destroyed them all. Even thus shall it be in the day when the Son of man is revealed   (Luke 17:26–30).

Thus upon Jesus' return the wicked will be destroyed. There will be no second chance. Indeed, we already have our second opportunity to accept Jesus. When we sinned we forfeited our first opportunity, but God in His love now calls all men to avail themselves of this second offer of salvation by accepting Him.

At a time when we hear so much about peace and unity for the third millennium of the Christian era, it is important to remember the words of Paul.

For when they shall say, Peace and safety; then sudden destruction cometh upon them, as travail upon a woman with child; and they shall not escape   (1 Thessalonians 5:3).

And the heaven departed as a scroll when it is rolled together; and every mountain and island were moved out of their places. And the kings of the earth, and the great men, and the rich men, and the chief captains, and the mighty men, and every bondman, and every free man, hid themselves in the dens and in the rocks of the mountains; and said to the mountains and rocks, Fall on us, and hide us from the face of him that sitteth on the throne, and from the wrath of the Lamb: For the great day of his wrath is come; and who shall be able to stand?
                   (Revelation 6:14–17).

Therefore prophesy thou against them all these words, and say unto them, The LORD shall roar from on high, and utter his voice from his holy habitation; he shall mightily roar upon his habitation; he shall give a shout, as they that tread the grapes, against all the inhabitants of the earth. A noise shall come even to the ends of the earth; for the LORD hath a controversy with the nations, he will plead with all flesh; he will give them that are wicked to the sword, saith the LORD. Thus saith the LORD of hosts, Behold, evil shall go forth from nation to nation, and a great whirlwind shall be raised up from the coasts of the earth. And the slain of the LORD shall be at that day from one end of the earth even unto the other

end of the earth: they shall not be lamented, neither gathered,
nor buried; they shall be dung upon the ground
(Jeremiah 25:30–33).

Now clearly these texts refer to the wicked who are alive when
Jesus comes, for John specifies that the wicked dead are not
raised until the end of the millennium. Speaking of the resurrection of the righteous in the first resurrection at Christ's coming,
John referred thus to the wicked:

> But the rest of the dead lived not again until the thousand
> years were finished. This is the first resurrection
> (Revelation 20:5).

Thus at the beginning of the millennium, the righteous dead together with the living saints are caught up to meet Jesus and His
angels in the air, and return with Him to heaven. On the other
hand, the living wicked are destroyed by the brightness of the
coming of Jesus, and with all the wicked of all ages are resurrected at the end of the millennium. During the millennium Satan
is as it were imprisoned upon earth.

> 1 And I saw an angel come down from heaven, having the
> key of the bottomless pit and a great chain in his hand. 2 And
> he laid hold on the dragon, that old serpent, which is the
> Devil, and Satan, and bound him a thousand years, 3 and
> cast him into the bottomless pit, and shut him up, and set a
> seal upon him, that he should deceive the nations no more,
> till the thousand years should be fulfilled: and after that he
> must be loosed a little season   (Revelation 20:1–3).

The word rendered "bottomless pit" is *abussos*. It is a Greek term
used in the Septuagint translation of the Old Testament in Genesis
1:2 (without form and void). For the earth will be without inhabit-
ant, in a state of desolation and chaos. It will be noted that verse
three states that Satan will be loosed for a little season. This event
takes place as soon as the wicked of all ages are raised at the
conclusion of the millennium; and it is then that Satan seeks to
rally the lost of all ages together in a great battle against Christ
and the saved.

> And when the thousand years are expired, Satan shall be
> loosed out of his prison, and shall go out to deceive the na-
> tions which are in the four quarters of the earth, Gog and
> Magog, to gather them together to battle: the number of whom
> is as the sand of the sea. And they went up on the breadth of
> the earth, and compassed the camp of the saints about, and
> the beloved city: and fire came down from God out of heaven,
> and devoured them   (Revelation 20:7–9).

At the end of the millennium, Satan is loosed and the wicked are
raised from the dead. It is evident that the nations Satan seeks to
deceive are the resurrected wicked. Obviously, he deceives them
to believe that they can overthrow Christ and the saints. But their
attack on the Holy City containing the saints is doomed to failure,
and in turn leads to their eternal death.

It will be seen that the New Jerusalem comes down from
heaven with Christ and the saints.

> And I John saw the holy city, new Jerusalem, coming down
> from God out of heaven, prepared as a bride adorned for her
> husband. . . . And he carried me away in the spirit to a great
> and high mountain, and shewed me that great city, the holy
> Jerusalem, descending out of heaven from God
>   (Revelation 21:2, 10).

It is at this time that efforts are made to overcome Christ and the
saints, but they fail.

> And they went up on the breadth of the earth, and compassed
> the camp of the saints about, and the beloved city: and fire
> came down from God out of heaven, and devoured them. And
> the devil that deceived them was cast into the lake of fire and
> brimstone, where the beast and the false prophet are, and
> shall be tormented day and night for ever and ever
>   (Revelation 20:9–10).

The above passage is followed by a brief exposition of the judgment and the fate of those who have not accepted Christ as their
Saviour.

> And I saw a great white throne, and him that sat on it, from
> whose face the earth and the heaven fled away; and there was
> found no place for them. And I saw the dead, small and great,
> stand before God; and the books were opened: and another

> book was opened, which is the book of life: and the dead were judged out of those things which were written in the books, according to their works. And the sea gave up the dead which were in it; and death and hell delivered up the dead which were in them: and they were judged every man according to their works. And death and hell were cast into the lake of fire. This is the second death. And whosoever was not found written in the book of life was cast into the lake of fire
> (Revelation 20:11–15).

It is at this time that the earth is recreated to be inhabited by the faithful of all ages, with Christ dwelling forever with them.

> And I saw a new heaven and a new earth: for the first heaven and the first earth were passed away; and there was no more sea. And I John saw the holy city, new Jerusalem, coming down from God out of heaven, prepared as a bride adorned for her husband. And I heard a great voice out of heaven saying, Behold, the tabernacle of God is with men, and he will dwell with them, and they shall be his people, and God himself shall be with them, and be their God. And God shall wipe away all tears from their eyes; and there shall be no more death, neither sorrow, nor crying, neither shall there be any more pain: for the former things are passed away. And he that sat upon the throne said, Behold, I make all things new. And he said unto me, Write: for these words are true and faithful
> (Revelation 21:1–5).

> For as the new heavens and the new earth, which I will make, shall remain before me, saith the LORD, so shall your seed and your name remain. And it shall come to pass, that from one new moon to another, and from one sabbath to another, shall all flesh come to worship before me, saith the LORD
> (Isaiah 66:22–23).

Thus the information contained in God's Word reveals that the millennium commences with the return of Jesus Christ and the angels. The saints of all ages are gathered together to go home to live with Jesus in heaven for one thousand years. The unfaithful are destroyed by the brightness of Christ's coming, and Satan and his angels are as it were in the bleak abyss of this earth for a thousand years, where they are afforded ample time to review their shameful works of evil and to contemplate their ultimate destruction. It is during the millennium that the saints review the records of the rebellious humans and angels. (See 1 Corinthians 6:2–3 and Revelation 20:4).

At the end of the millennium, all the wicked of the ages are raised. The New Jerusalem with the saints descends to the earth. Satan rallies the lost in a last effort to overtake the saints, but they are destroyed by the fire sent from God. The new earth is recreated in its perfect condition, and the saints live forever in the recreated earth. A beautiful description of this time is prophesied by Isaiah.

> And I will rejoice in Jerusalem, and joy in my people: and the voice of weeping shall be no more heard in her, nor the voice of crying. There shall be no more thence an infant of days, nor an old man that hath not filled his days: for the child shall die an hundred years old; but the sinner being an hundred years old shall be accursed. And they shall build houses, and inhabit them; and they shall plant vineyards, and eat the fruit of them. They shall not build, and another inhabit; they shall not plant, and another eat: for as the days of a tree are the days of my people, and mine elect shall long enjoy the work of their hands. They shall not labour in vain, nor bring forth for trouble; for they are the seed of the blessed of the LORD, and their offspring with them. And it shall come to pass, that before they call, I will answer; and while they are yet speaking, I will hear. The wolf and the lamb shall feed together, and the lion shall eat straw like the bullock: and dust shall be the serpent's meat. They shall not hurt nor destroy in all my holy mountain, saith the LORD
>
> (Isaiah 65:19–25).

God has provided for us in His Word a certain understanding of the events which will take place from the time of Christ's return until the restoration of the earth to its Edenic beauty. What a joy it will be to share eternity with our blessed Redeemer in the certainty of everlasting righteousness and unbroken joy!

THE DILEMMA OF
THE LORD'S DAY

For centuries the first day of the week, Sunday, has been acknowledged as the Lord's day, the day of special worship by evangelical Protestants. But in this custom there is a great dilemma. There is not the slightest evidence in Holy Writ that the first day of the week is the Lord's day. The common starting point for declaring the Lord's day to be Sunday is in the book of Revelation.

> I was in the Spirit on the Lord's day, and heard behind me a great voice, as of a trumpet   (Revelation 1:10).

This text in no way identifies which day is the Lord's day. Therefore we must search for those scriptures that identify the Lord's day.

> But the seventh day is the sabbath of the LORD thy God: in it thou shalt not do any work, thou, nor thy son, nor thy daughter, thy manservant, nor thy maidservant, nor thy cattle, nor thy stranger that is within thy gates   (Exodus 20:10).

> If thou turn away thy foot from the sabbath, from doing thy pleasure on my holy day; and call the sabbath a delight, the holy of the LORD, honourable; and shalt honour him, not doing thine own ways, nor finding thine own pleasure, nor speaking thine own words   (Isaiah 58:13).

It has frequently been argued that these are texts from the Old Testament period when indeed the seventh day of the week was the day of holy convocation. But Jesus confirmed the fact that the Sabbath is the Lords's day during His earthly ministry. Nowhere in Scripture is this statement rescinded, nor could it be; for it is embodied in the unalterable law of God.

> Therefore the Son of man is Lord also of the sabbath
> (Mark 2:28).

There is no scriptural validation for the claim that the Lord's day is the first day of the week, for neither Christ nor His disciples declared that a change of the day had occurred. On the evidence of God's Word, we must acknowledge that the Lord's day is God's seventh-day Sabbath. Much has been said about the Sabbath being Jewish, but this assertion is again unsubstantiated by Scripture. Indeed the Sabbath was established at Creation, long before there was an Israelite or a Jew.

> And God blessed the seventh day, and sanctified it: because that in it he had rested from all his work which God created and made   (Genesis 2:3).

The contention that the Sabbath was made for the Jews is wholly untenable. Jesus Himself declared that the Sabbath was made for mankind.

> And he said unto them, The sabbath was made for man, and not man for the sabbath   (Mark 2:27).

The unchanging nature of the Sabbath is indisputable for those who have pivoted their beliefs upon the Word of God. We have just noted that the Sabbath was instituted at Creation, God Himself participating in this sacred time. Down through the history of the Old Testament, God's faithful people kept the Sabbath. Even before God gave to Moses the Ten Commandments, the Israelites kept the Sabbath.

> Then said the LORD unto Moses, Behold, I will rain bread from heaven for you; and the people shall go out and gather a certain rate every day, that I may prove them, whether they will walk in my law, or no   (Exodus 16:4).

> And it came to pass, that on the sixth day they gathered twice as much bread, two omers for one man: and all the rulers of the congregation came and told Moses. And he said unto them, This is that which the LORD hath said, To morrow is the rest of the holy sabbath unto the LORD: bake that which ye will bake to day, and seethe that ye will seethe; and that which remaineth over lay up for you to be kept until the morning. And they laid it up till the morning, as Moses bade: and it did not stink, neither was there any worm therein. And Moses said, Eat that to day; for to day is a sabbath unto the LORD: to day ye shall not find it in the field. Six days ye shall gather it; but on the seventh day, which is the sabbath, in it there shall be none. And it came to pass, that there went out

some of the people on the seventh day for to gather, and they found none. And the LORD said unto Moses, How long refuse ye to keep my commandments and my laws? See, for that the LORD hath given you the sabbath, therefore he giveth you on the sixth day the bread of two days; abide ye every man in his place, let no man go out of his place on the seventh day. So the people rested on the seventh day   (Exodus 16:22–30).

There are references from time to time in the Old Testament to the keeping of the Sabbath, or to the violation by some of the fourth commandment. Of striking importance is the situation that occurred after the restoration of Judah under the leadership of Nehemiah. Nehemiah took strong action against those who were breaking the Sabbath and against those traders from Phoenicia who were offering their goods for sale to God's people on the Sabbath day.

In those days saw I in Judah some treading wine presses on the sabbath, and bringing in sheaves, and lading asses; as also wine, grapes, and figs, and all manner of burdens, which they brought into Jerusalem on the sabbath day: and I testified against them in the day wherein they sold victuals. There dwelt men of Tyre also therein, which brought fish, and all manner of ware, and sold on the sabbath unto the children of Judah, and in Jerusalem. Then I contended with the nobles of Judah, and said unto them, What evil thing is this that ye do, and profane the sabbath day? Did not your fathers thus, and did not our God bring all this evil upon us, and upon this city? yet ye bring more wrath upon Israel by profaning the sabbath. And it came to pass, that when the gates of Jerusalem began to be dark before the sabbath, I commanded that the gates should be shut, and charged that they should not be opened till after the sabbath: and some of my servants set I at the gates, that there should no burden be brought in on the sabbath day. So the merchants and sellers of all kind of ware lodged without Jerusalem once or twice. Then I testified against them, and said unto them, Why lodge ye about the wall? if ye do so again, I will lay hands on you. From that time forth came they no more on the sabbath. And I commanded the Levites that they should cleanse themselves, and that they should come and keep the gates, to sanctify the sabbath day.

> Remember me, O my God, concerning this also, and spare me according to the greatness of thy mercy
>
> (Nehemiah 13:15–22).

There is no question that Jesus was a faithful and regular Sabbath-keeper.

> And he came to Nazareth, where he had been brought up: and, as his custom was, he went into the synagogue on the sabbath day, and stood up for to read   (Luke 4:16).

Nor is there any doubt that Paul faithfully kept the Sabbath.

> But when they departed from Perga, they came to Antioch in Pisidia, and went into the synagogue on the sabbath day, and sat down   (Acts 13:14).

> And on the sabbath we went out of the city by a river side, where prayer was wont to be made; and we sat down, and spake unto the women which resorted thither   (Acts 16:13).

> Now when they had passed through Amphipolis and Apollonia, they came to Thessalonica, where was a synagogue of the Jews: and Paul, as his manner was, went in unto them, and three sabbath days reasoned with them out of the scriptures
>
> (Acts 17:1–2).

> And he reasoned in the synagogue every sabbath, and persuaded the Jews and the Greeks   (Acts 18:4).

Some have argued that Paul went into the synagogue on the Sabbath day because he was able to preach to the Jews there. But you will notice that in Acts 18:4 he not only went there for the Jews, he also spoke to the Greeks there, indicating that he was encouraging them to worship on God's Sabbath day also.

In the earth made new, God's saints will keep the Sabbath.

> And it shall come to pass, that from one new moon to another, and from one sabbath to another, shall all flesh come to worship before me, saith the LORD   (Isaiah 66:23).

Some have claimed Sunday sacredness as a memorial of the resurrection of Jesus, but this belief cannot be validated from Scripture. Indeed, Christ left us two ceremonies that commemorate His death and resurrection. The first is baptism.

> Know ye not, that so many of us as were baptized into Jesus
> Christ were baptized into his death? Therefore we are buried
> with him by baptism into death: that like as Christ was raised
> up from the dead by the glory of the Father, even so we also
> should walk in newness of life. For if we have been planted
> together in the likeness of his death, we shall be also in the
> likeness of his resurrection: knowing this, that our old man is
> crucified with him, that the body of sin might be destroyed,
> that henceforth we should not serve sin   (Romans 6:3–6).

And the second ceremony that Christ gave us is the communion
service:

> For I have received of the Lord that which also I delivered
> unto you, That the Lord Jesus the same night in which he was
> betrayed took bread: and when he had given thanks, he brake
> it, and said, Take, eat: this is my body, which is broken for
> you: this do in remembrance of me. After the same manner
> also he took the cup, when he had supped, saying, This cup is
> the new testament in my blood: this do ye, as oft as ye drink
> it, in remembrance of me. For as often as ye eat this bread,
> and drink this cup, ye do shew the Lord's death till he come
>   (1 Corinthians 11:23–26).

What is of striking evidence for the seventh-day Sabbath is the
record of the gospel writers concerning the resurrection of Jesus.
It will be noted that always they referred to the seventh day as the
Sabbath, and to Sunday as the first day of the week, even though
they were writing decades after the death of Jesus.

> In the end of the sabbath, as it began to dawn toward the first
> day of the week, came Mary Magdalene and the other Mary to
> see the sepulchre   (Matthew 28:1).

> And very early in the morning the first day of the week, they
> came unto the sepulchre at the rising of the sun (Mark 16:2).

> And they returned, and prepared spices and ointments; and
> rested the sabbath day according to the commandment. Now
> upon the first day of the week, very early in the morning, they
> came unto the sepulchre, bringing the spices which they had
> prepared, and certain others with them   (Luke 23:56–24:1).

> The first day of the week cometh Mary Magdalene early,
> when it was yet dark, unto the sepulchre, and seeth the stone
> taken away from the sepulchre   (John 20:1).

What an opportunity it would have been to refer to the first day as the Lord's day, had that been so proclaimed by Jesus! But that did not happen. What an opportunity it would have been to discard the Sabbath as the rest day of the Lord, but that did not happen either! There can be no question that evangelical Protestants have followed Roman Catholicism by continuing to worship on the first day rather than the seventh day of the week. Roman Catholics have been quick to taunt Protestants with this fact.

It is a shock to some Evangelicals to realize that Sunday was the counterfeit worship day of paganism, which acknowledged the deity of the sun. The counterfeit day of worship originated in Babylon, and through Babylon it came into Roman paganism, and has eventually found its way into Christianity.

The Christians in the nations of Eastern Asia did not accept Sunday sacredness, for they were protected from the Roman Catholic influence by the Muslim power in the Middle East. Neither did the Ethiopian Christians keep Sunday, because they also were protected from the Roman Catholic influence by the Muslim control of North Africa. Indeed, it took many centuries before Christendom even in Europe accepted Sunday sacredness. In Spain, Sunday sacredness was not accepted until the seventh century; in England also in the seventh century; in Wales and Scotland, in the eleventh and twelfth centuries. The Evangelicals who proclaim their acknowledgment of the lordship and sovereignty of Christ have failed to realize that the keeping of the Sabbath is the greatest and indeed the only true acknowledgment of the lordship and sovereignty of Jesus Christ, for He is Lord of the Sabbath.

The Roman Catholic Church has long claimed that its authority is confirmed by its change of the Sabbath from the seventh day to the first day of the week.

Listen to these words by C. F. Thomas, Chancellor of Cardinal Gibbons:

> Of course the Catholic Church claims that the change was her
> act. And the act is the *mark* of her ecclesiastical power and
> authority in religious matters.

The Convert's Catechism of Catholic Doctrine, by Reverend Peter Geirmann, says thus:

Question—Which is the Sabbath day?

Answer—Saturday is the Sabbath day.

Question—Why do we observe Sunday instead of Saturday?

Answer—We observe Sunday instead of Saturday because the Catholic Church, in the Council of Laodicea (A.D. 336) trans-ferred the solemnity from Saturday to Sunday
(Second Edition, p. 50. Rev.).

Question—Have you any other way of proving that the Church has power to institute festivals of precept?

Answer—Had she not such power, she could not have done that in which all modern religionists agree with her, she could not have substituted the observance of Sunday the first day of the week, for the observance of Saturday, a change for which there is not scriptural authority
(Stephen Keenan, *A Doctrinal Catechism*).

But since Saturday, not Sunday, is specified in the Bible, isn't it curious that non-Catholics who profess to take their religion directly from the Bible and not from the Church, observe Sunday instead of Saturday? Yes, of course it is inconsistent, but this change was made about fifteen centuries before Protestantism was born, and by that time the custom was universally observed. They have continued the custom, even though it rests upon the authority of the Catholic Church and not upon an explicit text in the Bible. That observance remains as a reminder of the Mother Church from which the non-Catholic sects broke away—like a boy running away from home but still carrying in his pocket a picture of his mother or a lock of her hair   (*The Faith of Millions*, p. 473).

Reason and sense demand the acceptance of one or the other of these alternatives: either Protestantism and the keeping holy of Saturday or Catholicity and the keeping of Sunday. Compromise is impossible
(Cardinal Gibbons, *Catholic Mirror,* December 23, 1893).

Many Protestant leaders have acknowledged the truth of the Roman Catholic claims.

There was and is a commandment to keep holy the Sabbath day, but that Sabbath day was not Sunday. It will be said, however, and with some show of triumph, that the Sabbath was transferred from the seventh to the first day of the week. . . . Where can the record of such a transaction be found? Not in the New Testament—absolutely not. . . . Of course, I quite well know that Sunday did come into use in early Christian history as a religious day, as we learn from the Christian Fathers, and other sources. But *what a pity* that it comes branded with *the mark of paganism,* and christened with the *name of the sun god,* when *adopted and sanctioned* by the papal apostasy, and bequeathed as a sacred legacy to Protestantism!

(Edward T. Hiscox, *Source Book,* pp. 513–514). (Baptist)

Centuries of the Christian Era passed away before Sunday was observed by the Christian church as the Sabbath. History does not furnish us with a *single proof* or *indication* that it was *at any time* so observed previous to the Sabbatical edict of Constantine in A.D. 321

(Sir William Domville, *The Sabbath Or an Examination of the Six Texts,* p. 291). (Church of England)

So some have tried to build the observance of Sunday upon apostolic command, whereas the apostles gave no command on the matter at all. . . . The truth is, as soon as we appeal to the *Litera scripta* (the literal writing) of the Bible, the Sabbatarians have the best of the argument

(*The Presbyterian Christian at Work,* April 19, 1883).

It is true, there is no positive command for infant baptism . . . nor is there any for keeping holy the first day of the week

(*Methodist Theological Compendium*)

It is quite clear that no matter how rigidly or devotedly we may spend Sunday, we are not keeping the Sabbath. The Sabbath was founded on a specific, divine command. We can plead no such command for the observance of Sunday. . . . There is not a single line in the New Testament to suggest that we incur any penalty by violating the supposed sanctity of Sunday

(Dr. W. R. Dale, *The Ten Commandments,* pp. 106–107). (Congregational).

The observance of the Lord's day (Sunday) is founded not on
any command of God, but on the authority of the church
(Augsburg Confession of Faith). (Lutheran)

The festival day of Sunday, like all other festivals, was always
only a human ordinance, and it was far from the intentions of
the apostles to establish a divine command in this respect, far
from them and from the early apostolic church to transfer the
laws of the Sabbath to Sunday   (Neander, *The History of
the Christian Religion and Church,* p. 186). (Episcopalian)

There are those who argue that the day of worship does not really
matter so long as one day in seven is observed. But when one
acknowledges that Satan has a counterfeit for every truth of God,
and that the pagan day of worship is Sunday, then no such sim-
plistic answer can be entertained. As we come to the close of this
earth's history, God provides a clarion call for all of God's faithful people to acknowledge His creatorship, His lordship, His sanctification and His sovereignty by keeping holy the seventh day of
the week. According to biblical principles, that is from sunset
Friday to sunset Saturday.

It shall be unto you a sabbath of rest, and ye shall afflict your
souls: in the ninth day of the month at even, from even unto
even, shall ye celebrate your sabbath   (Leviticus 23:32).

So important is the Sabbath that God made it a perpetual symbol
of sanctification.

Speak thou also unto the children of Israel, saying, Verily my
sabbaths ye shall keep: for it is a sign between me and you
throughout your generations; that ye may know that I am the
LORD that doth sanctify you   (Exodus 31:13).

Moreover also I gave them my sabbaths, to be a sign between
me and them, that they might know that I am the LORD that
sanctify them   (Ezekiel 20:12).

Perhaps the reason why some Evangelicals have diminished the
role of sanctification in salvation is due to their neglect of the
seventh-day Sabbath. We can never forget the words of Jesus,

But he answered and said, It is written, Man shall not live by
bread alone, but by every word that proceedeth out of the
mouth of God   (Matthew 4:4).

It is our experience that while many claim the day of worship to be a minor matter, they discover that when presented with God's claims for Sabbath worship, it provides the strongest test of their loyalty to God. It will take the utmost dedication and courage for Evangelicals to break the bonds of centuries of habits that have not been predicated upon the Word of God. But Christ, the Lord of the Sabbath, provides the strength for those who follow Him in every way.

THE DILEMMA OF
DISPENSATIONALISM

While the beginnings of dispensational teachings are vague, there is no question that the Brethren movement, especially as propounded by John Nelson Darby, gave profound impetus to popularizing the concept of dispensationalism among Protestants. Darby, in his six visits to the United States, planted the seeds of dispensationalism strongly into the minds of his hearers. Dispensational theology had its roots in the concept that the church had failed, and it would take a millennial reign of Christ to establish peace, unity and righteousness on the planet.

This theory was attractive to those who favored the disjunction of law and grace, separating the Old Testament from the New Testament eras into those who were saved by the law, and those who were saved by grace. It also had an attractiveness, therefore, to those who tended toward antinomianism—who believe in a carnal security, minimizing the role of the commandments of God, which were said to have been nailed to the cross. Dispensationalism gathered momentum in the last part of the nineteenth century and the early part of the twentieth. Joey R. Graves, a Southern Baptist minister, wrote a book, *"The Work of Christ Consummated in Seven Dispensations"* in 1883. But the real popularization of dispensationalism certainly came through Cyrus Ingerson Scofield in his Scofield Reference Bible, first published in 1909 and revised in 1917. Scofield divided the eras of sacred history into seven dispensations:

1. The dispensation of innocence which incorporated the span from Creation to the Fall;

2. The dispensation of conscience from the Fall to the Flood;

3. The dispensation of human government from the Flood to the choice of Abraham as father of God's people;

4. The dispensation of promise from the call of Abraham to the giving of the Ten Commandments;

5. The dispensation of law from the giving of the Ten Commandments to the death of Jesus Christ;

6. The dispensation of the church from the birth of Christ until the establishment of the eternal kingdom;

7. The dispensation of eternity when all God's people are redeemed.

This scheme is quite artificial. Many dispensationalists have simplified the scheme, rather addressing the dispensation of law covering the Old Testament and the dispensation of grace pertaining during the Christian era. Frequently the concept of dispensationalism has been connected with an understanding of the old and the new covenants. Some argue that the old covenant was a works-oriented covenant and the new covenant is established upon the grace of Jesus Christ. There is no question that the Bible details an old and a new covenant. The everlasting covenant, which is indeed the new covenant, is older than the so-called old covenant. The everlasting covenant, the covenant between God and man, was formulated in the eternity of the past.

> According as he hath chosen us in him before the foundation of the world, that we should be holy and without blame before him in love   (Ephesians 1:4).

It took effect when sin entered the world.

> And I will put enmity between thee and the woman, and between thy seed and her seed; it shall bruise thy head, and thou shalt bruise his heel   (Genesis 3:15).

It was ratified by the precious blood of Jesus Christ. The old covenant was mediated through the offering of animal sacrifices. Christ became the Mediator of the new covenant.

> And for this cause he is the mediator of the new testament, that by means of death, for the redemption of the transgressions that were under the first testament, they which are called might receive the promise of eternal inheritance. For where a testament is, there must also of necessity be the death of the testator. For a testament is of force after men are dead: otherwise it is of no strength at all while the testator liveth
> (Hebrews 9:15–17).

It is referred to as a "better covenant" because it is established upon the eternal promise that Jesus would be the substitute for man. The old covenant was built upon the fallible promises of man.

> But now hath he obtained a more excellent ministry, by how much also he is the mediator of a better covenant, which was established upon better promises (Hebrews 8:6).

The law of God was written on tables of stone by the finger of God.

> And the LORD said unto Moses, Come up to me into the mount, and be there: and I will give thee tables of stone, and a law, and commandments which I have written; that thou mayest teach them (Exodus 24:12).

In the new covenant these commandments are to be written on the hearts of all who accept the sacrifice of Jesus Christ.

> For this is the covenant that I will make with the house of Israel after those days, saith the Lord; I will put my laws into their mind, and write them in their hearts: and I will be to them a God, and they shall be to me a people:
> (Hebrews 8:10).

> This is the covenant that I will make with them after those days, saith the Lord, I will put my laws into their hearts, and in their minds will I write them (Hebrews 10:16).

Such a covenant is not simply outward form, but the fullness of the total submission of the life to Jesus, so that the law becomes a living principle of life and action.

Some have gone to the Scriptures to support the concept of dispensationalism, claiming that in the Old Testament the faithful were saved by keeping the law. But this concept is contrary to Scripture.

> Knowing that a man is not justified by the works of the law, but by the faith of Jesus Christ, even we have believed in Jesus Christ, that we might be justified by the faith of Christ, and not by the works of the law: for by the works of the law shall no flesh be justified (Galatians 2:16).

In the King James Version of the Bible, the word *dispensation* is used just four times:

> For if I do this thing willingly, I have a reward: but if against my will, a dispensation of the gospel is committed unto me
> (1 Corinthians 9:17).

> That in the dispensation of the fulness of times he might gather together in one all things in Christ, both which are in heaven, and which are on earth; even in him
> (Ephesians 1:10).

> If ye have heard of the dispensation of the grace of God which is given me to you-ward   (Ephesians 3:2).

> Whereof I am made a minister, according to the dispensation of God which is given to me for you, to fulfil the word of God
> (Colossians 1:25).

Frequently Ephesians 3:2 has been presented as a basis for a dispensation of grace separate from a dispensation of the law. But that cannot be substantiated. The word translated "dispensation," *oikonomia* does not mean dispensation in the manner that dispensationalists use the term today. It comes from the Greek word for steward, and therefore a better translation would be the *stewardship of grace*. In no way does this word support a dispensational concept of divine salvation. The concept of dispensationalism is built upon the thought that throughout the history of humanity, God continues to change His method of saving mankind. But that is contrary to Scripture.

> For I am the LORD, I change not; therefore ye sons of Jacob are not consumed   (Malachi 3:6).

> Every good gift and every perfect gift is from above, and cometh down from the Father of lights, with whom is no variableness, neither shadow of turning   (James 1:17).

Salvation has never been effected by anything that man could do. That is clear in both the Old and the New Testaments.

> Look unto me, and be ye saved, all the ends of the earth: for I am God, and there is none else   (Isaiah 45:22).

The transformation of the life through God is just as strongly enshrined in the Old Testament as in the New.

I will accept you with your sweet savour, when I bring you out from the people, and gather you out of the countries wherein ye have been scattered; and I will be sanctified in you before the heathen (Ezekiel 20:41).

And I will sanctify my great name, which was profaned among the heathen, which ye have profaned in the midst of them; and the heathen shall know that I am the LORD, saith the Lord GOD, when I shall be sanctified in you before their eyes (Ezekiel 36:23).

And the heathen shall know that I the LORD do sanctify Israel, when my sanctuary shall be in the midst of them for evermore (Ezekiel 37:28).

Peter's declaration at Pentecost focused upon Jesus as the only foundation of salvation, and is just as applicable to the Old Testament saints as New Testament saints.

Neither is there salvation in any other: for there is none other name under heaven given among men, whereby we must be saved (Acts 4:12).

One of the clearest evidences that the Old Testament believers were saved in the same way as New Testament Christians, is presented in Hebrews chapter 11. All the saints were saved by faith and not by works. But good works in obedience to God was the evidence of that faith. Here are a few examples:

By faith Abel offered unto God a more excellent sacrifice than Cain, by which he obtained witness that he was righteous, God testifying of his gifts: and by it he being dead yet speaketh (Hebrews 11:4).

By faith Noah, being warned of God of things not seen as yet, moved with fear, prepared an ark to the saving of his house; by the which he condemned the world, and became heir of the righteousness which is by faith (Hebrews 11:7).

By faith Abraham, when he was called to go out into a place which he should after receive for an inheritance, obeyed; and he went out, not knowing whither he went. By faith he sojourned in the land of promise, as in a strange country, dwelling in tabernacles with Isaac and Jacob, the heirs with him of the same promise: for he looked for a city which hath foundations, whose builder and maker is God   (Hebrews 11:8–10).

By faith Moses, when he was come to years, refused to be called the son of Pharaoh's daughter; choosing rather to suffer affliction with the people of God, than to enjoy the pleasures of sin for a season; esteeming the reproach of Christ greater riches than the treasures in Egypt: for he had respect unto the recompence of the reward   (Hebrews 11:24–26).

Since sin entered the world, the only way mankind could live was through the provision of the grace of Jesus Christ. Consistent with this fact is the revelation that Noah was saved from destruction in the deluge by accepting Christ's grace, and this was evidenced by his obedience to God's law.

But Noah found grace in the eyes of the LORD   (Genesis 6:8).

In this sense, the world from the time of the Fall has been under the dispensation of grace, and will so continue until the redemption of mankind at the Second Coming of Jesus, and even into eternity itself. It is surely time for Evangelicals to disassociate themselves from the unscriptural concept of dispensationalism, which snares them away from love for God evidenced in their obedience to God's commandments.

THE LEGACY OF
JOHN DARBY

Most Evangelicals today know little more than the name of John Darby. Yet they hold views concerning prophetic interpretations similar to those held by this man who was the founder of the Plymouth Brethren Church in England.

His influence upon fundamentalist Christianity is no coincidence. An understanding of the history of John Darby's life and teachings will help clarify the nature of those teachings which Evangelicals are borrowing from him today.

Darby was born in London in 1800. He graduated from Trinity College, Dublin, in 1819, and was called to the Irish bar in 1825. Almost immediately, he forsook the legal profession, and for two years served as the curate of the Anglican church in Wicklow.

In 1827 his questions concerning church authority led him to leave his curacy, and ultimately to leave the Church of England. Darby was greatly influenced by the Brethren movement. The Brethren movement had its origins in Dublin in 1825, where a small number of earnest men, dissatisfied with the state of the Protestant churches in Great Britain, met regularly. It should be remembered that of all of Southern Ireland (now the Irish Republic), Dublin is the most Protestant area, with about ten percent presently claiming membership in various Protestant churches. Trinity College, where Darby was educated, is a famous stronghold of Protestant post-secondary education in Dublin.

In 1827, about the time John Darby left the curacy of Wicklow, he joined the Brethren meetings, which was to be the foundation of his later teachings and prolific writings. Darby was soon traveling extensively. He visited the university centers of Paris, Cambridge and Oxford in the 1830s. It is of no little significance that his visit to Oxford was at the time of the development of the Anglo-Catholic movement at Oxford University, led by the theologians, S. R. Maitland, James Todd and William Burgh. It was just after this time that the Oxford movement, as it came to be called, had its origins. The Oxford movement was a natural development from the Anglo-Catholic movement. Most historians trace its origin to a sermon preached in St. Mary's Church (Oxford), July 9, 1833, by the well-known preacher, John Keble, then professor of poetry at Oxford University. His topic that day, "National Apostasy," focused on the moral failure of British society, and, by implication, of the Church of England. It is to be recognized that it was a time of growing concern in the Anglican Church. In the previous century, the Methodist movement had challenged the established church, and the nonconformists of the Congregational Church were still exerting a power influence.

In the congregation hearing Keble that day was John Henry Newman (1801–1890), the rector of St. Mary's Church. Newman had graduated from Oxford University in 1821 and had been ordained to the Anglican ministry in 1823. Up to that time the brilliant young Newman had spent most of his time as a tutor in the colleges of Oxford. Newman appears to have been profoundly influenced by Keble's sermon, and thus commenced a journey which led him to leave the Anglican priesthood in 1843 and to become a member of the Roman Catholic Church in 1845. In 1846 he made a pilgrimage to Rome where he was ordained to the Roman Catholic priesthood. Newman quickly became a strong force for Roman Catholicism in England. His influence not only affected the Roman Catholic Church, but also the Anglican Church and his alma mater, Oxford University. So indebted was the Roman Catholic Church to Newman that in a most unusual step in 1879 Pope Leo XIII elevated Newman directly from the priesthood, creating him a cardinal.

It was in this theological milieu that John Darby developed his prophetic perspectives. Though Darby barely escaped with his life in February 1845, in Vaud, Switzerland, when a revolution grounded in Jesuit intrigues broke out, he nevertheless accepted the Jesuit-inspired futuristic interpretations of prophecy, making them the foundation of his own prophetic interpretations.

After his visits to Paris, Cambridge and Oxford, Darby settled for a time in the southern seaport city of Plymouth. Soon Darby had formed an assembly of Brethren, and the city quickly gave its name to an influential branch of the Brethren movement. Though it is still known as the Plymouth Brethren Church today, in Europe the followers of this stream of the Brethren movement were more commonly referred to as Darbyites.

The impact of the Brethren movement was enhanced when John Harris, the perpetual curate of Plymstock, resigned his position in 1834 and became the editor of the Brethren's first periodical, *The Christian Witness*. However, significant divisions soon arose in the Brethren movement. Darby was at the center of the conflict and was accused of varying widely from the original teachings and principles of the movement.

To understand the split in the Brethren movement, we need to retrace our steps to Dublin. Soon after Darby joined the Brethren meeting in Dublin, the famous Powerscourt Conferences commenced, which later exerted a strong influence upon the theology of the Fundamentalist movement in America. Darby, though still in his twenties, soon showed himself to be a leader in prophetic interpretation. It was at these meetings that the pretribulation concept began to take shape. The pretribulation teaching is the foundation of the secret rapture. In essence, this teaching claims that before the great tribulation on earth, the church (God's true saints) is secretly raptured and is, therefore, spared the great persecution of this period that results from the wicked cruelty of the Antichrist of the end-time. It has been claimed that the idea of the secret rapture had its origins in Edward Irving's church in London, and that it was revealed by the voice of the Holy Spirit. It certainly did not arise out of the Word of God, though later rapturists attempted to use Scripture, including Matthew 24:44, to support this unbiblical concept. Others have seen the rapture as having its origins in Jesuit theology through Ribera, and still others trace its beginnings to the visions of a lass, Margaret McDonald, in Glasgow, Scotland. But in reality it is ultimately traced to the Spanish Jesuit missionary Manuel de Lacunza (see chapter twenty-two). Darby incorporated the futuristic interpretation of prophecy, the rapture, and pretribulation theology into his own teachings.

Just as influential was his emphasis upon the disjunction of law and grace. This separation arose out of the development of dispensational theology. Rather than recognizing that all are saved by grace through faith, whether living in the pre- or post-Christian era, Darby held that at different times God saved man in different ways. This concept was later to be fully developed in the early twentieth century by Cyrus Scofield. It was John Darby and his supporters who popularized the antithesis between law and grace, a concept that is now pervasive throughout fundamental Protestantism.

It is precisely this dispensational teaching that led to the concept that the Old Testament is of little significance to Christians today, for it was written for those who lived in a different dispensation. Even much of the New Testament is declared to have little value, and the more extreme dispensationalists claim that the relevant part of the Bible is limited to the imprisonment epistles of Paul.

But by no means did all Brethren leaders support the more extreme and speculative views of John Darby. The Brethren movement began to split, though two pillars remained common to all branches—premillennialism (the concept that the second coming of Christ occurs before the millennium), and futurism (that the time prophecies concerning the antichrist have their fulfillment at the end of time). However, some of the leaders of the Brethren rejected dispensationalism and pretribulationism. Among these were prominent Brethren leaders, B. E. Newton, H. A. Ironside and S. B. Tregelles. It is of interest to note that the famous man of faith, George Muller, joined the Brethren movement, though not accepting all of Darby's flights of speculative theology. Tregelles later was to say concerning the rapture, "it was not from the Holy Scriptures, but from that which falsely pretended to be the Spirit of God." Newton considered Darby's dispensational teachings as "the height of speculation," an evaluation shared by Ironside.

The teachings of Darby led to an irreconcilable split between the Brethren (though some attribute the major blame for the split to Newton). Two major Brethren groups emerged in the 1840s, the Darbyites, often known as the Exclusive Brethren, and the Bethesda or Open Brethren. However, it was the Darbyites who would have a major influence upon the Fundamentalist movement of the United States.

As early as 1838, Darby moved to Switzerland, where he made a surprisingly strong impact upon many young men who gathered around him. He became a vocal preacher against the

Methodist movement. Many Brethren congregations were established in the Swiss cantons of Vaud, Geneva, and Bern, and he had a significant influence in Lausanne. During his later years, Darby spent considerable time in translating the Scriptures in German and French.

Many accepted Darby's premillennialism as a fresh and vital approach, in contrast to the prevailing postmillennial views (that Christ's Second Coming occurs after the millennium).

But the greatest impact of Darby proved to be, not upon England or Europe, but upon the United States. It is important to recognize that his impact was not so much in the establishment of a strong Plymouth Brethren Church in the United States, but rather in the initial influence he exerted upon mainline churches, especially the Congregational and Presbyterian Churches. Later, by the influence of Cyrus Scofield and the Scofield Bible, an even greater influence was exerted upon the more Evangelical denominations: Baptist, Church of Christ, and Church of God.

All in all, Darby crossed the Atlantic six times to bring his innovative ideas to the New World: 1859, 1864–1865, 1866–1868, 1870, 1872–1873, and 1874. He also visited the West Indies, Italy (1871) and New Zealand (1875). Added to his frequent travels was the influence of his prolific writings and his hymn production. His impact upon America must not be minimized. He was often warmly received in the United States, especially in St. Louis (where Cyrus Scofield first accepted Christianity in 1879). His preaching stirred fresh interest in the Second Coming. It is believed that his teachings led directly to the establishment of prophetic conferences, which continued into the twentieth century. The first was held in an Episcopal church in 1878. In 1886, Chicago was the site of another such conference, but it was unquestionably the annual Niagara Conferences, held on the Canadian side of the falls from 1883–1897, that were the most famous. These attracted some of the leading Protestant theologians of the day. Other conferences were held in Northfield, Massachusetts, the home of Dwight L. Moody, and still others at Seacliff, Long Island, New York.

As in Britain, there was a split in the theological beliefs of those participating in these conferences. It seems they were united upon the premillennialist concept. Many, however, rejected the pretribulation view of the rapturists. The influence of Darby, however, was certainly not extinguished by his death in 1882, nor was it limited to the Plymouth Brethren. Though the exclusiveness of the Plymouth Brethren was apparently rejected in the United States, many of their prophetic interpretations were nonetheless accepted.

It is also of no little significance that dispensationalism has linkages with the seventeenth-century development of Calvinism. Most supporters of dispensationalism hold to a Calvinistic creed. Thus the doctrinal statement arising out of the first United States conference of 1878 stressed: (1) rigid verbal inspiration; (2) the absolute depravity of man and helplessness to assist in his own salvation; (3) the sovereign transcendence of the triune God. These concepts became normative for dispensational theology.

The crux of dispensational teaching is that each dispensation commences when God makes a covenant with man and ends when He intervenes in punishment of the disobedient. Each succeeding dispensation has little or no significance to the one that precedes it or the one that follows. God exercises His sovereignty in relation to nations by predestination, as He does with individual human beings. The Jews have a special election with God. Some Gentiles have an election with God, and there is nothing they can do that has any significance to this ordination. Thus dispensationalists perceive the New Testament through the eyes of these false theories.

Some dispensationalists hold that Jesus' teachings are not directly relevant to the Christian church, for He was speaking to the kingdom of the Jews. Thus Jesus' teachings reflect the dispensation of the law, whereas we are living under the dispensation of grace. Such believers hold that the present age is a parenthesis in history not mentioned in the Old Testament. They believe that the prophetic clock stopped at Calvary. Thus they justify the "gap theory" in their interpretation of Daniel's seventy-weeks prophecy. They explain that the sixty-nine weeks ended at Calvary and that halted the prophetic clock. It will not restart until the end of the age, when the seventieth week will be fulfilled during the reign of the Antichrist. Had the Jews accepted Christ, His millennial kingdom would have been established then on earth. These dispensationalists believe that when John the Baptist preached "The kingdom of heaven is at hand," Jesus was then ready to set it up; but the Jews rejected it, so God had to extend time to give the gospel to the Gentiles before He could set up His kingdom. One wonders, then, what Jesus meant when He said "If my kingdom were of this world, then would my servants fight." John 18:36.

During the seven-year rule of the Antichrist, the dispensationalists propose that he will covenant with the Jews who are restored to Palestine, the temple will be rebuilt in Jerusalem, the ten tribes will be regathered and the sacrificial system reestablished, and that these startling events will lead to many conversions among those not raptured. These are called the tribulation saints. After three and one-half years, Antichrist breaks his treaty with the Jews, and for the next three years, Antichrist inflicts fearful persecution on the new Christians and the faithful Jews. Then Jesus will appear to destroy Antichrist, and Christ will establish His visible kingdom for a thousand years (some say 360,000 years).

To a greater or lesser extent, this unscriptural concept is pervasive among the fundamentalist Christians. The two most common errors arising from Darby are (1) the disjunction of law and grace, denying the power of Christ to provide victory in the life of the dedicated Christian; (2) futurism—the end-time Antichrist thus denying the identity of the Papacy as antichrist.

These views of Darby are highly speculative. They are not based upon a *plain* Thus saith the Lord, but rather upon the conjectures of John Darby's fertile mind. Thus they must be rejected. The *plain* words of Scripture ask the rhetorical question, "Do we then make void the law through grace"—then *plainly* answer that question, which required no answer, lest our dull minds be confused, "Yea we establish the law." That is clear and plain. The apostle John in his first epistle *plainly* stated that the seeds of antichrist were present in his day. Let God's people seek *plain* evidence from Scripture, and ignore the guesswork provided by vain philosophy.

THE LEGACY OF
CYRUS SCOFIELD

A lthough the two men never met, no one did more than C. I. Scofield to forward the speculative and erroneous prophetic interpretations of John Darby, the founder of the Plymouth Brethren religion. Scofield embraced Christianity in St. Louis, Missouri, in 1879, just three years before the death of Darby. Darby's last visit to the United States was in 1874, but few cities were more responsive to his prophetic interpretations that St. Louis. Though Scofield traced his conversion to the 1879 St. Louis crusade of Dwight L. Moody, and while their ministries were to cross each other from time to time, and though Scofield was to preach Moody's funeral service in 1899, nevertheless, Scofield appears to have followed far more closely the prophetic directions of Darby than of Moody.

Cyrus Scofield, a convincing speaker and powerful protagonist for the dispensational theology, nevertheless, made his greatest impact through the publication of the *Scofield Reference Bible*, which has had a greater influence upon conservative Protestant theology than any seminary in the United States, or all seminaries combined. Scofield's influence resulted from the fact that this Bible was printed by the prestigious Oxford University Press, and the fact that it was sold by the millions by colporteurs throughout the United States, especially in the South.

Before his conversion, Scofield had a checkered career. He was born in Clinton, Michigan, well north of Detroit, in what can truly be described as frontier country. Never recovering from Cyrus' birth, his mother died a few months later. He was brought up by older sisters and his stepmother. In his youth he traveled to Tennessee to live with a sister and brother-in-law. There he joined the Confederate army and later was given a discharge on request when he revealed his Michigan birthplace.

Scofield found his way to St. Louis where, after a short experience as a law clerk, he assumed the role of lawyer. It was in St. Louis that he married his first wife, Leontine Cerre, a daughter of one of the wealthy French fur-trader families of St. Louis. Leontine was a Roman Catholic. Two daughters and a son were born of this marriage. The son died in infancy. At the time of the birth of the second daughter, Scofield was in the process of moving to Atchison in northeastern Kansas.

It was in Kansas, while still in his twenties, that Scofield experienced a meteoric rise and fall in politics and law. This venture into politics and law also proved to be the death of his marriage. In 1871 Scofield was elected the representative to the Kansas legislature as member for the fourth district. He was immediately assigned to the post of chairman of the judiciary committee of the lower house. He soon became embroiled in the seamy side of politics. He exerted remarkable skill in engineering the election of his senior law partner to the United States House of Representatives to replace the then-incumbent member. In appreciation for his help, the new representative was able to secure President Grant's appointment of Cyrus Scofield to the office of United States District Attorney for Kansas. Although the appointment was not a little controversial at the time, it appears that the youthful Scofield began to perform credibly.

However, the next six years of Scofield's life, from 1873 to 1879, are somewhat shrouded in mystery and are punctuated with not a little scandal. In December 1873, he suddenly resigned his post as District Attorney and fled to Canada. Evidence uncovered later indicates that his resignation was precipitated by a scandal (well covered up by the Republican Party of Kansas) that probably involved financial dealings. In leaving Atchison, Scofield left his wife and family, never again to return to them. Ultimately, after his conversion and at the beginning of his ministry, he divorced Leontine, and subsequently married his second wife, Hettie, who was to bear him one son.

Scofield resurfaced in St. Louis, where he faced a number of embezzlement and forgery counts. Although his wealthy sister seems to have bailed him out of some of these circumstances, evidence suggests that he did serve about six months in jail, and that may have been where he first began to look to Christianity for answers to the questions of life. In any case, he was in attendance at Moody's 1879 crusade, and during this time he made his first commitment to Christ.

In a remarkably short time, Scofield received and accepted the offer of the pastorate of the Dallas Congregational Church, then a struggling congregation. Soon, under Scofield's capable leadership, the church, basically a fortress for northerners who had migrated to the Southwest, began to attract southerners. It seems that Scofield was able to use his short stint in the Confederate army as a means of attracting some of the southerners to the church. The church also gained as members some of the more influential leaders of Dallas, and its future was assured.

Scofield became attracted to the Niagara conferences, held on the Canadian side of the falls annually between 1883 and 1897. Although it appears that Scofield was not at that time a major preacher at these conferences, he was increasingly in demand as a preacher across the nation and was less and less available to the pulpit of his Dallas church. By the 1890s he had spent time in Europe and had become well known in Great Britain. So beloved was he in Dallas that the Congregational church was willing to keep him as their pastor even when he was able to spend little time with them.

A significant change came when in 1896 Scofield accepted the pulpit in the Northfield Church in Massachusetts. Northfield was the birthplace of Dwight L. Moody and his lifelong residence, when not in Chicago or travelling. Moody was a member of the Trinitarian Congregational Church that Scofield came to pastor, and it is generally agreed that Moody was at least partially responsible for the call to Scofield. Scofield was able to minister to the students of the three schools which Moody had established— Northfield Seminary for Girls (1879), Mt. Herman School for Boys (1881), and the Northfield Bible Training School, operated during the winter months. It was in this church that almost four years later, Scofield was to preach the funeral service for Moody when the evangelist laid down his life at the age of 62.

Scofield was soon participating in many other conferences, and his fame and influence were increasing significantly, especially in and around New England and New York. While it is hard to say when Scofield conceived the idea of the Reference Bible, it is certain that it was on his mind very early in the twentieth century. By that time his Bible correspondence course was very popular around the United States, and it seems to have been a significant factor in the decision to produce the Reference Bible. Scofield was greatly encouraged by a well known Evangelical leader of the day, A. C. Gaebelein. A major thrust forward came when Scofield visited Oxford University in 1906. At Oxford there was some positive response to Scofield's proposed Bible notes, and on June 5, 1907, Scofield signed an agreement with the American branch of the university press in New York City. Two years later the work was ready for publication.

Although Scofield did not meet the two Cambridge scholars, B. F. Westcott and F. J. A. Hort, his 1909 edition of the Reference Bible acknowledges the influence of these men upon his work. Many readers will recall that Westcott and Hort were noted scholars in the tradition of the Anglo-Catholic movement of Oxford University, though they were professors at Cambridge University. They were the leading lights in the preparation of the 1881 Revised Version of the Bible, which forsook the Protestant tradition of Bible translation from the Received Text by following as primary sources the Codex Vaticanus and the Codex Sinaiticus. These Greek manuscripts from the Western Roman Church had evidence of tampering and are supportive of Roman Catholic theology.

By 1905, Scofield had left the Northfield Church in Massachusetts and had returned to his Dallas congregation. However, Scofield was now such a sought-after speaker that his local congregation saw him only sparingly. By 1914 he was one of the leaders of the famous Chicago Prophecy Conference. For the last few years of his life his activities diminished, yet in spite of recurring ill health, he was able to superintend the 1917 revision of his Reference Bible.

Of intense importance to readers is the long-term influence of Scofield and his Bible. It is self-evident that had the nonbiblical prophetic interpretations of John Darby been confined within the Plymouth Brethren Church, their impact would have been, at the most, localized. But by his six visits to the United States Darby was able to penetrate the denominational barriers, so that churches such as the Congregational. the Presbyterian, and the Baptist Churches began to be influenced by Darby's errors. But it was the *Scofield Reference Bible* which penetrated the minds of the laity in the pews, as many appeared to have uncritically placed the same level of authority on these human words as they did upon the words of inspiration.

What then are the basic errors of the Darby/Scofield system of Bible teachings and prophetic interpretation?

1. Theistic evolution. Though perhaps not so much a part of his prophetic system, Scofield nevertheless is responsible for the large-scale defection by the rank-and-file members of conservative Protestant churches from the biblical presentation of creationism. Commenting upon the very first text of Scripture, Genesis 1:1, Scofield assures the reader that it allows for the long geologic periods proposed by scientists. This obviously gives credence to the concepts of theistic evolution.

2. Dispensationalism. A pillar of Scofield's theology is dispensationalism. He was not the originator; for Augustine, bishop of Hippo in the fifth century, taught a form of dispensationalism. However, Scofield popularized this view. Scofield's scheme has identified seven dispensations:

1. *Innocence*—the pre-Fall period of man;
2. *Conscience*—the antediluvian period;
3. *Human Government*—the postdiluvian period until the call of Abraham;
4. *Promise*—from the time of Abraham to the giving of the law;
5. *Law*—from Sinai to the cross;
6. *Church*—from the cross to the rapture;
7. *Eternity*—the eternal existence of the saved.

There is some confusion in Scofield's seven dispensations, as he does not define the seventieth week of the prophecy of Daniel 9:24–27 as a separate period. Neither does he identify the millennium as a distinct dispensation.

A key issue in Scofield's dispensationalism is the fact that in each dispensation, God deals quite differently with man; therefore the lessons from one dispensation do not have direct relevance to another. Actually, the differences between the dispensations before the cross and the dispensation of the church after the cross are the most significant to Scofield's theology.

Yet we are reminded that Paul says,

All scripture is given by inspiration of God, and is profitable
for doctrine, for reproof, for correction, for instruction in righteousness   (2 Timothy 3:16).

3. Failed Kingdom. Scofield's dispensational teachings hold
to the view that the first coming of Jesus was designed to set up
Christ's earthly kingdom upon earth with His chosen people, the
Jews. Thus when John the Baptist taught that the kingdom of
heaven was at hand (Matthew 3:2), he was actually teaching that
Christ had come to establish His earthly kingdom. Therefore, the
dispensation of the church is seen as a parenthesis in which the
gospel was taken to the Gentiles after the failed kingdom. In light
of this theory it is hard to understand the words of Christ to
Pilate.

Jesus answered, My kingdom is not of this world: if my kingdom were of this world, then would my servants fight, that I
should not be delivered to the Jews: but now is my kingdom
not from hence   (John 18:36).

4. The Stopped Prophetic Clock. According to Scofield, when
Christ died, the prophetic clock stopped. Thus, the seventy-week
prophecy of Daniel 9 stopped at the end of the sixty-ninth week
when Jesus died. Students of prophecy will recognize the difficulty in establishing a valid starting year for the seventy-week
prophecy of Daniel chapter 9, that would end the sixty-ninth week
at A.D. 31, the year of the crucifixion. All sorts of complicated
schemes and reckonings have attempted to achieve this goal, but
none is convincing. The sixty-nine week period ended A.D. 27; 483
years after King Artaxerxes' decree of 457 B.C. to reestablish
Jerusalem and Judea. Thus the end of the sixty-nine week (483-
year) period coincided with the beginning of Christ's ministry at
His baptism.

5. The Gap Theory. The concept of the stopped prophetic
clock has led to the gap theory as the explanation for Daniel 9.
This theory places fulfillment of the first sixty-nine weeks of the
prophecy before the death of Jesus. Then, after an approximately
2,000-year gap, comes the fulfillment of the final week (7 years)

of the prophecy. This period is declared to be the reign of the antichrist. This error has led to dangerous new translations of Daniel 9:24–27 in some modern Bible versions, in an attempt to fit the futuristic antichrist theory. The following is an example of biased translation:

> Seventy "sevens" are decreed for your people and your holy city to finish transgression, to put an end to sin, to atone for wickedness, to bring in everlasting righteousness, to seal up vision and prophecy and to anoint the most holy.

> Know and understand this: From the issuing of the decree to restore and rebuild Jerusalem until the Anointed One, the ruler, comes, there will be seven "sevens," and sixty-two "sevens." It will be rebuilt with streets and a trench, but in times of trouble. After the sixty-two "sevens," the Anointed One will be cut off and will have nothing. The people of the ruler who will come will destroy the city and the sanctuary. The end will come like a flood: War will continue until the end, and desolations have been decreed. He will confirm a covenant with many for one "seven," but in the middle of that "seven" he will put an end to sacrifice and offering. And one who causes desolation will place abominations on a wing of the temple until the end that is decreed is poured out on him (Daniel 9:24–27, NIV). (Compare with the King James Bible.)

6. The Futuristic Interpretation of Revelation. Essentially, the book of Revelation is divided into sections, according to the dispensationalist. Chapters 1–3 are said to have been fulfilled in the early Christian church. Thus, John's statement indicated he is describing events that must shortly come to pass (Revelation 1:1) refers only to the first three chapters. Chapters 4–22 are said to detail events that take place immediately before the rapture, during the reign of the antichrist, and in the establishment of the kingdom.

7. The Disjunction of Law and Grace. Scofield's dispensationalism certainly calls for the separation of law and grace. The dispensation of the church is, he says, the dispensation of grace. Because men are "saved by grace through faith and not of works" (Ephesians 2:8–9), the law has no part to play in the

salvation of the church. Thus, Scofield opens the floodgate to antinomianism. This concept is now common in Evangelical teachings. Large numbers have lost faith in Jesus' power to provide victory over all of Satan's temptations. Yet the Bible constantly places the law and the gospel together.

> Here is the patience of the saints: here are they that keep the commandments of God, and the faith of Jesus
> (Revelation 14:12).

8. The Secret Rapture. It will be recalled from chapters 22 and 26 that at least three different persons are attributed as the source of the secret-rapture doctrine: Manuel de Lacunza, Margaret McDonald and Edward Irving. The theory has inspired authors to write such books as *The Twinkling of an Eye,* and musicians to compose such songs as "The King is Coming." It has also inspired such bumper stickers as "Beware! The driver of this car may be raptured at any time." Above all, it has stimulated much speculation more in line with science fiction than with earnest Bible study.

Briefly, the secret rapture concept proclaims that the church (the chosen saints) are raptured at the Second Coming of Jesus. It is visible to them, but unseen by those who remain upon the earth. This rapture takes place before the appearance of the antichrist. Thus the church does not experience the tribulation, and therefore the supporters of this view are called pretribulationalists. Immediately after the rapture, Antichrist (a satanically controlled individual) appears and sets up his kingdom upon earth. He makes a league with the Jews and reigns in the temple rebuilt in Jerusalem. His reign lasts for seven years, the final week of the seventy-week prophecy. After three and one-half years he breaks his covenant with the Jews, cruelly persecutes both them and the new generation of Christians who have arisen after the rapture of the church (these Christians are referred to as tribulation Christians), and reigns a further three and one-half years before Christ comes a third time to destroy Antichrist. To the careful student of Daniel 9:24–27, this interpretation of the seventieth week is wholly unjustified.

The concept of a church raptured before the tribulation is an especially attractive one for all members of the church. This concept also fits in snugly with dispensationalism and with the concepts of Calvinistic predestinarianism. The concept of an end-time Antichrist, first proposed by the Jesuit Francisco Ribera, is, however, gaining disturbing support, especially as futuristic interpretations of prophecy become commonplace in the church.

9. Pretribulationism. The secret rapture is indivisible from pretribulational concepts. Pretribulationism separates the church (the saints) who will be raptured before the tribulation, from those redeemed who, because of the mighty evidence of the fulfillment of prophecy, will accept Christ after the beginning of the reign of the Antichrist, and who will go through the tribulation (tribulation Christians). In essence, this doctrine provides what some call the second chance for salvation. In other words, the Second Coming of Jesus does not end the probation of the inhabitants of the world; there is another chance after the church has been raptured. The idea totally contradicts Scripture. Just before Christ returns, He declares,

> He that is unjust, let him be unjust still: and he which is filthy, let him be filthy still: and he that is righteous, let him be righteous still: and he that is holy, let him be holy still
> (Revelation 22:11).

10. Premillennialism. All rapturists and dispensationalists appear to be premillennialists; that is, they believe that the coming of Jesus precedes the millennium. To this extent they are consistent with biblical truth. However, they accept the error that during the millennium Christ sets up His earthly kingdom and reigns on earth for 1,000 years (some say 360,000 years).

11. Limited Authority of the Bible. The dispensational concept limits the relevance of most of the Bible. The Old Testament, covering dispensations in which it is claimed that God dealt with man differently from the way He deals with man today, has no binding authority for the church. The four gospels also have limited authority for today, because Jesus was addressing the Jews

during the dispensation of law, when He planned to set up his earthly kingdom. Some go so far as to say that only the prison epistles of Paul have full significance for today.

This concept is also inexplicable in light of the fact that the gospels were written about thirty to sixty years after the death of Christ. Surely, were the dispensationalists correct, the gospel writers would have indicated the irrelevance of Christ's teaching to the Christian church. By way of observation, it is well to recognize the implication when someone declares himself to be a New Testament Christian, or a church claims to be a New Testament church.

When by 1910 the movement had taken the name of Fundamentalist, the intent was to project the claim that the movement is true to the fundamental or pillar truths of the Bible. Often, verbal or word-by-word inspiration was claimed. Further, extraordinary efforts were exerted in futile attempts to prove that the prophetic scheme of the movement was a reestablishment of the teachings of the apostles and the early church. But neither dispensationalism nor the secret rapture could be thus validated. Unfortunately, many who use the Scofield Bible have tended to accept Scofield's comments as almost equally authoritative as the divine Word itself. Our counsel is to treat these comments as of human rather than inspired origin, and return to the mighty Protestant principle which bases all doctrine upon the Bible alone. This standard would protect against deception by the fanciful concepts of faulty human beings.

THE DILEMMA OF
THE FUTURE

Almost half a millennium has passed since the spectacular birth of the Evangelical movement. In that period of time the wonderful promise of this movement has not materialized. Indeed to a great extent the Evangelical movement at the end of the twentieth century is in a state of chaos. Eclecticism, pluralism, ecumenism, Pentecostalism, compromise, impotency, doctrinal confusion and spiritual inertia are much in evidence. Surely the Evangelical movement needs a new focus, a focus riveted upon the unchanging principles of the Word of God.

In a futile effort to regain meaning in the Evangelical movement some have vainly sought after the false unity offered by the ecumenical movements. Others have sought to refill their increasingly deserted pews by the introduction of Pentecostal and Charismatic forms of worship. But the true power of the Word is missing in these futile efforts. These forms contain the chaff and discard the grain.

Evangelical Protestantism began with a single-minded focus upon the power of Scripture, and its highest purpose can be reached only by an even greater return to the concepts of the Bible and the Bible only as the basis of faith and practice. The present direction of evangelical Protestantism can never achieve the great unity for which Christ prayed in His prayer. The ecumenical movement is the enemy of unity, for it calls for unity based upon a false platform of compromise and of doctrinal de-emphasis. One has only to read the epistles of Paul to Timothy and to Titus to realize the centrality of truth and doctrine.

> If thou put the brethren in remembrance of these things, thou shalt be a good minister of Jesus Christ, nourished up in the words of faith and of good doctrine, whereunto thou hast attained   (1 Timothy 4:6).

> Till I come, give attendance to reading, to exhortation, to doctrine   (1 Timothy 4:13).

All scripture is given by inspiration of God, and is profitable for doctrine, for reproof, for correction, for instruction in righteousness: that the man of God may be perfect, throughly furnished unto all good works   (2 Timothy 3:16, 17).

Holding fast the faithful word as he hath been taught, that he may be able by sound doctrine both to exhort and to convince the gainsayers   (Titus 1:9).

In all things shewing thyself a pattern of good works: in doctrine shewing uncorruptness, gravity, sincerity (Titus 2:7).

Not purloining, but shewing all good fidelity; that they may adorn the doctrine of God our Saviour in all things
(Titus 2:10).

In Jesus' prayer for unity we often ignore the central key of that unity.

Sanctify them through thy truth: thy word is truth (John 17:17).

And for their sakes I sanctify myself, that they also might be sanctified through the truth   (John 17:19).

There is no sanctification aside from truth, and it is the truth that has sanctified that leads to real unity. Unity is not a *goal,* it is not an *objective,* but it is a *result.* When God's people are united in the truth that sanctifies, there is unity, which is clearly seen in the new-birth principles enunciated by Peter.

Seeing ye have purified your souls in obeying the truth through the Spirit unto unfeigned love of the brethren, see that ye love one another with a pure heart fervently: being born again, not of corruptible seed, but of incorruptible, by the word of God, which liveth and abideth for ever   (1 Peter 1:22–23).

In his great unity chapter, Paul has also emphasized the centrality to unity of sound doctrine and a sanctified life.

And he gave some, apostles; and some, prophets; and some, evangelists; and some, pastors and teachers; for the perfecting of the saints, for the work of the ministry, for the edifying of the body of Christ: till we all come in the unity of the faith, and of the knowledge of the Son of God, unto a perfect man, unto the measure of the stature of the fulness of Christ: that we henceforth be no more children, tossed to and fro, and carried about with every wind of doctrine, by the sleight of men, and cunning craftiness, whereby they lie in wait to deceive; but speaking the truth in love, may grow up into him in all things, which is the head, even Christ

(Ephesians 4:11–15).

> **There is no sanctification
> aside from truth,
> and it is the truth *that has sanctified*
> that leads to unity**